D1806940

BIGGER THAN LIFE

BIGGER
than Life

*The History of Gay Porn Cinema
from Beefcake to Hardcore*

BY JEFFREY ESCOFFIER

RUNNING PRESS
PHILADELPHIA • LONDON

© 2009 by Jeffrey Escoffier
All rights reserved under the Pan-American and International Copyright
Conventions
Printed in the United States

*This book may not be reproduced in whole or in part, in any form or by any means,
electronic or mechanical, including photocopying, recording, or by any information
storage and retrieval system now known or hereafter invented, without written permission from the publisher.*

9   8   7   6   5   4   3   2   1
Digit on the right indicates the number of this printing

Library of Congress Control Number: 2008939356

ISBN 978-0-7867-20101
Cover design by Whtney Cookman
Interior design by Stewart A. Williams
Typography: Excelsior

Running Press Book Publishers
2300 Chestnut Street
Philadelphia, PA 19103-4371

Visit us on the web!
www.runningpress.com

A Note about References:
*Videographies and information about many the movies, directors and performers
mentioned in the book can be found online at The Gay Erotic Video Index
www.wtule.net/Intro.*

*Information can also be found on the mainstream movie database Internet Movie
Database (IMDb) at www.imdb.com/search.*
Please note that neither site is totally comprehensive.

To Rod Barry, my muse

Jerry Douglas, my mentor,

and Wash West, who gave

me the passport

CONTENTS

Introduction

Hardcore porn—both the straight and gay varieties—entered mainstream American culture in the 1970s as the sexual revolution swept away many of the cultural inhibitions and legal restraints on explicit sexual expression. The first porn movie ever to be previewed by *Variety*, the entertainment industry's leading trade journal, was Wakefield Poole's *Boys in the Sand* (1971), a sexually explicit gay movie shot on Fire Island with a budget of $4,000. Moviegoers, celebrities, and critics—both gay and straight—flocked to see *Boys in the Sand* when it opened in mainstream movie theaters in New York, Los Angeles, and San Francisco.

Within a year, *Deep Throat*, a heterosexual hardcore feature, opened to rave reviews and a huge box office—exceeding that of many mainstream Hollywood features. It was quickly followed by *The Devil in Miss Jones* and *Behind the Green Door*. *Variety* reported that between June 1972 and June 1973, these three movies earned more—on a screen-by-screen basis and in terms of gross revenues—than all but a handful of mainstream Hollywood releases. This was the era of "porn chic." Ironically, 1972 was also the year of *The Godfather*—and the beginning of Hollywood's renaissance.

The first signs of a "sexual revolution" appeared in the mid-sixties. In January 1964 *Time* magazine announced the arrival of a "second sexual revolution," signaled, in the magazine's view, by an increase in what it called "Spectator Sex"—representing a new degree of sexual explicitness in books, movies, and Broadway plays. Over the next few years, articles also appeared in many other publications, ranging from *America* (March 6, 1965), a magazine published by the Catholic Church, to *Ebony* (August 1966), a mass market magazine with a predominately African-American readership.

These reports identified a number of trends and developments taking place throughout American society. The cultural atmosphere of the sixties—particularly what was referred to as "the counterculture"—had begun to emerge at around the same time. The popularity of rock music, the increased use of marijuana, LSD, and other drugs among youth, widespread public displays of nudity, and a new openness about sexuality contributed to the widespread awareness of radical cultural change. Public interest in sex had been growing since the late forties and by the sixties the flood of novels, magazine articles, and advice books dealing with sexuality grew to epic proportions.

Yet the sexual revolution of the sixties and seventies would never have taken place without a series of extended legal and political battles over obscenity and pornography. They were not only struggles over free speech and the First Amendment; they were also business overtures. Nevertheless, these battles helped to create a public space in American culture for sexual speech, a space where it was permissible not only to discuss patterns of sexual behavior but also to portray sexuality honestly and bluntly in fiction, on the stage, and in movies.

Freedom of sexual expression was the necessary condition for the later emergence of sexual liberation, the women's movement, and the civil rights of gay men, lesbians, and transgendered people—implying an odd coalition among principled First Amendment activists, porn entrepreneurs, sex radicals, feminists, LGBT (lesbian, gay, bisexual, and transgender) activists, and sexual minorities.

Pornography and pornographic films were an integral part of the sexual discourses that emerged during the sexual revolution's two decades. The sexual explicitness of pornography ranges from soft-core images of attractive models posing or running in the woods to gritty depictions of kinky sex acts in alleyways. Pornography can reinforce the crudest stereotypes of sex roles, standards of beauty, or power dynamics, or it can contribute to the education of desire. It can be a fantasy machine or a form of discourse about sex—or it can be all these things at the same time.

Supreme Court decisions, in particular, changed the social and economic context for sexual expression in the United States. Justice Brennan's definition of obscenity in *Roth v. United States of America* in 1957 profoundly shaped subsequent developments: "[1] Whether to the average person, [2] applying contemporary community standards, [3] the dominant theme of the material taken as a whole [4] appeals to prurient interests." Brennan declared "obscenity" as "utterly without socially redeeming importance," and ruled that it was not protected by the freedoms of speech and press. However, he also created an opening for the freedom of sexual speech when he noted that "sex and obscenity were not synonymous ... obscene material having a tendency to excite lustful thoughts," and that "All ideas, even ideas hateful to prevailing climate of opinion—have the full protection" of the First Amendment. The *Roth* decision, however, had created an enduring double bind—it continued to pose an enormous obstacle to free and honest expression of sexual thoughts by defining obscenity as "utterly without socially redeeming importance"—thus declaring in effect that the public expression of sexual fantasies and thoughts was not protected by the First Amendment. However, subsequent decisions such as *Miller v. California* (1973) helped to create an opening in which it became possible to discuss sex and to represent it both literarily and visually—and without which the sexual revolution is difficult to imagine.

3

As the sexual revolution moved into high gear, nudity and pornography were at the forefront of the period's cultural battles. Avant-garde movies had anticipated these developments. Jack Smith's *Flaming Creatures* was one of the first. Andy Warhol made a series of experimental films that explored New York's gay sexual underground. Using a hand-held camera and adopting a documentary film style, he made movies that portrayed sexual outlaws—male hustlers, drag queens, and gay men—with some nudity but without any hardcore sexually explicit behavior. Warhol's *Blow Job*, made in 1963, showed only the face of the man being fellated. *My Hustler*, made a year or two later, shows a male hustler sitting on a beach while on the soundtrack three people quarrel about his sexual appeal. In *The Chelsea Girls* (1966) and then in *Lonesome Cowboys* (1969), which became smash hits at mainstream movie theaters, Warhol used nudity and included soft-core expressions (and soft penises) of "perverse" sexuality.

By the seventies, newspapers with names like *Screw*, offering sexual information, personal ads, and sexually explicit photos and art, were available on street corners in larger American cities, demonstrating increased public interest in sex and suggesting that perhaps sexual behavior was undergoing changes as well. The legal victories often translated into phenomenal economic success for the publishers, filmmakers, and distributors of sexually explicit materials. Most of these materials were aimed at male audiences, and sought to satisfy many of the traditional male sexual fantasies, thus contributing to the enormous success of magazines like Hugh Hefner's *Playboy*, Bob Guccione's *Penthouse*, and Larry Flynt's *Hustler*.

Russ Meyer's 1959 film, *The Immoral Mr. Teas*, was another major turning point in popular culture's attitudes toward sex. Following its release, desperate theater owners turned to other such sexploitation movies—soft-core sex films—to fill the void left by the collapsing market for mainstream Hollywood movies. Known as nudies or nudie-cuties, they were usually produced on a low budget and took the place of the classic "exploitation" movies that had focused on tabloid themes. Instead, the nudies, as their name suggests, focused more or less entirely on nudity, sexual story lines, and simulated sex acts. And unlike the classic exploitation movies, there was no pretense of "education"; instead they provided titillation and entertainment. The first nudie, Meyer's *The Immoral Mr. Teas,* told the story of Bill Teas, who while under sedation for a tooth extraction fantasizes that the dentist's assistant is naked. Afterward, on his rounds as a delivery man, every woman he encounters appears naked to him.

Pornography created space for increased experimentation with a whole range of sexualities not organized around procreation and reproduction, desires that included oral and anal sex, homosexuality, sadomasochism, and various fetishes. Under the banner of sexual intercourse outside of heterosexual marriage, pornography harnessed voyeurism and exhibitionism to portray sex with multiple partners, group sex, fellatio and cunnilingus, anal intercourse, lesbianism, male homosexuality, sexual fetishisms, sex toys, BDSM, and other sexual practices. Thus the sexual revolution helped emancipate men and women who were stigmatized for their sexuality.

Though the sexual revolution was at first largely a heterosexual phenomenon, it also had a profound effect on homosexual men. The intense stigma attached to homosexuality before Stonewall blocked any open discussion of gay male sexuality and forced gay men's sexual expression deep underground. Consequently, the increasing acceptance of pornography during the sixties and seventies played a significant role in the sexual lives of gay men, even more than it did among comparable groups of heterosexual men. The increasing social acceptance of pornography helped to legitimize visual representations of homoerotic images and gay sex as well. Before 1962, homosexual materials, even those without any sexual content, were considered obscene by definition. The emergence of gay hardcore films provided explicit representations of gay sexual behavior not otherwise available. And the availability of such images helped to affirm the nascent gay identity.

Since most gay men become adults without learning the social and sexual codes of their community, film pornography contributes, as film critic Richard Dyer has observed, to their "education of desire." Erections, orgasms, and the performances of sexually desirable, masculine, and energetic performers helped to create positive images of gay male sexuality and identity. Gay hardcore also reinforced the new style of gay masculinity—it recorded (almost like a "documentary") and codified the new masculine sexual ethos that was emerging among gay men. Gay porn, as a genre, portrayed "straight" men engaging in homosexual acts. It thus served to situate homosexual *desire* within masculine territory irrespective of heterosexual or gay identities. The commercial success of gay porn emerged from the cultural and economic significance of gay identities, and not—however widespread it may be among males—homosexual desire.

Almost all of those involved in making "commercial" gay pornographic movies began as amateurs in a field that had virtually never existed before, either as art or commerce. Many of their "underground" predecessors had repeatedly suffered arrest and other forms of legal harassment. There was no developed gay market, and any films made commercially were shown in adult X-rated theaters. After the Stonewall riots and the emergence of the gay liberation movement in 1969, a number of entrepreneurs began to make gay adult movies for the new mail-order market. The gay porn film industry grew dramatically during the next thirty years and transformed the way men—gay men in particular—conceived of masculinity and their sexuality.

Desire, psychologists have found, is not something given to us out of the blue; it is constructed through fantasy—and it is through fantasy that we learn how to desire. Pornographic movies are passports to a *fantasy world* where sex exists without the everyday encumbrances of social convention, endurance, or availability. To imagine a sexual performance in a fantasy or to see one in a porn movie enables us to experience sexual excitement without the side effects of anxiety, guilt, or boredom—and for many of us the erotic excitement is heightened when the fantasy includes an element of risk, danger, mystery, or transgression. Porn lets us explore those new fantasies. [Cowie, 132-52]

———————

REFERENCES

David Allyn, *Make Love, Not War: The Sexual Revolution: An Unfettered History* (Boston: Little, Brown and Company, 2000).

Edward de Grazia, *Girls Lean Back Everywhere: The Law of Obscenity and the Assault on Genius* (New York: Vintage, 1992).

Elizabeth Cowie, "Pornography and Fantasy: Psychoanalytic Perspectives," Lynne Segal and Mary McIntosh, *Sex Exposed: Sexuality and the Pornography Debate* (New Brunswick: Rutgers University Press, 1993).

Jeffrey Escoffier, *Sexual Revolution* (New York: Thunder's Mouth Press, 2003).

Joseph Slade, *Pornography in America* (Santa Barbara: ABC-CLIO, 2000).

PART ONE

PASSPORTS
TO FANTASY

CHAPTER ONE

Blue

Obviously, blue is a through-the-looking-glass word, a word of many (and often contradictory) meanings, some of which are dead, some of which are very much alive, and at least one of which—blue, meaning "indecent" or "obscene"—seems, after an existence of more than one hundred years, to be moving from the limbo of argot toward general usage.

—JOSEPH P. ROPPOLO, "'BLUE': INDECENT, OBSCENE," *AMERICAN SPEECH, 1953*

Summer 1962: It's hot and muggy, and a little hazy, too, on the beach at Coney Island. Under the boardwalk where it's dark and cool, groups of teenagers sit huddled on blankets and towels. Music blares from small transistor radios, their long antennas poking into the air. Sitting nearby, a thin, gaunt man listens to the teenagers talk and makes mental notes of the Top 40 songs coming out of the small handheld radios: "Leader of the Pack," "My Boyfriend's Back," Elvis Presley's "Devil in Disguise," and "Wipeout." Popular disk jockeys Cousin Brucie and Murray the K issue a constant stream of commentary, jokes, and self-promotion. The listener is Kenneth Anger, a filmmaker from Los Angles who had been living in France for the past eight years. [Hutchison, 125]

Anger chose the hit song "Blue Velvet" as the centerpiece of *Scorpio Rising*, the short experimental film he was making. The movie prefigured the powerful social forces that would threaten to disrupt the United States over the next two decades. Inspired by *The Wild Ones*, the 1953 movie that starred Marlon Brando as the leader of a motorcycle gang that rides into a small town and terrorizes it, Anger both worshipped and deconstructed the mythology of the American "barbarian." "Blue Velvet" became the "dressing adagio," played as a motorcycle gang dresses in leather and chains. "The dark erotic imagination," Gregory Markopoulos hypothesized, was "palpable in the images of hulking male physiques." Filmed in Brooklyn and edited in San Francisco, Anger's film was an attack on middle-class American values and a subversive glorification of the homoerotic film images that shaped American notions of masculinity—exemplified by Brando and by James Dean in *Rebel Without a Cause*.

One of the first American filmmakers to explore homoeroticism and its cultural mythologies, Kenneth Anger shot a short film called *Fireworks* (1947), a homosexual dream/nightmare that was inspired by the 1943 zoot suit riots in Los Angeles—in which gangs of sailors attacked and beat zoot suit–wearing Latino youth because they were not serving in the armed forces. The film portrayed a young man who, awaking from a dream with a monstrous erection creating a tent in the bedsheet, rises to go out into the night in search of sexual adventure. He goes to a men's room and comes upon a sailor flexing his bare chest and muscles. When the young man asks the sailor for a light, the sailor physically rebuffs him. Then he is set upon and beaten by a gang of the sailor's mates. The film is permeated with surrealistic sexual symbolism—statues under sheets representing erections and a Roman candle spewing white sparks from a sailor's crotch.

Born and raised in Los Angeles, Anger grew up in a family closely tied to the movie industry. As a young boy, he collected photographs and newspaper clippings about various stars while he listened to adults gossiping about the scandalous goings-on of Hollywood. Later, he recounted many of these sordid stories in his best-selling book *Hollywood Babylon*. "A perverse prayer to the heyday of Hollywood," wrote Mick Brown of the book, "a terribly thorough and thoroughly terrible record of the seamy underbelly of Tinseltown's dreamlike façade, with skeletons wrenched out of closets, peccadilloes mercilessly unearthed and corpses scattered liberally." [Hutchison, 198] Like *Hollywood Babylon*, Anger's films chart the underworld—both the sordid and the occult realities—of the American myths of glamour, beauty, power, and eroticism.

Scorpio Rising, his 1963 masterpiece, paid homage to the macho rites of a motorcycle gang and extended Anger's exploration of homoerotic imagery—juxtaposing and inter-cutting images of a motorcycle gang and costumed but partially undressed revelers, of policeman and Nazi flags—the flags hinting at the well-known brutality of the Los Angeles Police Department that terrorized Latinos and African-Americans as well as lesbians and gay men for so many years. The motorcycle gangs represent the forces of rebellion still unformed and mixed with fascist elements and violence. It is pervaded by homoeroticism, erotic images of male physiques, nudity, and violence. [Hutchison, 2004]

• • •

That same summer Jack Smith shot *Flaming Creatures* on the roof of New York's Windsor Theater downtown on Grand Street. Made for a mere $300, it was a transvestite extravaganza rather than an idolization of machismo and violence. More an abstract montage of the human body—of penises (limp and erect), nipples, feet, and lips—it was a campy and bizarre tale of orgies, vampires, and transvestites rather than a recognizable movie.

Flaming Creatures created a huge sensation in New York in 1963 and 1964. No avant-garde film had ever generated such a huge public outcry. Intentionally shocking as so many of the avant-garde films of the era were, it was considered the most offensive of them all. When it was shown at the Gramercy Arts Theatre the following March, along with *Un Chant d'Amour,* Jean Genet's portrayal of two men stealthily flirting between jail cells, the police raided the theater, confiscated the print, and arrested the program's director for obscenity. "It is a brilliant spoof on sex," wrote Susan Sontag, "and at the same time full of contradictions ... in which bodies, some shapely and convincingly feminine and others scrawny and hairy, tumble, dance, make love." [Sontag, 230] Proclaiming the film as a milestone in the sexual revolution, critic and avant-garde film advocate Jonas Mekas wrote: *"Flaming Creatures* [was] ... a manifesto of the New Sexual Freedom riders." Though seemingly slapdash and by today's standards a little silly, the film's surrealistic and sexually suggestive style influenced directors as different as Federico Fellini and John Waters. [Watson, 72; Banes, 172]

Andy Warhol first saw Jack Smith's film at a private screening at the Film-Maker's Co-op in 1963, and it motivated him to explore film as a medium. Already a famous painter, Warhol was known especially for his *Campbell's Soup Can* paintings and *Brillo* boxes. Pale and appearing frail, Warhol was a leader of the nascent Pop Art movement. Born and raised in Pittsburgh, Pennsylvania, in 1928, Warhol was a sickly youth who had suffered from St. Vitus' dance—a neurological disorder that caused involuntary movements—a complication of scarlet fever. He was frequently bedridden and unable to attend school, so he turned to art to occupy his time. He studied commercial design at the Carnegie Institute of Technology and upon graduation moved to New York City. There, he embarked upon a successful career in magazine illustration and advertising. Despite his financial success as a commercial artist, he wanted to be recognized as a serious artist. Nevertheless, effeminate and "obviously" homosexual, he had difficulty achieving acceptance in the macho art world of the 1950s.

In his early thirties he began to make paintings of various consumer products—the most notorious being the *Campbell's Soup Can* paintings that were the subject of his first one-man show in July 1962 at the Ferus Gallery in Los Angeles. The show received a great deal of publicity—most of it critical or sardonic. Art critic and philosopher Arthur Danto felt that Warhol's paintings of Campbell's soup cans and Brillo boxes marked a new era in the history of art and initiated a "post-historical" era in which "high" and "low" art blended together—from which a new pluralism emerged that changed the way art was made. [Danto, 3–12]

Throughout his life, Warhol explored erotic themes, frequently making "explicit homoerotic works" for his own private enjoyment. In the late fifties, he once proposed a show of drawings of "boys kissing boys." The artists who ran the gallery rejected the proposal because, as one explained, "the subject matter was treated ... too aggressively, too importantly, that it should be sort of matter of fact and self-explanatory." A rather mystifying explanation, typical of its time, but obviously homophobic. [Meyer, 95] At around the same time, he also made a series of "cock drawings." His assistant Nathan Gluck recalled:

> "Andy had this great *passion* for drawing people's cocks, and he had pads and pads and pads of drawings of people's lower regions: they're drawings of the penis, the balls and everything, and there'd be a little heart on them or tied with a little ribbon ... every time he got to know somebody, even a friend sometimes, he'd say 'Let me draw your cock'." [Meyer, 121]

He made many such drawings in the 1950s and often told friends that he was compiling a *Cock Book*. He was also a foot fetishist and just as often asked his friends and acquaintances if he could make drawings for a *Foot Book*. During the same period, Warhol made a series of collages of shoes representing some of his most cherished celebrities—among them Truman Capote, Judy Garland, Christine Jorgenson, Elvis Presley, and Zza Zza Gabor. [Meyer, 111–15]

BEEFCAKE

To some degree, the films of Kenneth Anger, Jack Smith, and Andy Warhol took for granted the gay male erotic culture that had begun to emerge in the 1950s. It started as an underground phenomenon, with small magazines containing photographs of almost nude men being sold on newsstands in the larger cities. These "physique magazines" and the mail-order businesses based upon them were the primary source of erotic male images for gay men.

Bob Mizer, an amateur photographer living in Los Angeles, played a major role in developing the business of publishing homoerotic images. At the time, most photographs of nude men or drawings of erotic scenes were available only through private networks or to "select mail-order customers." Long aware of his attraction to men, Mizer had taken nude photographs of attractive male friends since he was a teenager and developed the film in a closet set up as a dark room.

Mizer initially organized a modeling agency that would book attractive young men to pose for artists and photographers. He called it the Athletic Models Guild and set it up in the garage of his family's home in a residential neighborhood south of Hollywood. He usually photographed the men unclothed and had no difficulty recruiting young men to model. While some of them were available for sex, Mizer, in those early years, apparently took his own erotic pleasure primarily from the act of photographing them. It was a family business: both Mizer's mother and brother worked with him. His brother, who was heterosexual, handled the bookkeeping, and Mizer's mother knitted the posing straps for the models. [Hooven, 62]

Mizer particularly favored young streetwise toughs who exhibited rough masculine attitudes together with a degree of naiveté and cynicism. Many had just gotten out of prison; most had no stable residence or means of contact. Few ever showed up for their bookings—and other photographers soon ceased to rely on AMG models. But Mizer's photographs sold rather well. He placed ads in the back of physical culture and weightlifters' magazines.

In 1948, however, the United States Post Office conducted one of its periodic campaigns to clean up the mail-order advertisements in men's magazines—clamping down on sales of naughty sexually suggestive heterosexual cartoons, recordings of risqué night club acts, and novelty items, as well as images of nude women and men. The Post Office warned the magazine publishers that if they did not exclude such advertising they would not be able to use the mails. Though the ads were technically not illegal, the magazines quickly banned all physique ads.

In response, Mizer suggested to the other physique photographers that they pool their mailing lists and send out their catalogues jointly—thus minimizing the Post Office's opportunities for harassment. A couple of years later, when Mizer was experimenting with grouping the pages together, it occurred to him to create a magazine. He decided to call it *Physique Pictorial*. It featured photographs of young men wearing only posing straps, bathing suits, or loincloths and almost no editorial content—except that is, for the long and deceptively chatty, highly opinionated captions that often functioned implicitly more like editorials. [Nealon, 99–139]

Mizer took copies of the first issue to a popular newsstand on the corner of Cahuenga and Hollywood boulevards—known as a very cruisey corner for sexual pickups. It quickly sold out; soon other newsstands agreed to carry it as well. *Physique Pictorial* was a smash hit and soon spawned many imitators. By the mid-fifties there were more than a dozen small-scale format (five-by-eight-inch's) beefcake magazines—*Physique Pic-*

torial, Grecian Guild Pictorial, Tomorrow's Man, Body Beautiful, Young Adonis—all publishing photographs and illustrations centering on attractive, almost nude young men, often posed as sailors, centurions, wrestlers, and body builders. [Hooven, Waugh] In their back pages, photographs of tanned and oiled bodybuilders were available by mail order.

As F. V. Hooven points out in *Beefcake*, his history of the physique magazine, the magazines were not merely one aspect of a wider gay male culture, "they virtually *were* gay culture." [Hooven, 74] One writer estimated that the total circulation of the beefcake magazines in those oppressive times was over 750,000—probably the largest audience of gay male readers and consumers assembled to that point. [Waugh, 215–19]

The cult of male beauty that the physique magazines fostered helped shape gay men's physical ideals before there was any common culture. "A minuscule magazine featuring a bunch of guys with their clothes off but not completely naked may not seem like much of a revolution in the history of sex," argues Hooven. "But to the men who bought them, they were something new and daring. It took courage to purchase one of those little magazines in 1955." [Hooven, 52]

By 1958, Mizer decided to branch out and began to shoot short 8mm black-and-white films of the same young men cavorting by the pool or dressed in Greek tunics. Made in Mizer's Los Angeles home-based studio, a fortress-like compound of seven buildings protected by fences lined with razor wire and numerous attack dogs, the films employed simple story lines in which the youthful performers usually played stock characters—athletes, sailors, prisoners, and blue-collar workers. Cowboy and Indian motifs, leopard-skin loincloths, and Grecian pillars were frequent costumes and props. The wrestling film in particular was an AMG staple. [Waugh, 255–73; Watson, 237–38]

By the mid-sixties Mizer had photographed more than five thousand male models, many of them street kids, hustlers, body builders, actors, soldiers, and sailors. One young man who showed up on Mizer's doorstep in 1965 was Joe Dalle-sandro, a young runaway from upstate New York.

Only sixteen years old, he had escaped from a juvenile home in the Catskills and hitchhiked to California where he supported himself by hustling. Taken in by an African-American man who lived in Watts, Dallesandro also worked as a dish-washer in a pizza parlor. He was an attractive and well-built youth. Apparently, "an admirer" had suggested that he contact AMG to earn a little extra money posing. He told Mizer that he was nineteen years old and gave his occupation as "short order cook." His greatest ambition was to own his own Italian restaurant. Mizer taught him how to oil his body, comb and part his hair, and thrust his hips forward in order to show off his abs. In Dallesandro's one session with him, Mizer shot twenty minutes of film as well as numerous stills.

Dallesandro was grateful for his introduction to Mizer and the world of beefcake. Years later he told Steve Watson:

> "My introduction to the gay world did two
> things ...[o]ne, it saved me from life in prison for
> murder, which is probably where I would have
> wound up. How? Because the gay world showed
> me that you didn't have to beat up every man you
> saw or hurt people to make a point. Two, it
> taught me never to be homophobic, even before
> there was such a term." [Watson, 238.]

In 1966, *Drum* magazine, published in Philadelphia, and the San Francisco-based magazine *Butch* published photographs of frontal male nudity. Clearly intended as deliberate provocations, they resulted in Clark Pollak, the editor of *Drum*, being quickly arrested for obscenity. Joined by the American Civil Liberties Union, he fought the case all the way to the U.S. Supreme Court. After several years, during which time Pollak lost control of the magazine, the court ruled that the nude male body is not obscene. This is all quite ironic, since *Playboy*, founded in 1953, had of course already published hundreds of female nudes.

By the mid-sixties, virtually all of the physique studios, many of them based in Los Angeles where models were plentiful, had faced legal prosecution for obscenity. Mizer was extremely cautious and declared publicly that he had never photographed frontal nudity and had managed for a long time to avoid any legal problems. After his death the man who bought the AMG archives revealed that Mizer had actually photographed men frontally nude and made hardcore sex films.

Prostitution and nude modeling for artists and photographers have a long shared history. Mizer regularly recommended AMG models to other photographers and to "collectors" even though he must have realized that the young men were probably being hired for sex. But since he had never directly benefited from the exchange of sex for money from any of his referrals, he did not consider himself vulnerable. At the same time, over the years he had developed an elaborate set of codes to summarize information about each of his models: temperament, honesty, and physical traits, as well as sexual characteristics and interests. He offered the key to the code to various "trusted" customers. Nevertheless, the secret code seemed suspicious to the LAPD Vice Squad, which arrested him for running a prostitution ring. He was convicted and, though he never revealed it to anyone, he seems to have spent some time in 1968 in jail—the very profitable *Physique Pictorial* failed to appear throughout most of 1968. By the time he returned to his studio, the world of gay male pornography had dramatically changed. [Hooven, 124]

SEX FACTORY

In the same summer that Kenneth Anger lurked under the boardwalk at Coney Island eavesdropping on teenagers listening to Top 40 and Jack Smith shot *Flaming Creatures*, Andy Warhol made *Kiss*. He setup a Bolex camera on a tripod, turned on the lights, and two people kissed until the camera's three-minute magazine ran out. It was very simple—usually a black-and-white close-up of a man and a woman kissing. Full lips, mouths wet, their tongues sliding and energetically probing each other. The man's eyes are closed, the woman's open. The kiss is interrupted every three minutes with the flicker of a white screen, then the kissing resumes again. In each "episode," different pairs of women and men are kissing. But it is often difficult to tell the couples apart. The whole film lasts about an hour and is silent, without even any music. The camera almost never changes position. [Koch, 17–21; Watson, 117–19]

While it was being filmed, *Kiss* provoked a degree of competition among its participants. "Smart and original people realized it was an opportunity to do something clever," recalled Stephen Holden, who was one of the kissers. Critic Parker Tyler agreed, saying the competition was "forcing them to fresh prodigies of osculative style to justify, it seems, the camera time being spent on them." [Watson, 118]

Later that year Warhol made *Blow Job,* whose title alone creates "pornographic" expectations. The entire course of the thirty-minute film focuses on the face of a handsome young man who is presumably getting his cock sucked. We never see the fellatio itself, or who is giving the man a blow job. We don't know whether it is a man or a woman nor can we even be sure that it is a "real" blow job. It is a pure reaction shot. Again, the camera is immobile, focused only on the man's face. We see him gaze into space, look down, drift off into an erotic reverie; we see him wince and relax; now and then he seems about to have an orgasm. Finally, after a moment of apparent ecstasy, he lights a cigarette. We assume that he's had an orgasm. "Perhaps the greatest film Warhol ever made," writes Wayne Koestenbaum, "*Blow Job* [is] a film of almost unbearable intimacy—unbearable, because one realizes watching it, that one has never before spent forty minutes without pause unselfishly looking at a man's face during the course of his slow movement toward orgasm." [Koch, 47–51; Koestenbaum, 72]

Warhol made a third "erotic" film in that same period: *Couch*. Though it has been screened very rarely, it's more sexually explicit than either *Kiss* or *Blow Job*. Filmed in 1964, *Couch* consists of various scenes of people engaged in sex play with each other on a couch. Its title is a play on the ideas of both the psychoanalytic couch and the casting couch. Naomi Levine, who had participated in *Kiss* and had kissed more performers than anyone else in it, was also in *Couch*. She was filmed gyrating naked on a couch in an attempt to attract the interest of a young man who pays more attention to his motorcycle than to her ample breasts. Another young woman was fucked in the ass by Warhol's assistant Gerard Malanga as she lay on top of a black dancer. Malanga, though straight, was also shown getting a hand job from Warhol "superstar" Ondine (whose real name was Robert Olivo). There are many awkward or comic moments in the film, as when Ondine throws a scarf over Malanga's body or wears his glasses while performing fellatio. Sex is treated as an everyday activity, much like eating or sleeping. As in *Kiss*, some viewers saw *Couch* as an exposé of the poverty of heterosexual sex—and implicitly the acceptance of homosexuality as a normal sexual practice. [Bockris, 203; Koestenbaum, 75–76; Watson, 159–160]

In *Kiss*, *Blow Job*, and *Couch,* the camera's immobility transforms these erotic acts into abstractions. Sex becomes impersonal. The "real" action takes place outside the frame. Time slows down. The close-ups create a powerful sense of intimacy. The voyeur becomes a machine. In both *Kiss* and *Blow Job* Warhol withholds our direct engagement with the sexual activity implied by each film. They require us to imagine or fantasize the sex. The films' perversity lies in creating that intimacy, stimulating our arousal, and then denying our voyeuristic impulses and thwarting release from our excitement. But then we wait; we wait for the "end." They incite the "itch" but not the "scratch" of sex: the pleasure of arousal, not the pleasure of release. It is this that makes Warhol's nonexplicit "pornography" so deeply perverse.

Each of the films he made that year drew upon the "voyeurism" that Warhol believed was the foundation of film as a medium. The "erotic" films like *Kiss, Blow Job,* and *Couch* were only a handful of the films—all in the same style—that Warhol made in the early sixties of people performing such banal tasks as applying makeup, making coffee, talking on the phone, gossiping, having casual sex, drinking, arguing, kissing, getting a haircut, sleeping, and eating. "My first films using the stationary objects," Warhol noted in an interview at the time, "were made to help the audience get more acquainted with themselves. Usually, when you go to the movies, you sit in a fantasy world, but when you see something that disturbs you, you get more involved with the people next to you." [Bockris, 191]

Years later, in 1969 after he had ceased making films like these, Warhol compared his style of shooting these early erotic films to "beavers," soft-core pornographic films made during the sixties of young woman nude and showing only their pubic areas. Beavers were a milestone in the development of pornographic films. These movies were initially made and sold through mail order, but sometime around 1967 they started playing in peep show arcades and theaters in San Francisco. According to Kenneth Turan and Stephen Zito in *Sinema*, their book about the beginnings of the American pornographic film business, beavers were made with "a staggering artlessness, and there was, at first, no overt sexual content. The performers were not strippers but rather young girls who were earning a little spare cash to put themselves through San Francisco State or Berkeley." [T&Z, 77]

Warhol considered "beavers" kindred films to *Kiss, Blow Job,* and *Couch,* his early erotic movies, as he explained in a 1969 interview:

> INTERVIEWER: It's been suggested that your stars are all compulsive exhibitionists and that your films are therapy. What do you think?
>
> WARHOL: Have you seen any beavers? They're

where girls take off their clothes completely. And they're always alone on a bed. Every girl is always on a bed. And then they sort of fuck the camera.

INTERVIEWER: Have you actually made a beaver yet?

WARHOL: Not really. We go in for artier films for popular consumption, but we're getting there. Like sometimes people say we've influenced so many other filmmakers. But the only people we've really influenced is that beaver crowd. The beavers are so great. ... It's always on a bed. It's really terrific. [Koestenbaum, 77–78]

In 1964, Warhol moved into a new studio on East 47th Street in Manhattan, which was christened The Silver Factory—called that because Billy Linich (aka Billy Name), one of his assistants, had covered its walls entirely in silver foil. It was in the Factory, at its various locations, that Warhol assembled a loose group of people—speed freaks, drag queens, poets, artists, fashion models, and "Superstars." Most of the work produced in the Factory was collaborative. There, more than five hundred movies were made, a novel and other books were published, and a record and hundreds of photographs were produced. "I don't really feel all these people with me every day at the Factory are just hanging around me," Warhol explained. "I'm more hanging around them." [Watson, xii–xiii]

In 1965, Warhol returned to erotic subject matter again in *My Hustler*. It is a more psychological film than Warhol's earlier erotic films. The movie has a loose narrative, and perhaps most importantly it has a sound track—allowing for a degree of character development. Set at Fire Island Pines, the film opens out with a panoramic view of a beach, the ocean in the background. As we move closer, we see a handsome young man, Paul America, sitting in a beach chair. On the sound track, we hear the voices of a man (Ed Hood), another man, and a woman. The camera represents their gaze. Paul America is viewed close-up, handsome, and muscular, with dyed blond hair. Off screen, the men and the woman are quarrelling:

> "Don't even try to look innocent," we hear a snappish, queeny voice say. "You can't fool me. I know what both of you are here for and what you're after. I know you, you're not exactly complex, neither one of you has anything better to do with your time except to go around vamping a faggot's tricks. Well, I'm sorry to tell you you're not going to get away with it this time. He's mine. Mine."

> "Where'd you find him?" the other male voice queries.

> "What on earth *can* you mean, where'd I find him?" Hood replies.

> "I mean, like did you pick him up on the street?" Hood's male interlocutor asks.

> "The street! Hardly, my dear. That sort of thing is more your style. Street pickups are for aging out-of-work hustlers like you who've decided they've got to like it. Oh no—the streets indeed."

So the conversation goes. Hood ultimately reveals that he got Paul America, his hustler, from an agency called Dial-a-Hustler. Throughout this conversation the camera's eye remains steadily on Paul, without moving.

Cut to three people—Ed Hood, the man, and the woman—sitting on the deck of a beach house, having a drink. Hood's friends propose a bet—they will try to seduce the hustler away from the Ed Hood character. He accepts the challenge. First the woman, Genevieve Charbon, goes out onto the beach to seduce the hustler. Very quickly she is smoothing suntan oil over Paul America's back; then a white flickering screen appears and the first reel ends abruptly.

The second reel opens with two hustlers standing together in a bathroom—an older hustler (perhaps in his early thirties) shaves, washes his hands, and combs his hair as the handsome young hustler watches, waiting for his turn. Two men vie for their primacy in front of the mirror. The hustlers exchange beauty tips and discuss prostitution as work.

By the film's end nothing is settled—no one wins the bet made in the first reel. As the film closes, Hood and Charbon are arguing over Dial-a-Hustler's newest delivery. Warhol's friend Dorothy Dean interrupts the dialogue of the hustlers and makes another offer: "I'll get you educated. After all, why be carved up by these old faggots?"

Dean and her friend Chuck Wein—he is credited as "director"—had originally suggested making the movie. Dean had wanted another friend, Joe Campbell, to play the young hustler. Long infatuated with Campbell, Dean had repeatedly asked him to be the father of her child—not only because he was so handsome, but also so sweet-tempered.

When she proposed the project to him, she told him: "You're going to be a star, the movie's about hustling."

"That's a big subject," Campbell replied, remembering his own quite extensive experience as an escort. Eventually Campbell was cast as the "older" hustler. For many years he had had a relationship with Harvey Milk before the future politician moved to San Francisco. After they broke up, he had drifted from New York to Florida and back again, finding it difficult to make a living and get on with his life.

There was no scenario, so Wein had invited two friends of his from Cambridge, Hood and Chabron, who would be able to sustain the bitchy repartee that Wein thought was necessary for the film. The last addition to the cast was Paul Johnson, a muscular and handsome man whom one of Warhol's friends had picked up hitchhiking from the end of Long Island. Johnson was soon rechristened Paul America.

In contrast to Warhol's earlier movies, Wein had proposed making a narrative movie. Just before shooting started, Wein told Paul Morrissey, who was relatively new to Warhol's circle, "We can't let Andy just turn the camera on and let it run—we're not just going to waste this whole trip. You operate the camera, and I'll tell them what to do, and we'll make something like a real movie with stops and starts." [Watson, 233–34]

Morrissey hesitated. "It's not realistic," he explained, "to take two or three people out on a boat and think you're going to make a movie that's going to go out into theaters.... At that point I didn't think these things were possible." [Watson, 234–35] At first, Warhol didn't want to move the camera. He asked Morrissey to do it, so Morrissey panned the camera from Ed Hood and Genevieve Chabron to Paul America on the beach.

The interchange between Johnson (Paul America) and Campbell is hustlers' small talk, neither witty nor even bitchy. On screen there was clearly no chemistry between the two. Warhol had told them that the scene should be sexy, but the only direction he gave to Campbell was to open the medicine cabinet and read the brand names of what was there. It hadn't helped that Campbell didn't know he wasn't playing the hustler at the center of the film until they all had arrived at the Pines. Instead Campbell played the over-the-hill hustler—a role that resonated all too personally. Campbell found Paul America completely uninteresting. "He had nothing," Campbell recalled. "I guess he was a shape, but there was nothing inside. He had no lust, no desire, no agenda of any kind, even in drugs." The scene came off more jaded than sexy. "I sure wish it could have been someone responsive," Campbell concluded. "It was like talking to a dead person." [Watson, 235]

My Hustler, so different from Warhol's slow and silent minimalist films of people eating, sleeping, kissing, or getting blow jobs—or of films like *Empire,* which was of the Empire State Building over the course of twenty-four hours—was a hit at the small theaters showing avant-garde films. It is a movie about "sex" or at least as much about sex as movies of that period allowed—that is, no explicit sex—and definitely about homosexual desire between men. Pornographic films of the time had not yet begun to show explicit sex, nor were there any gay-themed soft-core movies in theaters then. Warhol's movies encapsulate, as Wayne Koestenbaum argues, "what it feels like to wait for sex; to wait, during sex, for it to end; to wait, during sex's prelude, for 'real' sex to begin; to desire a man you are looking at; to endure postponement, perhaps for a lifetime, as you wait for the man to turn around and look back at you." [Koestenbaum, 12]

Pornography as it came to develop in the very late sixties and after was less about waiting per se than it was about fantasy as a prelude to desire. As the first Warhol film to reflect the influence of Paul Morrissey, *My Hustler* does not push the film to its limit as a medium, but instead is the first of Warhol's cinematic explorations of the male body—and the emotional preoccupation with time, waiting, and homosexual desire.

My Hustler closely resembles a documentary film in its *cinema verité* style—a documentary of homosexual desire at one historical moment. Porn filmmaking, as it developed after 1969, included a strong documentary impulse—ultimately documenting and authenticating male sexual arousal and release. Warhol's *cinema verité* of desire focused almost exclusively on foreplay as a prelude to orgasm.

Despite the lack of explicit sex in his movies, Warhol remained obsessed with sex and male sex organs, very much in the spirit of the beaver films.

> "During this period [the sixties] I took thousands of Polaroids of genitals.... Whenever somebody came up to the Factory, no matter how straight-looking he was, I'd ask him to take his pants off so I could photograph his cock and balls. It was surprising who'd let me and who wouldn't." [Warhol, 294]

The Polaroids were obviously a continuation of his passion

for the "cock drawings" he made in the 1950s.

During this period, Paul Morrissey emerged as Warhol's primary artistic partner for his film projects. Unlike many of Warhol's other collaborators, Morrissey had no interest in the art world and was hostile to the drug use of the Factory's other denizens. He had always wanted to make commercial films and had persuaded Warhol that it was possible to make money from the sort of films he was shooting. [Bockris, 239]

In 1966 Warhol and Morrissey decided to make a movie on a larger scale than any they'd done before. They wanted to film a big hit. Warhol began to shoot short half-hour sequences of various people in his entourage exposing their most intimate feelings or in conflict with one another. The film had no overall plot, no scripts except perhaps some notes or sketches. Like his other films, each segment was shot in one take until the thirty-five-minute reel of film ran out. As Warhol explained, "This way I can catch people being themselves instead of setting up a scene and shooting it and letting people act out parts that were written.... It's better to act naturally than act like someone else. These are experimental films which deal with human emotions and human life." [Bockris, 255]

This "directorial" philosophy put the burden of performing an interesting scene on the performers themselves. Personal animosities among the performers and the extensive drug use fed into the process. Warhol and Morrissey primed the pump by circulating rumors of what performers had said about one another. They shot between twelve and fifteen reels—including scenes with Robert Olivo (aka Ondine), the fast-talking and vitriolic ranter playing the "Pope of Greenwich Village"; Brigid Berlin in the role of a drug dealer shooting up amphetamine through her blue jeans; Gerard Malanga playing an irresponsible hippie being reprimanded by his mother, acted by experimental filmmaker Marie Menken; drag queen Mario Montez being reduced to tears by two bitchy gay men; sweet-natured hippie Eric Emerson telling the story of his life and stripping naked; Hanoi Hannah as a dominatrix with two lesbians; and the idle chatter of a middle-aged homosexual in bed with a hustler. [Bockris, 255; Koch, 90–91]

When it came time to put *The Chelsea Girls* (as Warhol and Morrissey decided to call the film) together for screening at the Cinematheque, New York's premier venue for avant-garde filmmakers, they had six and half hours of film consisting of at least twelve to fifteen different segments. It was much too long for any screening, so they decided to show two reels next to each other at the same time. "The juxtaposition of actors and action, color and black and white, sound and silence," Victor Bockris noted, "gave *Chelsea Girls* a visually beautiful impact as well as a schizophrenic effect, particularly when the same players appeared in two reels running next to each other exposing different aspects of their personalities, and turned it into something much greater than any of the individual films alone." [Bockris, 256] Yet it was also a devastatingly harsh self-portrait of Andy Warhol's world. "It's our godless civilization approaching the zero point." wrote Jonas Mekas in the *Village Voice*. "It's not homosexuality, it's not lesbianism, it's not heterosexuality: the terror and hardness that we see in *Chelsea Girls* is the same terror and hardness that is burning Vietnam and it's the essence and blood of our culture, of our way of living: this is the Great Society."

Chelsea Girls is considered one of Warhol's masterpieces. It was an immediate and stupendous hit. It moved from the small, cramped, underground showcase at the Cinematheque to leading mainstream movie theaters uptown. Both praised and reviled, it gave Warhol the highest public profile and the largest audience he had ever achieved. [Bockris, 256–59]

Bosley Crowther, the *New York Times* movie critic, attacked *Chelsea Girls* as the harbinger of civilization's end:

> More disturbing than the contagious lethargy of the movie is the deeper message: these dreamy swingers, playing their games, clearly question the most basic assumptions of our culture—

namely that heterosexual coupling, happy or unhappy, moral or immoral, is a socially significant enterprise worthy of the closest possible scrutiny. Hollywood's tinsel titillation and art house film's hard bedrock fornication are replaced by a new sexual mythology, a cool low-keyed playful polymorphism. The message flashed ... is utterly subversive. [Bockris, 264]

Writer Gore Vidal took the opposite tack. "To make fun of the art of the cinema," he wrote, "by just showing boys taking their pants down just because everybody wanted to see their cocks, and doing it over and over and over again and really blowing the minds of those people who write about the movies, I thought that was really genius." [Bockris, 264]

• • •

After the success of *The Chelsea Girls*, Warhol was contacted by the manager of the Hudson Theater, just off Times Square, for something that he would be able to show there. Morrissey suggested *My Hustler*: "They want to show something, and the title will make them think it's a sex film like all the girl films being shown there." [Watson, 336] *My Hustler* opened there in July 1967 and grossed $18,000 in its first week. The gossip magazine *Confidential* magazine reported, "*My Hustler* has touched off the trend toward full homosexual realism in the movies. The reason according to the film critics, is that it is the first full length film to take a look at the lavender side of life without pointing a finger in disgust or disdain, but concentrating instead on the way life really is in the limp-wristed world." [Watson, 336–37]

Considering that it didn't even have any soft-core sex scenes, *My Hustler* did surprisingly well. Maura asked Warhol for something more like the Swedish art film *I, a Woman*, which was about a woman's sexual development. Morrissey and Warhol decided to make a film called *I, a Man* and asked the "pan-sexual" Doors singer Jim Morrison to star in it. When Morrison declined, they used his friend Tom Baker. It was to show a series of sexual encounters between Baker and eight different women. For commercial reasons, they sought to appeal to both gay and straight men. But Baker refused to engage in intercourse, fearing that it would jeopardize his acting career—which never materialized in any case. In the end, Baker was the only nude performer and did nothing more than caress or massage his clothed female costars.

Warhol and Morrissey's next "big" movie was *Lonesome Cowboys*. Warhol and Morrissey had conceived of the project during a visit to Tucson, Arizona. They started shooting in January of 1968. The production involved transporting the whole Warhol entourage to a small town in Arizona—including Warhol "Superstar" Viva along with stalwarts Taylor Mead, Eric Emerson, and Louis Waldon and newcomer Joe Dallesandro. Viva starred as a rich rancher battling a local gang of cowboys led by Louis Waldon.

In this film Warhol abandoned his signature method of setting up a camera and focusing it on a group of people until the film ran out and instead turned the camera over to Paul Morrissey, who gradually assumed the directorial role. Morrissey's strong directorial hand changed the dynamics between the camera and the actors. With Morrissey giving directions like "You gotta fight!" or "Take your pants down!" the actors gradually ceased to react to one another directly and this had the effect of minimizing the improvisatory chaos that gave Warhol's performers their distinctive personas.

Morrissey and Warhol had very different philosophies of filmmaking. Morrissey believed that "movies are a medium that are traditionally and necessarily grounded in a literary and dramatic framework and has only an incidental connection to poetry and painting," [Watson, 222] while Warhol worked with static images, repetitions, and single words as concepts to organize a film. While neither believed in premeditated scenarios, they differed on the method of editing. For Warhol the "reel" was the unit of editing; Morrissey, however, was willing to change the camera's location and use the zoom.

The artistic differences between Warhol, who was reluctant to abandon the immobile camera and minimal editing, and Morrissey, who wanted to make commercial, more narratively oriented films, generated a great deal of tension among the actors on the set. Many of them preferred Warhol's position. Almost in a reversal of their ordinary roles in a Warhol movie, the characters they played spilled over into their behavior behind the scenes. Eric Emerson, ordinarily so gentle and sweet natured, got carried away and initiated an unplanned simulated gang rape of Viva while filming—believed to be a punishment for her being temperamental. She was outraged, and although she allowed filming to continue, she stormed off the set when the filming was done. Rumors of a "rape" brought local police and "vigilantes" around to investigate. Surveillance by the local officials, first provoked by rumors of the "rape," became so disruptive that Warhol decided to stop shooting in Arizona and return to New York to finish the movie. [Bockris, 285–93] But someone had also filed a complaint with the FBI. Warhol discussed the situation with Billy Name, one of his assistants:

> WARHOL: Oh, you know the FBI ... think Viva was really raped in the cowboy movie.

> NAME: that FBI man said, you know, you know what it was, he told me someone had complained that guys were going down on her and she was going down on the guys. That's the thing that upset ... that got some people to get the FBI on us. It's not the rape thing, it's that supposedly people saw her going down on guys.

> WARHOL: We don't have that in the movie, do we?

NAME: No, she didn't do it. [Bockris, 292–93]

After the shoot in Arizona was interrupted, neither Warhol nor Morrissey worked on the movie until the following year.

When *Lonesome Cowboys* was released in May 1969, it was widely perceived as Warhol's most popular movie at the box office—though critics saw it as flawed, even a bad movie, and a real failure in light of Warhol's early films and especially *The Chelsea Girls*. Yet *Lonesome Cowboys* represented a shift in Warhol's approach to cinema and his portrayal of sex. It is a cowboy movie—a traditionally macho genre dominated by actors like John Wayne. Like many Westerns, the cast is mostly men. But in *Lonesome Cowboys* the relations between men in nature—that is, out in the open, without any clothes on—are portrayed as tender and free. Machismo is merely a front, something you put on like your clothes. Nudity is freedom and joy. Nakedness is almost utopian.

HUSTLERS AND SUPERSTARS

In the summer of 1968, the British director John Schlesinger came to New York to film *Midnight Cowboy*. Based on Leo Herlihy's novel, it told the story of a naïve young man from Texas who comes to New York City to make a living escorting wealthy women.

Schlesinger had originally asked Warhol to play the role of an underground film director. But Warhol suggested instead that Schlesinger hire Viva and cast various other Warhol stars as extras—Ondine, Taylor Mead, and Joe Dallesandro were among those cast as participants in a typical sixties party scene.

While Warhol was in the hospital recuperating from an attempted assassination by Valerie Solanis, he and Morrissey regularly discussed the making of John Schlesinger's *Midnight Cowboy*, which was being shot in New York at the time. They both felt that Schlesinger had moved into their own territory.

Only in Schlesinger's case, United Artists was paying three million dollars to make the story of a hustler. When Paul relayed that only a few of Warhol's players were working as extras, Warhol suggested, "Why don't you go out and make a movie like that, and we could have it out before theirs? And you could use all the kids that they didn't bother to use." Morrissey loved the idea, and since Warhol was still in the hospital he thought "I finally won't have Andy operating the camera.... So this was a good chance to disengage from Andy having to be there to push the button." [Watson, 386–87]

Morrissey quickly assembled a cast. Many were regulars at Max's Kansas City, a popular bar and restaurant frequented by Warhol regulars. Others were Warhol stalwarts such as Louis Waldon, transvestites Jackie Curtis and Candy Darling, and Joe Dallasandro, who played a male hustler who must raise two hundred dollars to pay for an abortion for his wife's best friend.

Flesh opened with a long shot of Dallesandro lying in bed sleeping nude—a reference back to Warhol's first movie, the six-hour-long *Sleep* in which Warhol's boyfriend John Giorno slept through the entire movie. But in *Flesh* there was a plot and the camera was engaged in it. The beautiful and sweet Joe Dallesandro emerged as an exalted object of adoration. As happened with porn stars later, many fans assumed that the young man named Joe in his movies was the same person they saw on the screen; and they were not completely mistaken. *Flesh* was the first American film to have full-frontal male nudity and Dallesandro played much of it in the nude.

Hustler, athlete, photographer's model, Dallesando had a presence that evoked the world of the physique magazines and the 8mm movies. At one point, a prospective hustler protests to Joe that he is straight. Dallesandro replies with a worldly fatalism: "Nobody's straight—what's straight? You just do whatever you have to do. It's hard to learn how to do that but once you got it down pat, don't even think about it no more ... he's only going to suck your peter."

Flesh made Joe Dallesandro into an international movie

star—the first who achieved fame as a nude actor in what some people called at the time a pornographic movie. [Watson, 387–89] He was also the first male sex symbol to be openly eroticized—as much by gay men as by women—and was counted as one of the ten most beautiful men that the well-known fashion photographer Francesco Scavullo had ever photographed. Dallesando's crotch was photographed for the album cover of the Rolling Stones' *Sticky Fingers*.

Dallesandro was only eighteen when Paul Morrissey and Andy Warhol discovered him. Living at the time in New York City with his wife, he heard that the "Campbell's Soup guy" was making a movie in a friend's apartment building. Warhol was shooting *The Loves of Ondine*, his homage to the brilliant amphetamine-driven ranting transvestite, Ondine. Dallesando and his friends went to watch, but when he poked his head in the door, Morrissey invited him to join the moviemaking. Dallesandro improvised a twenty-three-minute scene in the movie wearing only his jockey shorts.

Morrissey cast Dallesandro in the three movies of his *"Flesh* trilogy." The movie after *Flesh* was to be a "picaresque account of the life of a drug addict." He proposed pairing an addict on a downward spiral with a survivor—someone who was ruthless to "get something out of life." [Watson, 402] It was to be called *Trash*. It also starred Dallesandro, who was paired with one the Factory's drag performers, Holly Woodlawn, as Dallesandro's girlfriend. There was some uncertainty as to whether Woodlawn and Dallesandro would click. But as Morrissey recalled after the first afternoon of filming, "I knew within minutes of filming that my hunch was right and my instinct had paid off. I knew I had my two basic characters and I would have a movie." There was nothing sexual about their chemistry. Dallesandro thought that the scrawny brunette was ugly, but he treated her with a degree of masculine chivalry. Nor was she attracted to Dalle-sandro; Woodlawn was quite devoted to her sixteen-year-old boyfriend. The third installment, again starring Dallesandro, was *Heat*—a campy remake of *Sunset Boulevard*.

Flesh had moved Warhol and Morrissey fully into the realm of commercial soft-core pornography, and in some ways beyond it—it not only included nudity, lesbians, and voyeurism, but also fetishism, transvestitism, and even an erection. It was enthusiastically reviewed by *The Advocate*, the national gay newspaper:

> At last a perfect film has emerged from the Warhol Factory ... Paul Morrissey has added the heretofore missing ingredients—a strong direc- torial touch and superb camera-artistry, along with judicious editing.... Dallesandro is a man of a thousand faces—the shifting of a lock of hair changes his appearance.... Prediction: Joe Dalle- sandro will be a top American film star.

The films Morrissey made under the Warhol aegis extended Warhol's longtime preoccupation with his erotic worship of the male body. Their movies enshrined "the hustler" and "the transvestite" as iconic male figures. Both the hustler and the transvestite divorce their bodies from conventional male social roles. The hustler offers his body for sale; he cedes his sexual preferences, whatever they are, to his customer—in today's parlance, he is gay-for-pay. The transvestite rejects his/her male body (transsexual surgery was not as available and affordable in the sixties as it is today) and the identity that "normally" goes with it.

INTO THE BLUE

Warhol was familiar with the X-rated world of Times Square. He regularly attended peep shows in the arcades, and bought his beefcake magazines there.

> "Personally I loved porno," he wrote in *Popism*, "and I bought lots of it all the time—the really dirty, exciting stuff. All you had to do was figure

out what turned you on, and then just buy the
dirty magazines and movie prints that are right for
you, the way you'd go for the right pills or right
cans of food. (I was so avid for porn that on my
first time out of the house after the shooting I went
straight to 42nd street and checked out the peep
shows with Vera Cruise and restocked on dirty
magazines." [Warhol, 294]

After *Lonesome Cowboys* was released and Paul Morrissey's
Flesh received such a popular reception, Warhol made one last
movie, more or less on his own. The original idea came from Viva
while she was tripping on LSD. She had decided that she wanted
to make a movie about "real sex"—just two people spending time
together and then having sex. She approached Warhol with the
idea during his recuperation from Valerie Solanas's assassination
attempt, and he asked Louis Waldon to be in the film. Waldon
had in fact appeared in some porn movies several years before
hardcore was introduced. They were probably nudies. "In T&A
[tits and ass] movies," Waldon explained, "the woman was
always the focus, the man was just a prop. When Andy said he
wanted us to make love, I knew it wasn't going to be a dong-
and-balls movie, it was going to be sensitive." [Watson, 393]

It was a return to basics, a classic Andy Warhol movie—
fixed camera, no editing, no script, just a man and woman
before, during, and after having sex. "I'd always wanted to do
a movie that was pure fucking," Warhol wrote in *Popism*,
"nothing else, the way *Eat* had been just eating and *Sleep* had
been just sleeping."

Warhol had come full circle. The experiments with scripts
and narratives failed to achieve what he had identified as the
pleasures of watching. In an interview with Leticia Kent from
Vogue magazine, he offered a manifesto for his approach to
movie making—and by virtue of its generality, the cinematic
portrayal of sex:

Scripts bore me. It's much more exciting not to

know what's going to happen. I don't think plot is important. If you see a movie of two people talking you can watch it over and over again without being bored. You get involved—you miss things—you come back to it.... But you can't see the same movie over again if it has a plot because you already know the ending ... Everyone is rich. Everyone is interesting. Years ago, people used to sit looking out of their windows at the street. Or on a park bench. They would stay for hours without being boring although much was going on. *This is my favorite theme in movie making—* just watching something happening for two hours or so ...

Fuck, or *Blue Movie* as it was later called, was shot in a single day. As in the past, Warhol set up the scene—he placed the bed in the middle of his friend David Bourdon's living room— and did the filming himself.

It opens with Viva and Waldon lying clothed on the bed. As they undress, they talk and joke. A running theme is whether or not Viva would suck Waldon's cock. The badinage ends when Viva takes Waldon's cock out of her mouth and declares: "Okay, that's it. This is really boring." [Watson, 392–93] Through most of the movie Viva and Waldon played around in bed and then finally fucked. When the sex was done, they had something to eat.

Morrissey was hardly involved at all during the filming— and in fact, he left during the climactic sex scene, which Malanga attributed to Morrissey's chagrin at failing to successfully "sanitize" the movie—i.e., failing to make it without any sexually explicit activity.

When Viva saw the film, she disliked it intensely. She thought the sex scene was "flat, perfunctory and quite unlike the beautifully choreographed balletic mystical love scene she had envisioned." [Bockris, 315] Warhol had to beg her to sign the release in order to show it in a theater. Waldon, on the other hand, felt differently. He and Viva had previously been in a relationship together. "I really loved Viva," he said, "but I knew we could never make it together. For me, this situation was two people having their last fuck. We meet for the last time, and we do everything backward. We meet, we fuck, we eat." [Watson, 393] Later, Viva thought that the film's ultimate message had more to do with Warhol: "I think my own idea about *Blue Movie*, wasn't, as I believed at the time, to teach the world about 'real love' or 'real sex' but to teach Andy." [Bockris, 315]

Whatever Viva or Morrissey thought of it, *Blue Movie* was a landmark film in the era of the sexual revolution. It was the first sexually explicit feature-length movie with sound to have a theatrical release. [Williams, *Screening Sex*, 104–110] Warhol himself seemed ambivalent about it as well. He told one interviewer that it was about the war in Vietnam. "The movie is about … uh—love not destruction," he said. It was ironic because only the year before, the "soft-core" box office hit *I Am Curious (Yellow)*, which was really about opposition to the war in Vietnam, had been released. Yet it was frequently seized at theaters around the country for obscenity merely on the basis of a few seconds of male frontal nudity and simulated cunnilingus.

Warhol recalled that "when … *Lonesome Cowboys* … began to die pretty quickly, we had to think about what to replace it with, and I wondered if it should be *Fuck*. It was released as *Blue Movie*."

> I was still confused about what was legal in pornography and what wasn't, but at the end of July, what with all sorts of dirty movies playing around town and dirty magazines like *Screw* on every newsstand, we thought, oh why not, and put *Fuck* into the Garrick Theater after changing the title to *Blue Movie*. It ran a week before getting seized by the cops. They came all the way down to the Village, sat through Viva's speeches

about General MacArthur and the Vietnam War, through Louis calling her tits "dried apricots," and through her story about the police harassing her in the Hamptons for not wearing a bra, etc., etc., etc.,—and *then* they seized the print of our movie. Why, I wondered, hadn't they gone over to Eighth Avenue and seized things like *Inside Judy's Box, Tina's Tongue*? Were they more "socially redeeming" maybe? It all came down to what they wanted to seize and what they didn't, basically. It was ridiculous. [Warhol, 294–95]

On September 17, 1969, a judicial panel, deliberating for no more than half an hour, ruled that *Blue Movie* was hardcore pornography on three counts: it aroused prurient interest, it offended community standards, and it had no redeeming social value.

With *Blue Movie*, Warhol's five-year artistic project of pushing against the limits of representing erotic images and showing sex had at last begun to overlap hardcore pornography. A week after filming *Blue Movie*, he proclaimed that "the people who used to do girlie movies copy our movies now and they're really good.... It's real dirty, I mean I've never seen anything so dirty. They copy our technique." [Bockris, 315]

"What's pornography anyway?" Warhol asked rhetorically of *Vogue* reporter Leticia Kent.

> "The muscle magazines are called pornography, but they are really not. They teach you how to have good bodies.... I think movies should appeal to prurient interests. *Blue Movie* was real. But it wasn't done as pornography—it was an exercise, an experiment. But I really do think movies *should* arouse you, should get you excited about people, should be prurient. Prurience is part of the machine. It keeps you happy. It keeps you running." [Watson, 394; Bockris, 327]

By the end of the sixties, many of the underground streams that fed explicit sexual expression in American culture—the underground cinema of Kenneth Anger and Jack Smith, the physique magazines and the gay male subculture, and soft-core erotica, beaver films, and nudies in the peep shows—had begun to surface and flow into one major current. None of these were local phenomena. Each cultural achievement attained a degree of national recognition. Warhol took from these smaller-scale achievements; he improvised, imitated, and experimented with different ways of creating erotic images in film as a way of exploring *the medium's potential to represent sexual experience*. He stopped short of identifying the pornographic possibilities of film as medium.

Novelist and screenwriter Terry Southern, coauthor of the *New York Times* best-seller *Candy*, a pornographic takeoff of Voltaire's *Candide*, and an Oscar-nominated screenwriter whose credits included *Easy Rider*, Stanley Kubrick's *Dr. Strangelove,* and the Jane Fonda vehicle *Barbarella*, summed up Warhol's contribution to pornographic film in his novel *Blue Movie*. About a Hollywood director making a pornographic movie that portrays the entire spectrum of human sexuality, including incest and homosexuality, the novel was published in 1970 just as hardcore movies began to be shown in theaters in San Francisco, New York, and Los Angeles. Early in the novel Boris Adrian, known as B. (widely believed to be based on Stanley Kubrick, to whom the novel is dedicated), a prominent director of "arty" movies, and Sid, a producer, discuss the state of erotic moviemaking at the end of the sixties:

> "I've got to find out," B. said … "how *far* you can take the aesthetically erotic—at what point, if any, it gets to be such a personal thing that it becomes meaningless."
>
> "I got news for you," said Sid, firm and terse, "they been doing it for years—*'underground*

movies' they're called, ever hear of 'em? Andy Warhol? They show *everything*—beaver, cock, the whole store! It's a fucking *industry*, for Chrissake!"

Boris sighed, shaking his head. "They don't show *anything*," he said softly, even sadly, "that's what I'm trying to tell you. They haven't *started* to show anything. No *erection*, no *penetration* ... *nothing*. And besides that, they're *Mickey Mouse* .... *amateurish*, just like the stuff we were looking at tonight—bad acting, bad lighting, bad camera, bad everything. At least in the stag films you actually see them fucking ... in the underground movies, it's only *represented, suggested*— erections and penetration are never shown. So the underground films don't even count. But what I want to know is, why are the other ones— the stag films—always so ridiculous? Why isn't it possible to make one that's really *good*—you know, one that's genuinely poetic and beautiful." [Terry Southern, 28]

REFERENCES

Sally Banes, *Greenwich Village 1963: Avant-Garde Performance and the Effervescent Body* (Durham: Duke University Press, 1993).

Victor Bockris, *Warhol: the Biography, 75th Anniversary Edition* (Boston: Da Capo, 2003).

Arthur Danto, *Beyond the Brillo Box: The Visual Arts in Post-Historical Perspective* (New York: Farrar, Straus and Giroux, 1992).

F. Valentine Hooven, III, *Beefcake: The Muscle Magazines of America 1950-1970* (Köln: Taschen, 2002).

Alice Hutchison, *Kenneth Anger: A Demonic Visionary* (London: Black Dog Publishing, 2004).

Stephen Koch, *Stargazer: The Life, World and Films of Andy Warhol, revised and updated* (New York: Marion Boyars, 2002).

Wayne Koestenbaum, *Andy Warhol* (London: Phoenix, 2003).

Richard Meyer, *Outlaw Representation: Censorship and Homosexuality in Twentieth-Century American Art* (New York: Oxford University Press, 2002).

Christopher Nealon, "The Secret Public of Physique Culture," *Foundlings: Lesbian and Gay Historical Emotion Before Stonewall* (Durham, N.C.: Duke University Press, 2001).

Terry Southern, *Blue Movie* (New York: Grove Press, 1970).

Kenneth Turan and Stephen Zito, *Sinema: American Pornographic Films and the People Who Make Them* (New York: Praeger, 1974). [identified as T&Z]

Steve Watson, *Factory Made: Warhol and the Sixties* (New York: Pantheon, 2003).

Thomas Waugh, *Hard to Imagine: Gay Male Eroticism in Photography and Film from Their Beginning to Stonewall* (New York: Columbia University Press, 1996).

Andy Warhol and Pat Hackett, *Popism: The Warhol Sixties* (San Diego: Harcourt, 1980).

Linda Williams, *Screening Sex* (Durham: Duke University Press, 2008).

Maurice Yacowar, *The Films of Paul Morrissey* (New York: Cambridge University Press, 1993).

CHAPTER TWO

Beefcake in Babylon

"And there's more to sex in L.A. than just sex."

—EVE BABITZ IN *SEX, DEATH AND GOD IN L.A.*

It was June 26, 1968. The sun was bright and the sky cloud-less. Not a typical Los Angeles day in June, which are often grey and sunny at the same time. The storefronts along Alvarado Avenue, across from MacArthur Park, resembled the small shops on the main street of a prosperous suburban com-munity. Only MacArthur Park itself seemed a bit shabby, though ironically it, too, was having a prosperous moment—as a bustling market for pot, acid, cocaine, and heroin.

"A Most Unusual Film Festival," stated the marquee of the Park Theatre. The program listed in the *Los Angeles Free Press* announced Jack Smith's *Flaming Creatures*, Andy Warhol's *My Hustler*, and a Kenneth Anger trilogy. Other films billed for the series included gay soft-core titles like Pat Rocco's *Love is Blue, Nudist Boy Surfers, Boys Out to Ball,* and "Warhol's B-J (call theatre for title!)" This "most unusual film festival" was the first theatrical screening ever—in the United States or even the world for that matter—devoted to all-male, sexually explicit (although not yet hardcore) films.

The Park's film festival was the first public sign of gay erotic filmmaking. It drew upon the local physique photographers to show their 8mm short films theatrically. Its origins lay not so much in a gay political or cultural awakening, but in the economic troubles of the movie industry caused by the rise of television. Of course, America was also in the midst of a sexual revolution and straight Americans had been going to softcore erotic movies for a decade.

• • •

For years, homosexuals in Los Angeles had lived lives of secrecy, pervaded by fear. The LAPD had systematically harassed, entrapped, arrested, and brutally beaten the city's gay men and lesbians. On New Year's Eve 1966, for example, patrons at the Black Cat on Sunset Boulevard, many dressed in drag after the annual costume party at New Faces, another gay bar up the street, were attacked by undercover and uniformed vice cops after a number of customers exchanged the customary kisses with one another at midnight. Numerous patrons were brutally beaten and more than a dozen arrested and forced to lie face down on the sidewalk until squad cars arrived to take them away. Several plainclothes officers chased one patron back to New Faces, where they trampled the woman owner and beat the bartenders unconscious; one was hospitalized for more than a week. The hospitalized bartender was charged with assault and the men who kissed were charged with lewd conduct. A jury found them all guilty.

On February 11, 1967, L.A.'s first gay demonstration to protest police brutality took place. Organized by PRIDE (Personal Rights in Defense and Education), an organization of younger gay men and lesbians, this event occurred more than two years before the famous demonstrations protesting a police raid of the Stonewall in Greenwich Village in New York

City that launched the gay liberation movement in June 1969. [Dawes, 60–61; Faderman & Timmons, 154, 156–57]

Beginning in March 1968, a series of Gay-Ins—modeled on Be-Ins, the counterculture's celebrations of drugs, nudity, and rock music—took place in Griffith Park, a notorious cruising ground made famous by John Rechy's 1963 novel, *City of Night,* and the location of the observatory in James Dean's movie *Rebel Without a Cause,* to protest police entrapment tactics.

Later that year, police harassment at The Patch, another gay bar, provoked further responses from gay men and lesbians. The Patch's owner had been warned that he had to prohibit drag, same-sex groping, and dancing or risk closure by the LAPD. When business dropped off, the owner decided to reinstate these activities. Then one weekend night in August, vice officers burst into the bar, demanded IDs, and arrested several patrons. [Faderman & Timmons, 157–58; Thompson, 6]

Many of the city's lesbians and gay men knew of these events from stories in *The Advocate.* Starting out as a newsletter clandestinely printed in the basement of ABC Television's headquarters, it served as the gay community's newspaper. In the wake of the police brutality and other indignities, L.A.'s gay men and lesbians slowly began to organize politically.

THE PARK THEATRE

"By the Sixties," wrote Kenneth Anger in *Hollywood Babylon,* his sordid chronicle of sexual scandal among the glamorous, "Old Hollywood has died. The battlements of those feudal fiefdoms, the studios, fell one by one to the enemy... television." [Anger, 279] Grand movie palaces fought for the few blockbusters, which often lost money; smaller theaters stood empty.

The trouble had started in 1948 when the U.S. Supreme Court's decision in the Paramount case forced the major Hollywood studios to divest their theater chains. No longer the property of the studios whose films they screened, theaters ceased to be routinely provided with films. Moreover, television had cut deeply into weekly ticket sales. Movie audiences shrank from 78 million ticket buyers a week right at the end World War II to barely 16 million a week by the end of the sixties—a drop of 80 percent in twenty-four years. By the late sixties, movie theaters were so sparsely populated that owners were desperate to bring people back.

The Supreme Court's decision had also reduced the power of the Production Code. For years, strict moral guidelines had been enforced by the studios, making it virtually impossible to exhibit films that failed to pass the censors—including themes only remotely dealing with sexuality. In 1956 the Supreme Court, in another landmark decision, ruled that nudity without sexual behavior itself was not obscene. [Schaefer, 327–30]

The Park Theatre, originally a first-run movie venue, opened in 1911 as the Alvarado Theatre. It was renamed The Park in the mid-sixties, when it started showing nudie-cuties. By 1964, the market for sexploitation movies was flooded. Exhibitors started showing double bills in order to attract audiences, and producers spent more to improve the movies' production values and to promote star names. [Turan & Zito, 17]

Like other theaters, the Park went through all these changes, yet by early 1968 it was not doing very well. Three or four other theaters in that part of town were also playing soft-core films, but there was a gay community in the Westlake district and neighboring Silver Lake. And no one—in LA or anywhere else—was showing erotic movies for them. Ed Kazan, the theater's manager at the time, had previously run a couple of gay bars, and was aware that soft-core gay porn had often been screened in the back rooms of local bars. He suggested running gay soft-core to Shan Sayles and Monroe Beehler, the Park's owners. [Siebenand, 12, 78]

Beehler was enthusiastic about the idea. "Hey, we can get a whole new audience. All I need is to find some filmmakers."

At the time there weren't many gay-oriented films that included an explicitly sexual component. Sayles and Beehler immediately set out to find local gay filmmakers to supply the Park and the other theaters they owned with gay-themed soft-core pornographic movies. They faced a considerable challenge: only 1.4 percent of the thousands of stag films made between 1920 and 1967 were exclusively male homosexual. [Hollis and Knight 56] What *was* available were the films of Kenneth Anger, Jack Smith, and Andy Warhol—the first films with homoerotic imagery to be shown in public. Yet most of these films had been made in the context of avant-garde art scenes, and none of them showed explicit sexual action.

However, Sayles and Beehler soon found a number of local photographers and filmmakers who had already made erotic films. One was Pat Rocco, who had worked as a physique photographer before he started shooting three-minute short films of his models posing. He soon undertook more ambitious and sophisticated narrative shorts that he sold by advertising in the *Los Angeles Free Press,* and built up a substantial mail-order business.

Sayles and Beehler asked to see his work.

"I showed them a few hours of these films," Rocco said in a 1974 interview.

Sayles told Rocco, "These don't belong in a private collection, these belong on the screen. They're good enough to show, and we'd like to start the Park Theatre with them." [Turan & Zito, 110]

In contrast to the sexually charged symbolism of Kenneth Anger or the rough-hewn bohemianism of Warhol, Rocco's movies were more conventionally sentimental. His films usually showed attractive boys holding hands, walking through shady woods, and kissing behind chiffon curtains. They rarely even showed simulated sex. Nevertheless, showing two males kissing was considered daring. One of Rocco's favorites was *Discovery.* Made in 1968, it was shot entirely in Disneyland and followed two young men, naked and kissing on Tom Sawyer's Island. The movie ends with them walking out of Disneyland hand in hand. [T&Z, 109–11]

The Park screened more than sixty of Pat Rocco's soft-core homoerotic short films—"naked boys on the beach films" as director Jerry Douglas later characterized them—in the first year of its gay programming. Business was very good that first year. The theater was pretty full no matter what was showing. Altogether, Rocco made more than a hundred films over the next few years—for the Park and other theaters.

Another local filmmaker was the legendary Bob Mizer of Athletic Model Guild fame. "Most of Mizer's films," noted *Advocate* film reviewer Jim Kepner, "had guys wearing trunks or briefs getting out in the yard to do their daily exercises. Then eventually they took their briefs off and then what they did, while looking like ordinary muscle exercises, was actually intended to get the maximum of flopping." These films were called "danglies" or "backyard cock danglers." Yet, Kepner explained, "there would be hints of sadomasochism. There would be wrestling where they would get into near sodomy positions or slave market situations." [Siebenand, 17]

Mizer and Rocco represented two very different perspectives on the gay male erotic culture that had developed before the sexual revolution of the 1960s. Mizer's beefcake photos and the illustrations he published in the *Physique Pictorial* by artists like Quaitance, Etienne, or Tom of Finland focused on the male figure as sexually desirable: muscles, bulging crotches, dressed in skimpy or tight clothes. Rocco's movies portrayed gay male romance and love, usually of attractive young men; they down-played the sexually desirable masculine figure and the sexual aspect of gay relationships.

Sayles and Beehler realized they would also need to produce new movies if they wanted to keep their theaters busy. Sayles, a large and boisterous man, fancied himself an old-style movie mogul. "He was so flagrant," observed adult film director Scott Hanson, who had once worked for him. "I wouldn't say he was effeminate, but he was so grandiose. Shan was so overpowering that you missed the gay thing. All you saw was some guy acting like a movie producer.... [You would be] sort of stunned by him." [Douglas, *Manshots*, 12/94, 12]

He and Beehler set up Signature Films as a production unit and gutted one of their theaters, converting it into a sound stage and office. They became the founding fathers of the gay porn business in southern California, and sought to establish it in the image of the Hollywood movie studio, but each had a very different style. Sayles modeled himself on the studio boss; Beehler was the practical head of production. Initially they were partners or colleagues managing the Continental Theater chain; Beehler, according to Bob Mizer and Tom DeSimone, left Signature, Continental's production units, to start his own company, Jaguar Productions. Both were considered gay by those they worked with, but there is little evidence either way. One of Beehler's colleagues at Jaguar Productions, the company he started after leaving Signature, mentions that he had a girlfriend.

Brash, ruthless, and flamboyant, Sayles rode roughshod over directors, performers, and theater managers; Beehler was smoother and had a more professional style. "I always had a good relationship during the period when I was under contract to work with [Shan Sayles] and make pictures for him," Rocco recalled.

> "At times though he is a difficult man to get along with. He is a very headstrong man. A man who knows what he wants. He is very definite. He is not often right, but at least he is definite.... [Monroe Beehler] is an unusually fine gentleman, the nicest and most qualified man I know in this business. He is extremely qualified in all areas of filmmaking, production, distribution, and so on. He is easy to deal with, honest, intelligent, and just generally tops in my book." [Siebenand, 77–78]

Many thought that Sayles was unscrupulous—"If it will make a buck, he will do it, no matter what," DeSimone said. For instance, when the Juan Corona killings—Corona, a labor contractor in Texas, raped and murdered twenty-five men and buried their machete-hacked bodies in the orchards owned by local farmers—were in the news, Sayles proposed rereleasing DeSimone's *The Collector*, a controversial soft-core film about a man who kidnapped boys and kept them chained. DeSimone was turned off by the idea of cashing in on such a gruesome event.

"What can I say? He is one of the sharpest people I know," Jim Cassidy observed of Sayles.

> "Very sharp, very clever, very crafty. He has fucked over a lot of people and he is still fucking over a lot—always will.... Shan probably did more to fuck up gay films than anyone else in the country. He would do things like selling high-powered, funky, shitty films. But he made more money than anyone else in gay films, too." [Siebenand, 186–87]

Many of the filmmakers who had come from the still photography and physique magazine side of the business were suspicious of both Sayles and Beehler. Cassidy preferred Sayles over Beehler.

> "I don't like the guy at all. I have more respect for Shan Sayles than I do for [Beehler]. A lot of people would probably say the opposite—Shan is a dog and Monroe a god. At least you can talk to Shan. He is all business and you can get a deal across. You know ahead of time Shan will exploit you or your film.... Monroe is a sneaky, shady 'nice guy,' a lot of honey on his lips." [Siebenand, 186–89]

In 1968, Sayles launched an ambitious effort to produce gay soft-core feature films. He had purchased the rights to *Song of the Loon*, a sentimental gay male romance novel set in the wilderness of the American West. He hired Scott Hanson and Joe Tiffenbach, the director and cinematographer respectively of a technically adept short film called *The Closet*, which Sayles had played in his theaters.

"It's a go," Sayles told Hanson, "We're going to make the movie. This is going to be a spectacle! There will never be a movie like this! There's never been anything like this! You're going to write the screenplay."

In a production memo to Sayles, Hanson and Tiffenbach characterized the novel as "flowery, nellie, gooey."

"We have removed some of the flagrant homosexuality," Hanson wrote, "and have substituted instead a fantasy of masculine relationships, against a background of visual beauty.... These effects were intended primarily and legitimately to serve as a means of portraying sexual acts. The eroticism is still there. The desire will be tastefully disguised. We know that we can handle this in such a way as to make overt homosexuality understandable and sincere to today's audiences."

"We cannot reproduce the book," Hanson told him. "It's ridiculous."

"You *must*," Sayles exclaimed. "You cannot change too much, because the audience wants the book and you've got to try to recreate it." Sayles had apparently agreed to keep the exact wording of the novel's dialogue when he'd purchased the rights from the author. [Douglas, *Manshots*, 12/94, 10–11]

Before production started, Sayles called Hanson and producer Tiffenbach to his office. "I want you to watch this." he told them, and showed clips from Hollywood Westerns such as *The Big Sky*, *Stagecoach*, *The Last of the Mohicans*. "This is what I have in mind," he said.

Hanson and Tiffenbach ran ads in *Variety* and *The Hollywood Reporter* casting for "rugged frontier-type, non-union movie. Some nudity involved." The response was overwhelming—"guys in full Indian drag, coonskin caps with glitter on them ... we brought every queen—drag queen, transvestite—out of the closet."

At the auditions, Hanson and Tiffenbach explained to the actors that it was going to be a "gay movie" but not a pornographic one. It would involve holding, hugging, kissing, and whatever was necessary to convey the romantic relationships. Most of the actors who showed up stayed for the audition. Selected for the two leads were Morgan Royce and John Iverson, who as far as Hanson and Tiffenbach knew were both heterosexual.

Shooting on the film started during the summer of 1969. Most of the outdoor scenes were shot on location in northern California near Mt. Shasta. But even before the shoot was finished, Sayles showed up with his entourage, including his bookkeeper, concerned that Hanson and Tiffenbach were over budget.

"I smell a rat here." Tiffenbach told Hanson, "Suddenly we're over budget when we're not over budget."

Within three weeks Sayles had shut down the entire production. The actors and the production team were forced to return to Los Angeles. A tug-of-war ensued over the finished footage and scenes that hadn't yet been shot. Hanson and Tiffenbach were fired and never paid. Sayles finished the film himself and edited it to obscure the fact that it was incomplete.

It was never completely clear why Sayles closed production on the movie. Hanson cynically believed that Sayles had "screwed so many people over the years that his way was, that if he didn't screw you he was not functioning the way he wanted to function." [Douglas, *Manshots*, 12/94, 15] But in fact, Sayles may have wanted to cut his losses since he had recently decided to start producing hardcore films. *Song of the Loon* eventually opened in 1970 at a number of Sayles's theaters around the country. Despite its truncated production, patchwork editing, and soft-core sex, *Song of the Loon* was viewed as a landmark.

During the first six months, the gay programs at the Park did very well, but over the next twelve months interest in the soft-core movies began to wane. Audiences wanted to see more explicit sexual activity on screen, although even full frontal nudity was still relatively rare. However, men in the audience at the Park as well as other theaters showing porn often managed to find some hardcore action among themselves.

"[T]here was grumbling from two sides." Kepner recalled, "As the stories developed, some complained that too much time was being wasted on meaningless action and the actors should get their clothes off and get to it as soon as they could. The others wanted more story line and more sentiment." [Siebenand, 18] Theater owners in particular pushed for more hardcore action.

When Sayles and Beehler urged Rocco to incorporate more explicit sexual action, he refused. Rocco "didn't really want to do hardcore," recalled Barry Knight, who worked for him briefly, "he was really against the hardcore part of it." He only wanted to do "the loving and the kissing and the touching." [Douglas, *Manshots*, 6/96, *11*].

> "It was not an easy decision to make," Rocco later explained. "I was offered great sums of money to make certain films. I really feel however that showing the complete sexual action—hardcore—is not necessary to make a story real or believable. It can be indicated without going into explicit or clinical detail. Yet this is what the distributors wanted. They demanded that you stay up close and show everything down to the last drop. They wanted seventy-five percent of the film to be sexual action. I just thought they were unreasonable." [Siebenand, 65]

GOING HARDCORE

Meanwhile, distributors and exhibiters clamored for more sexually explicit movies in order to bring audiences back into their theaters. San Francisco was the first city where hardcore features were played extensively. It had happened almost overnight—by 1969 the city already had twenty-five theaters offering hardcore movies. Estimates at the time placed the number of theaters nationally showing sex films between one and four hundred in cities from Indianapolis to Dallas, Houston, and New York. [T&Z, 77–80]

During 1968, the Park's owners had decided to produce their own gay hardcore material. Straight porn filmmakers refused to make gay films, and the older generation of gay physique photographers, especially those who had made 8mm or 16mm movies—such as Bob Mizer and Dick Fontaine—were not willing to take the risk. Many of the physique photographers had suffered legal persecution at one time or another during the sixties—Bruce of L.A. and others had even gone to jail for periods of time. Mizer, who had managed to escape earlier attempts, was finally arrested in the mid-sixties on prostitution charges, primarily on the basis of his referrals of models to other "photographers."

What degree of nudity a film had and how sexually suggestive the behavior accompanying it could be were changing very quickly. Early soft-core films had strict but informal "guidelines" governing what could be shown—the penis had to be soft, not be even slightly enlarged. No one was allowed to touch his own penis. According to Bob Mizer, it changed week by week. But by the middle of 1969 Sayles wanted "heavy, hard stuff." At that point Mizer chose to bow out. [Siebenand, 48]

The AMG Story was Mizer's last project for Sayles and Beehler. It was a pseudodocumentary that showed Mizer at work in his studio. Jim Cassidy, a straight or bisexual man who had first posed for physique photographer Jim French (later the founder of Colt Studios) and had recently been a finalist in the 1970 Groovy Guy Contest, was cast in a nonsexual role as the host/narrator. The movie showed photos and film clips of Mizer's work going back to 1946. In addition to the clips from the 8mm posing and wrestling films, it included a relatively new spanking scene and one hardcore episode—an orgy scene, according to Cassidy, "with twenty young men sucking and fucking around a pool."

Casting for these films was a relatively simple process.

Mizer's casting director would pick up hustlers along Selma Avenue in the seedy stretch of Hollywood off Santa Monica Boulevard. Before hiring them he would ask to see how large their penises were. "[T]hose kids were making $20 a day" working for AMG, Cassidy recalled.

> "When it came time to get paid (I was getting $150) I was ashamed to say what I was getting near them. They did all that work for $20. And they were so goddamn hungry looking. Mizer had a little picnic lunch set up. He had beans and hot dogs and a couple of loaves of bread and some Kool-Aid. And to keep these kids back from the table just about took a whip and chair. It was all gone in a minute. It was pitiful." [Siebenand, 172]

Cassidy found Mizer's treatment of models disconcerting and the idea of working in gay porn unappealing. After finishing *The AMG Story*, he went on to make numerous straight hardcore movies before returning to gay porn, where he became a popular star.

If Cassidy was put off by Mizer's treatment of models, Mizer himself was taken aback by Shan Sayles's treatment of Monroe Beehler. He "treated [Beehler] like a lackey. I asked him once how he took all that. He did all the work and [Sayles] just sat around." [Siebenand, 49] However, during the making of *The AMG Story*, Beehler abruptly left Signature. Sayles brought in a new producer to finish the movie. When Beehler left Signature, Mizer took out some of the hardcore material that Beehler had insisted on but that he thought was detrimental to his image of AMG.

After *The AMG Story*, Mizer had no incentive to continue making movies for theatrical release. "The whole films-for-theaters venture was a big financial loss for me," Mizer concluded. "It almost wrecked our mail-order business and diverted time and energy from our regular work. I regret that I ever got involved. I am glad I got out of it without getting my fingers burnt more badly than I did. And I never want to be part of it again." [Siebenand, 50]

• • •

In early 1969, Tom DeSimone, a young film professional in his early thirties, went to see the gay program at the Park. A graduate of the UCLA film program, he had worked for several years in the film industry as an editor and had directed a low-budget exploitation horror movie.

"I was very disappointed" with films shown at the Park, he recalled later. "I remember seeing a lot of young kids in them jumping around on pogo sticks and other such nonsense. The quality of the films was terrible. They were badly photographed and the projection was lousy.... I wanted to make one of these films and really show some quality work." [Siebenand, 50] Sayles suggested that the young man shoot a pilot short to see if he could handle shooting sex.

DeSimone went out with a 16mm camera and two friends and shot a scene in someone's backyard. Titled *Yes*, it screened at a number of film festivals and was included in DeSimone's 1974 anthology film, *Erotikus*.

"What I shot was all simulated and very artsy," DeSimone recalled. "I cut it together, put some classical music on it and brought it to him." [DeSimone, *Manshots*, 6/93, 11] When Sayles saw the pilot short, "he flipped."

"Come work for me and I'll give you anything you want," he reportedly told DeSimone.

DeSimone started working right away for Signature Films, Sayles' production unit. He hired a crew and began to put out about four features a month—both straight and gay softcore—in 16mm and with sound. One of his first projects was to finish making *The AMG Story* after Beehler was fired.

DeSimone's first film for Signature was *The Collection*. Far beyond the sentimental style of Pat Rocco's movies or the boisterous boyishness of Bob Mizer's wrestling films, it told the story of a gay man who kidnapped young men and kept them locked in cages for his sexual pleasure. While there was nudity and simulated sex, there were no erections. Nevertheless the theater was routinely harassed by the police because of the S/M-styled subject matter. Later it was even cited by the very liberal U.S. Commission on Obscenity and Pornography in 1970 as an unhealthy example of pornographic films. [DeSimone, *Manshots*, 6/93, 12]

Around June 1969, only months after DeSimone had set up shop, Sayles called Signature's employees into the conference room and announced that the company was changing its production policy. From that point on they would make hardcore movies, and if anyone was uncomfortable with that, they were invited to quit. He would stand by his staff and get them the best lawyers. But he told those assembled that if he were asked, he would deny any knowledge of what they were doing.

"When the decision came that we should switch to hardcore," DeSimone remembered years later, "it was like: stay with it or get out. And of course, we all knew that we'd have to go even further underground, because everything was getting busted." [DeSimone, *Manshots*, 6/93, 12]

Making hardcore was against the law, according to Captain Jack Wilson of the LAPD: "You cannot make a hardcore film without violating the prostitution laws. When you pay actors to engage in sex or oral copulation, you've violated the laws. You've solicited individuals to engage in prostitution by asking them to exchange sex for money." [T&Z, 127–28]

Because hardcore producers in the early seventies operated outside the law, many were fly-by-night operations. "Stories [were] written on matchbook covers and dialogue is made up by performers more noted for looks than talent," one producer observed at the time. "Filming takes place on a single day, and the results are sometimes little more than records of sexual activity framed by the collective sexual fantasies of the people who film and edit one film a week, every week of the year." [T&Z, 127–28]

"We had always made our films very carefully," DeSimone remembered.

> "Even when they were only simulated, we did them quietly and out of the way because I didn't want people nosing around. So I felt confident we could make the switchover without too much problem. But I didn't like having to switch to hardcore. I knew it meant the quality of the film and everything else would go down. We had been making decent films, I thought, and even though they were sex films they were nicely done." [Siebenand, 84]

Even Sayles had been reluctant to make the switch, but Signature began to shoot hardcore sex scenes to replace the simulated sex scenes in its soft-core features to compete with the San Francisco and New York exhibitors. [Siebenand, 85–86]

The switchover to hardcore dramatically altered how sex movies would be made. Tom DeSimone believed that having to perform "real" sex changed who would be cast in hardcore movies. "When you get into hardcore," he noted, "you are dealing with a different class of people. You can't get actors or actresses anymore, but pimps and whores." [Siebenand, 85] Sex films were no longer merely products made on the margins of the Hollywood film industry—they were both outside the law and outside the film industry.

The defining characteristic of hardcore was "insertion." During the soft-core era, since it was unclear what would be enforced, every film tested the limits. Soft-core porn films sometimes showed erections. They showed people who appeared to be sucking penises and getting fucked, but they never showed oral or anal penetration. Actors could not put their faces close to an erect penis and lick it. Thus there was a lot of licking the stomach, dry humping, and humping each other without showing the penetration. [DeSimone, *Manshots*, 6/93, 12]

The switch from simple nudity to hardcore took place

almost seamlessly. "[It] just sort of seeped in, that is why the date is so hard to pinpoint," observed porn reviewer Harold Fairbanks. "[Tom DeSimone's] *The Collection* came out in 1969, but it was soft core, all simulated sex. Stories were a little earthier. For example, *The Collection* was about a man who kidnaps boys and makes them sex slaves. I think that plot is a little grittier than something Pat Rocco would have done. In Pat's films the boys are always just running down hillsides." [Siebenand, 27]

Straight soft-core porno had already established routines when it came to narrative structure and simulated sex acts. Since the first soft-core movies (also called "nudie cuties") ten years before, they had evolved a very rigid formula: first the boy/girl scene, then girl/girl scene, the orgy scene, and finally the kiss-off. The sequence, producers believed, was necessary for the films to succeed commercially. The boundary between nudity and obscenity was constantly shifting. In the beginning it was considered "pornographic" to show pubic hair. It wasn't until 1968 that any nudie-cutie showed public hair. "Pickle and beaver" shots—the penis and the female crotch—soon followed. [McNeil and Osborne, 10–11] Gay soft-core movies, by contrast, were a more recent development; the narrative structure had not yet evolved a strict formula.

Straight hardcore sex fit easily into the existing narrative formulas—dealing with erections and getting cum shots were the new challenges. But in gay films, hardcore sex posed somewhat different obstacles: erections, anal penetration, and ejaculations (whose?) were seen as essential, but a standard sequence of sexual action had not yet emerged. Who sucked or fucked whom, in what order, remained an open question. Initially the approach was purely quantitative: "Generally, I keep my actors to about six people," Signature director Tom DeSimone explained, "and that gives me three sex scenes and six cum shots." [Siebenand, 92]

Hardcore had, nevertheless, emerged very quickly as a commercial imperative. Sexually explicit hardcore films were already being shown in San Francisco and New York City in 1969. Audiences in L.A. had also tired of the sentimental and soft-core gay films. Distributors and exhibitors, according to Pat Rocco, wanted sexual action to take up at least 75 percent of the film's running time. They also wanted sexual action to start within the first five minutes. These demands imposed significant constraints on the narrative arc of a pornographic film. Making such films for theatrical release posed major challenges to producers and filmmakers—not only casting (always more difficult than for straight sexploitation movies), but directing, establishing narrative conventions, and performance.

The shift to hardcore raised another challenge: developing the professional technique and conventions for filming explicit sex acts. The gay soft-core films shown in the Park and other theaters had barely moved beyond frontal nudity and kissing. Some of the physique photographers such as Bruce of L.A. or Bob Mizer had made 8mm hardcore shorts for special customers—with oral and anal penetration—but they were not shown in theaters.

One of Signature's early gay hardcore films, *Desires of the Devil*, aptly illustrates the transitional phase of the new film genre. Probably made sometime during 1971, it was directed by Sebastian Figg, a former actor who had appeared in soft-core films (*Escape to Passion*, 1970) and who directed *The Specimen*, a straight hardcore feature, released a year later.

The movie has five scenes, but there is only one cum shot in the entire film. For example, in the first sex scene Jim Cassidy, the film's star, meets a man at a theater and is invited home for a drink. Eventually they go into the bedroom and undress. They embrace naked on the bed and the man sucks Cassidy's dick, but the camera does not focus on the fellatio. They shift position and the man lies on his back as Cassidy inserts his penis, but we never see the penis penetrating the man's ass. They fuck for a few minutes, then separate, embrace, and fall asleep—the fucking looks faked; neither man has an orgasm. Cassidy wakes up and sneaks out after taking some cash from the man's wallet.

After he leaves the first man's apartment, Cassidy meets another man on the street and goes back to that man's apartment. Very quickly, they undress and they move from the man sucking Cassidy's cock to sixty-nine to Cassidy fucking the man. There is no penetration in this scene either, but it is much more convincing, and it looks as though there was real fucking. The man comes while he's being fucked, although again, Cassidy doesn't himself reach an orgasm. The last three scenes have very little sexual action—only oral sex—no anal penetration and no orgasms.

It's not clear why neither penetration nor the money shot was portrayed. Virtually none of the formulas used in today's porn was in evidence. It is possible that the film was originally conceived as a soft-core feature film and incorporated some explicit sex while in production during the period's chaotic transition to hardcore. And that the film's director and producer assumed that the story, the nudity, and the quasi-hardcore and simulated sex put it satisfactorily into the hardcore category. It may also reflect the fact that the conventions surrounding penetration, erections, and the cum shots were not yet firmly established.

The director's role also changed from that of directing actors in simulated sex scenes that included dialogue and had some character development to that of directing and choreographing sexual performances, which required coaching the performers through a series of sex acts, offering them encouragement, monitoring erections, and eliciting and photographing successful cum shots.

As Tom DeSimone explained at the time: "You have to be a real psychologist."

> "Your mind is constantly clicking about how to solve a million and one problems. You realize what they are going through on the bed. We try to treat it as gingerly as possible. When it is time for the scene we try to introduce the two people,

> because lots of times they don't meet each other until the day of the shooting. I introduce them and tell to go over in the corner and run over the scene—not the sex scene—and they generally work the chemistry out, if they know they are going to have to get it on."

It sometimes took hours to regain erections or shoot a cum shot. "A couple of times it has been a disaster," DeSimone explained in 1974.

> "One of the actors will come up to me and say, we just can't do it. And then there is a fast reshuffling—and then the other person is insulted because he realizes the reshuffling is going on.... Often I have had scenes that were total disasters and we had to re-match people or fake things as best we could.... And by then the whole picture is lost."[Siebenand, 90–5]

In a very short time, gay hardcore movies included cum shots. When did the convention emerge that visually displayed cum shots would serve as the narrative conclusion of the sexual action? DeSimone has claimed that his film *One*, which consisted of a series of solo masturbation scenes, was the first commercial hardcore film to show cum shots. What's interesting about the "cum shot" as the concluding moment of a penetrative sex act, now an accepted convention of the entire genre, is that it is not, of course, a "realistic" representation of the male orgasm—except when withdrawal before orgasm is considered a form of contraception.

Unlike in heterosexual hardcore, where only the male performers are able to display their states of arousal and orgasms, the female performers are able to fake both arousal and orgasms. In gay porn, states of arousal of all performers are always visible. In contrast to the active and passive participants in straight porn, in gay porn the orgasms of both the performer fucking and the one getting fucked were equally important.

Much as the early years of gay hardcore involved pioneering content and technique, so, too, was it a time of creatively dealing with erections or lack thereof. Many performers needed to be attracted to their partners in order to get an erection and perform. Others were able to get erections without regard to whether they were attracted to their partner in a scene. Porn star Jim Cassidy's advice to aspiring performers was "you have to be able to get it up manually. Like stroke it to get up and do it under any conditions and circumstances. That is the prime requirement for getting into this field. And if you can do it in gay porno you should be able to do it in straight porno, too." [Siebenand, 183] He reported that "I have gotten many jobs because I would come through under any conditions." [Siebenand, 177]

Since there was no way to fake an erection, if the lack of one became a problem, tricks and stopgap measures had to be worked out. Performers sometimes asked for a magazine or book to help them get aroused. When the performers lost their erections because they had to wait for lighting to be adjusted or the camera to be moved, a "puffer" was brought in to fellate the performers and get them aroused. The terminology was not yet settled—some insiders referred to "the resident c.s." (Rocco) and others to "fluffers" (Cassidy)—the term that is still used. Jim Cassidy occasionally substituted his hard-on for an actor unable to get an erection. According to a number of insiders, many performers used marijuana and poppers (amyl nitrate) to help them with their on-camera performances. Some would bring cocaine and snort it. [Siebenand, 177–78]

If it was necessary to fake an ejaculation, egg whites or hand cream were used. "We just squirt a little or … put some in their mouths and let it dribble out." [Siebenand, 95] In one scene, a performer had swallowed Cassidy's cum shot prematurely. Rather than wait to reshoot it, Cassidy filled his mouth with condensed milk and pretended that someone was coming in his mouth. "I let the milk ooze out and it kept coming and coming…. I saw Dakota a few months later and he said, 'Cassidy that was really a good cum scene.' I told him, 'Sorry I really can't take credit for it. It was some cow's big moment.'" [Siebenand, 180]

Casting also became much more complicated with the shift to hardcore. Hard-core production in California always took place in the shadow of the state's tough pandering law, under which a paid performance of sex was considered to be prostitution and it carried a three-year prison term. [McNeil & Osborne, 405, 407–14]. "The vice squad used to send people out there posing as models," DeSimone recalled. "Very sexy guys. So you had to be very careful when you interviewed these people what you said, because you were hiring them to perform sex for money and that was pandering. And that was how they used to get you." [Siebenand, 93]

For the most part, casting relied on the filmmakers' personal grapevine. Once a film was cast, the performers were assigned to a designated spot and then driven to the location of the shoot. No one was allowed to make phone calls from the film's location. As DeSimone remembered it, "There was always that fear when you were starting to do a scene, because stories were that these people would pose as models and just as you were about to do the sex, you'd get busted. So, there was always that moment or turning point before they actually got into the action. Once they started kissing and fondling and got erect, you pretty much knew that they were into the scene." [DeSimone, *Manshots*, 6/93, 13]

Casting in the early days was governed by a mix of criteria based on physical appearance, trial and error, and personal sexual experience with the performers—as it is today as well. Pornographic film performances relied upon the physical and imaginative capabilities of individual performers, directors, and editors to create a convincing fantasy world on film—and a credible sexual performance was a very important part of it.

Ultimately, direction and physical setup were necessary to organize the sexual performances and set the stage to create a believable *fantasy world* on film. The sexual fantasy worlds of these films were stitched together from a hodgepodge of story fragments, cultural myths, clichéd plots, fetish objects, and physical settings, all melded together through the sexual choreography envisioned by the scriptwriter or the director. The shift to hardcore required new conventions of performance to make the porn film's fantasy world convincing.

STARS IN THE FIRMAMENT

Whether the fantasy world created by hardcore porn succeeded or failed with its viewers ultimately depended upon whether the performers were able to give believable sexual performances. Worshiped as models of masculine beauty, treated like sexual athletes, porn stars are more than objects of desire. Porn stars embody the sexual ideals of gay men. It is the porn star's sexual performance that is the portal through which viewers engage with a pornographic movie. Director Fred Halsted considered hardcore porn a performer's medium—as well as the cameraman's.

Most of the gay men who went to see porn at the Park looked to the performers to represent their sexual ideal of a gay man. They were "all butch or macho—or try to be," according to Jim Kepner, who was *The Advocate*'s film critic in 1968; performers were expected to be "very good looking, very masculine. … A few filmmakers have tried 'drag' characters, and it just doesn't work. It turns people off…. [T]hey will not pay [money] to be confronted with it on the screen. They want a Marlboro man." [Siebenand, 34]

Gay male culture at the time (and since) put the most attractive models on a pedestal and paid homage to them. While many of the attractive young men who posed for the beefcake magazines were idolized or considered "stars" by their fans, they were for the most part worshiped in closeted privacy. Few made the transition to film. Warhol's Joe Dallesandro, who had posed for Bob Mizer's AMG, was the most notable exception.

The existence of "stars" in porn movies owes a great deal

to Hollywood and the idea of the star system that originated in the film industry in the 1920s and 1930s. The star was and is both a featured performer and an iconic presence. Like movie stars or other celebrities, porn stars embody exalted ideals of beauty and personality—they are utopian erotic fantasies. Star personas crystallize both fantasies of identification—who the spectator wants to be—and fantasies of sexual desire—whom the spectator wants to have sex with—a psychological dynamic that is central to both gay films and gay pornographic films [De Angelis, 2001]. Most spectators of porn, whether gay or straight, vacillate between imagining themselves as the top and the bottom. [Cowie, 1993]

Porn stars are more like screen actors in general—as opposed to stage actors—in that they do not create a role, but instead build their personas and the roles they play as actors from their own psychological and physical characteristics—constantly projecting the same thing: "themselves." The emphasis is on the screen "persona" with its sense of immediacy and its suggestion of "authenticity"—a trait vitally important to porn films. The porn star's persona, and its meaning to his fans, is established not only through the star's own sense of self, through his physical appearance and attributes, but also by his style as a male and the kind of sex he performs. It is a characteristic that must be projected in a number of different films. [Escoffier, 2003]

DeSimone had worried that the switch to hardcore and the necessity of casting for explicit sexual performances would mean that performers were less likely to be actors and more likely to be hustlers, prostitutes, and drifters. Casting for gay hardcore productions was of course more difficult, since homosexuality was still relatively stigmatized. Most straight hardcore performers were not willing to appear in gay movies, so gay directors often recruited from among friends, acquaintances, hustlers, and casual sexual partners.

Given the kinds of concerns voiced by DeSimone, it's surprising that stars emerged so quickly in early gay porn. In fact, many of the most prominent performers in gay porn were not the hustlers or pimps DeSimone anticipated—though some of the more marginal players were. And others moved from porn *to* hustling. Since homosexuality was a stigmatized form of behavior, it did attract young, somewhat aimless working-class men.

Ironically, porn stars were first created by a "beauty" contest. Starting in 1968, *The Advocate*, then a local gay newspaper, sponsored the Groovy Guy contest. Contestants backed by local bars were judged on physique, facial features, and grooming. Often, the winning contestants were approached by the photographers and filmmakers to pose for pictures or to appear in a pornographic film. [Thompson, 8]

Only a few performers achieved a degree of renown in the early gay hardcore films made in Los Angeles—Jim Cassidy and Jimmy Hughes were the best known. The earliest star to emerge was Jim Cassidy. He grew up in Pennsylvania and spent two years in the Navy. After he got out he modeled for physique photographer Jim French in New York—posing in leather and motorcycle gear. In 1969 Cassidy moved to Los Angeles, and in the following year, entered the Groovy Guy contest. Though he came in third, he was approached by Pat Rocco to pose for a number of local gay publications. At the same time, Monroe Beehler approached him to appear in *The AMG Story* as the host and narrator for the faux documentary. When Beehler left in the middle of filming, Tom DeSimone took over and completed it.

Meanwhile, around the same time, Cassidy also made a short film called *Drilled Deep*. Originally to be called *Wrong Number*, it was about a telephone repair man fixing a phone. Cassidy thought the story a bit clichéd and the night before the shoot, he wrote a short script. The cast consisted of three people: Dakota, another rising gay porn star, a young woman named Judy Coleman, and Cassidy himself. Dakota plays a handyman drilling the door. Judy Coleman comes by and gets Dakota interested in "drilling" her, then Cassidy shows up and expresses interest in "drilling" Dakota while Dakota "drills" Judy.

Cassidy's career lasted for a number of years and spanned both straight and gay films. "I never wanted to work in films that bad," Cassidy recounted.

> "I did them not because I was out looking for them, but because they came to me.... [I]t was just a thing that was happening.... The hardcore films just came my way. The simulated kind were a little harder to get and I wanted to work in them more because they were a little bit more fun. You could act to a greater extent. It was more fun throwing dialog than sex." [Siebenand, 173–174]

Performers in gay porn never earned much money over the course of their "careers," which were never too long to begin with. While Cassidy had made hundreds of straight porn movies between 1970 and 1974, he only appeared in ten gay films.

> "I haven't made that much from gay porno," he explained. "I made a lot more in straight porno. I got paid more in gay porn because they wanted my name and I held out for more. But there was more straight porno going on. When I was living up in Hollywood I would often be working five or six days a week at it. In gay porno I might do a film every few months. I didn't want to do everything, because I might easily get overexposed.... I have made only ten gay films, but they have been played and played and replayed and replayed. Already from ten films I am overexposed. Straight porno is a different matter. You aren't the famous Jim Cassidy, you are just there. The chicks are the stars." [Siebenand, 183]

Jimmy Hughes was another performer who achieved short-lived star status before being entangled in rape and kidnapping charges in 1974. Like Cassidy, he, too, was approached to make gay films after winning the Groovy Guy contest (1971). He appeared in loops (short sexual scenes with minimal set-ups) and for a number of companies in San Francisco and New York for a flat fee of $300 to $350. He achieved some renown in a couple of Jaguar productions, a short sex scene in *The Experiment,* and in *Greek Lightning,* where as the star he was paid $1,000, a fairly substantial amount.

> "When I am filming," Hughes explained, "I don't give the slightest thought to the people who some day may see the film.... If I think about anything, it is the money I will be getting. If I thought about the audience I probably wouldn't even get a hard-on. I am not an exhibitionist. Filming is hard work ... there are too many retakes on the no sex scenes. It is a lot of work just to be drooled over later by a bunch of dick-happy queens. ... The only reason I made these loops and films was for the money. There was nothing I did on camera that I had not done many times before. I would guess that everyone in gay porno—actors, directors, right on down the line—are gay. But masculine gay."

Hughes regretted making gay porn. "Sex is important and precious," he told one reporter from prison, "and I have been exploiting myself for frogs [i.e., older, unattractive men] and faggots." [Siebenand, 140–41]

There was little discussion among filmmakers or gay journalists at the time about Cassidy's or Hughes's sexual orientation. Neither performer intentionally sought to perform in gay hardcore films, but both named money as a significant motivation. They would appear to be bisexual or perhaps what in following decades was called "gay-for-pay."

At the time of his arrest, Hughes was living in a romantic relationship with Kim Christy, a well-known female impersonator in Los Angeles. How the criminal charges for rape at gunpoint and the forced oral and anal copulation of nine young women fit into his sexual identity is not known. The original charges were eventually reduced through plea bargaining to two counts of rape at gunpoint of two young women.

Cassidy and Hughes were the two most notable stars to emerge on the L.A. porn scene in the early years. They achieved limited recognition but were soon surpassed by Casey Donovan, the star of Wakefield Poole's *Boys in the Sand*.

LA PLAYS ITSELF

Fred Halsted's *LA Plays Itself* premiered at the Paris Theatre in June 1972. Located on the corner of Santa Monica Boulevard and Crescent Heights, the Paris Theatre was, like the Park, owned by Shan Sayles's Continental Theaters. Halsted had no connection to either the physique photographers or the local film productions funded by Shan Sayles and Monroe Beehler. If anything, Halsted took hardcore gay erotic film down a path that had been opened up by Kenneth Anger.

Born in Long Beach, California, in 1941 and raised in Oakland, Fred Halsted moved to Los Angeles to attend college. He dropped out after three years and went into business, successfully developing a chain of wholesale nurseries. Halsted had taken up the study of Zen and had begun to think about his sexuality. He decided then to make a porno film in which he would create a part for himself, and then refashion himself to be that part. It was in this same period that he also began to explore his sadism. He started writing the script for *LA Plays Itself*. It was to be an "autobiographical" film exploring his philosophy of sex. When Halsted started filming *LA Plays Itself* in 1969, he had never seen a gay pornographic film.

LA Plays Itself opens with the camera moving quickly in the countryside outside Los Angeles. Zooming to wildflowers, rocks, and insects, it comes to rest on an idyllic sexual encounter in the Malibu Mountains: two young men kiss, suck each others' cocks, and casually fuck. The second scene opens on a gritty street in a run-down neighborhood of Los Angeles. Fred Halsted himself drives through seedy side streets in Hollywood—lined with young men hustling, porn theaters, and shabby store fronts. On the sound track a young man with a Texas drawl is reading a porno story. As we cruise the streets of Los Angeles, we overhear a conversation between two young men, one just arrived, the other coyly offering to show him around and warning the newcomer to avoid certain kinds of men.

In the third scene, we look down at a young man standing at the foot of a long stairway. Halsted stands at the top, pale, shirtless, wearing only jeans and boots. For a moment, we are suddenly prowling with Halsted again among half-naked men standing in the shadows in Griffith Park. Then just as suddenly we are back on the stairway again; Halsted pushes the young man into a bedroom and throws him on the bed. He ties up the young man, whips him, and finally puts his fist up the young man's ass. That scene introduced the practice of "fisting" to the American public as a form of sexual play.

Halsted had started working on the script for *LA Plays Itself* in 1969 and finished it shortly before its premiere in the spring of 1972. It was essentially the first installment of a trilogy of films summarizing his philosophy of sex. The second work of the trilogy, *Sex Garage*, was shot over the course of six hours in December 1971. Then, after prolonged work on the script, he started shooting *Sextool*, the third installment, during the summer of 1974.

Shot in high-contrast black and white—*LA Plays Itself* was shot in color—*Sex Garage* opens with a young woman giving a blow job to a garage mechanic. Then a macho biker replaces her, but he seems more interested in fucking his motorcycle; he literally fucks the motorcycle's exhaust pipe. *Sex Garage* was confiscated by the NYPD, purportedly for the latter scene.

Halsted intended *Sextool* to be "an encyclopedia of sex"—it was to include many different types of performers. But unlike Halsted's other films, *Sextool* has a psychological narrative. And like *LA Plays Itself*, he considered it "autobiographical." The lead is played by Charmaine Lee Anderson, a transsexual.

"I wrote Charmaine's role for me." Halsted explained. "I wrote this fucking film for Charmaine as Gloria, and I am Gloria. Gloria is a completely liberated person. She is a male ... [who] becomes a functional female and hits all the sailor and marine bars down in Long Beach.... she picks up straight studs and fucks them." [Siebenand, 218]

LA Plays Itself and its sequels were very different films from any of the other hardcore films shown at the Park. "In my films," Halsted explained, "I am not that interested in cum shots or erections or sucking or fucking. I am more interested in what is going on in the psyche and not the action itself." [Siebenand, 221–22] They made an artistic and philosophic statement about sex—in particular about S/M sex. *LA Plays Itself* had no narrative structure and the sex scenes were interrupted by unrelated images; there was only one somewhat half-hearted cum shot.

Halsted conceived his films as contributions to a philosophy of sex. "Sex is not 'coming,' that is superficial sex," Halsted said, explaining his philosophy.

> "Mine is personal cinema. I don't fuck to get my rocks off. In the best scenes I've ever had, I haven't come. I am not interested in coming.... I am interesting in getting my head off, my emotions off—and if I get my dick off, my rocks off, it really doesn't matter that much to me.... I am interested in emotional satisfaction and intellectual satisfaction." [Siebenand, 207]

Halsted seems to have anticipated Foucault's celebrated view of S/M as a "creative enterprise" that imagined "the desexualization of pleasure." [Bersani, 19]

Halsted believed that the erotic is both transgressive and sacramental. In the erotic encounter the physical barriers between people are breached, if only briefly, through the other's bodily orifices. "Stripping naked is the decisive action," wrote Georges Bataille. "Nakedness offers a contrast to self-possession.... Bodies open... through secret passages to give us a feeling of obscenity. Obscenity ... upsets the physical state associated with self-possession." [Bataille, 15–18]

Sex in Halsted's films violates the male characters' sense of self-possession. The result of this destruction is a sacred experience—"Coming is not the point. The point is revelation—the why." [Siebenand, 211] There is also no clear sense of homosexual identity in Halsted's films. "I consider myself a pervert first and a homosexual second," he said. [Siebenand, 222] The men in his films are not even necessarily gay men; some are straight men, and Charmaine is a man who became a woman. The sadist is only an instrument—the "sextool"—that opens the way to the sacred. He did not believe in the purely recreational aspect of sex:

> Sex as fun doesn't interest me.... I am interested in the broader ramifications of sex ... the mind-fucking aspects of sex. I like to make sex films because it gives me the opportunity to state my views.... I don't do it for the money.... I don't particularly view sex as fun. To me sex is not fun. To me sex is not enjoyable. To me sex is an emotional release. [Siebenand, 206–7]

Halsted believed that the S/M perspective was of particular importance to homosexual men. In fact, he considered "sadism ... more basic to my personality than homosexuality." [Siebenand, 222] "There is ... a mind-fuck element," he noted, "that goes into gay sex and gay relationships. The biggest gay porno hits always have S & M themes running through them.... Everybody does on some level, because it is the whole macho, male domination thing. Most homosexuals want to be dominated by another male." [Siebenand, 218]

LA Plays Itself opened in New York in the fall of 1972; it was a huge sensation. Recognized immediately for its artistic and philosophical vision, it was selected by the Museum of Modern Art, one of the world's leading art museums, for its permanent film collection. And like *Boys in the Sand*, which had premiered the previous December, it was one of the first porn movies—not just gay porn movies—reviewed in mainstream newspapers. Both movies helped to define the "porn chic" cultural trend of the early seventies and each was an example of an artistically serious hardcore film. Moreover, both films preceded *Deep Throat* as a pornographic film that played to general movie-going audiences.

EROTIKUS

In 1974—though commercial gay porn had emerged no more than five years earlier—filmmaker Tom DeSimone released *Erotikus,* a documentary history of gay erotic movies, both soft-core and hardcore. It captured the brief historical moment when gay porn was born in Los Angeles. Fred Halsted served as the narrator, slowly peeling off his clothes over the course of the movie and, at the film's conclusion, seemingly masturbating to orgasm—perhaps the first documentary with a "money shot"! Though in fact, it was widely reported that the orgasm was not Halsted's.

Making a "documentary" movie about pornography was a widely used strategy in the early 1970s for pushing the permissible limits of nudity and sexual explicitness on the screen in movie theaters. Documentary films, even with explicit sex, could be considered educational or "scientific."

Throughout the early seventies the legal status of pornography was in flux. In 1970, the Federal Commission on Obscenity and Pornography had recommended decriminalizing porn for adults. In 1973, the Supreme Court made its landmark decision in *Miller v. California,* where it declared that a work was obscene if it was "utterly" without redeeming social worth *and* if it lacked "serious" literary, artistic, political, or scientific value. In the wake of *Miller v. California*, plot offered the adult industry a basis for legally defending sexually explicit film productions because plot or a "documentary" format allowed adult filmmakers to claim that their films—like *Deep Throat*, *The Devil in Miss Jones*, or *LA Plays Itself*, all strongly narrative porn movies—had some redeeming social worth and "serious" artistic or scientific value. [Slade, 216–17]

Even before the *Miller* decision, straight pornographer Alex de Renzy was the master of the "documentary" ploy. Several years earlier, de Renzy had released a documentary called *Pornography in Denmark*, which had cost $15,000 to make and ended up grossing more than $2 million. In 1970, soon after hardcore started showing in the theaters of San Francisco, de Renzy released *A History of the Blue Movie* (1970)—a documentary history of erotic films, a compilation of stag movies dating from 1915 and clips of hardcore porn made in San Francisco in the late 1960s. Other documentaries, such as *I Am Curious (Yellow)* or pseudo-documentary movies, for example *I, a Woman*, dealing with sex or pornography, had routinely provoked censorship and controversy that attracted audiences into the theaters.

Gay pornographic films were far scarcer historically than the films de Renzy included in his compilation, and the recent cycle of production of gay porn wasn't even five years old. DeSimone's film retells the story of the Park Theatre and birth of gay hardcore cinema in Los Angeles. Starting from the physique photographers and their 8mm shorts, through the sentimental soft-core of Pat Rocco, and culminating in Wakefield Poole's *Boys in the Sand* and Halsted's *LA Plays Itself*, *Erotikus* portrayed DeSimone's own films as the cinematic bridge to Poole and Halsted's popular and critically acclaimed works. But DeSimone's films—*Yes*, the short pilot film that he shot for Sayles, *One* (1970), a documentary about adolescent sexuality; *The Collection* (1970), *Dust Unto Dust* (1970), *Tarzan the Fearless* (1971), *Assault* (1971), *Confessions of Male Groupie* (1971), *Duffy's Tavern* (1973)—were less cultural or artistic statements than porn simulations of commercial Hollywood feature films. *Erotikus* epitomized the first phase of the gay porn industry—barely five years old—at which point both Poole's *Boys in the Sand* and Halsted's *LA Plays Itself* had emerged as critical and commercial successes—though each of them was less technically polished than any of DeSimone's films.

• • •

In the summer of 1971, Monroe Beehler, who had been the first head of production at Signature, formed Jaguar Productions, one of the first film production companies intentionally set up to produce gay pornographic feature films for theatrical release. Like Signature, Jaguar also included a distribution arm that leased its films to a fixed circuit of twenty-two theaters. [Turan and Zito, 193] Modeled after Hollywood studios, Beehler assembled a team of people to do production and postproduction on all his films. The entire production operation was run out of Beehler's basement—editing, sound mixing, everything.

Jaguar made gay hardcore films with story lines—not only because feature-length films with stories were what he and his team believed in, but because after the *Miller v. California* decision, story and plotlines provided an alibi for hardcore porn. That way it could escape being classified as obscene.

Beehler had finally persuaded Pat Rocco to add explicit sex scenes to his films. Their first production was Pat Rocco's *Coming of Age,* and despite the hardcore action, it still resembled, as editor Barry Knight recalled, Rocco's earlier "lovey-dovey movies except for the sex added to it." After it opened at New York's Park Miller Theater in October 1971, the manager called the day after it opened and complained "There's no fucking in the first five minutes." [Douglas, *Manshots,* 6/96, 13]

Nevertheless, Beehler continued to produce hardcore movies with significant story lines. *The Experiment* (1972) was one of Jaguar's most successful and is considered Jaguar's best movie. Directed by Knight with a script by his friend Groton Hall, *The Experiment* told the story of a young man's first sexual encounter with another man and culminates in the young man's confession to his father about being gay—and his father accepting him. More than twenty-five minutes of character development occurred before the film's sexual action began.

Barry Knight, who had moved to the L.A. area earlier that year, was hired by Beehler to edit Pat Rocco's *Coming of Age*. Knight had worked in television before moving to Los Angeles. Probably the most memorable thing that Knight remembered was Beehler's warning, at their first meeting, about the possibility of police raids.

"Now when you come here," Beehler told him, "to edit in my basement in my beautiful home in the Hollywood Hills, if anyone knocks on the door, do not answer the door for anything." [Douglas, *Manshots*, 6/96, 10]

Jaguar not only produced its own hardcore features, but produced the films of a number of other young aspiring hardcore filmmakers. One of the earliest of these productions was the first work by the prominent director later known as Scott Masters. In 1973, he was using the name Robert Walters. The film was *Greek Lightning*—a gay hardcore takeoff of a James Bond movie starring Jimmy Hughes. Another aspirant who approached Beehler was John Travis, one of the leading directors in the history of gay porn, best known as the man who discovered gay porn superstar Jeff Stryker. In 1990, he and Scott Masters founded Studio 2000. Like Masters, Travis, one of the most important directors in the history of gay porn, started in the 1970s and continued to make gay porn films for almost forty years. John Summers was another, an influential figure in the development of the gay porn industry in San Francisco during the 1970s. William Higgins, one of the most influential directors of the late seventies and early eighties, made his first gay hardcore feature films for Jaguar before he went off and started Catalina Studios.

There were no standard mechanisms for recruiting performers to be in hardcore movies—no agents, referrals from other producers, or networking in the industry. Knight recalls that they would often go down to "central casting," which in the early seventies was the Gold Cup Coffee Shop on the corner of Hollywood Boulevard and Las Palmas—a notorious gay hangout in those years. [Douglas, *Manshots*, 6/96, 11; Faderman & Timmins, 150]

Distribution was set up through small chains of theaters. In 1973, Beehler decided to purchase the Century Theater in Los Angeles to show Jaguar films. Previously Jaguar had rented them to the Las Palmas Theater, one of the local porn houses that showed gay films. The Century was a big 1920s movie palace with six hundred seats. Beehler ran it like a regular movie palace, not like one of the many small 16mm porn theaters that had sprouted p 1968.

SOMEWHERE IN THE DARK

In the sixties and early seventies, sex between men took place in almost any porn theater. It did not matter if the theater showed gay or straight movies. Whether or not the men identified as queer or gay, they engaged in public sex in parks, bathhouses, saunas, locker rooms, public toilets, highway rest stops, and cheap movie theaters. The rise of theaters showing sexploitation movies in the 1960s—with their predominately male audiences—provided new opportunities for sexual activities: masturbation as well as sexual encounters.

Pornography, whether soft-core or hardcore, is a film genre designed to stimulate sexual excitement and pleasure. Thus, as in other genres that provoke intense physiological reactions—horror movies (fear) or melodramas (weeping)—the male audience in a theater showing pornographic films coexists in a state of arousal. It is a state "marked ... by the prolongation of desire and by the lack of a fixed position with respect to the objects and events fantasized." [Williams, 154]

While female prostitutes also worked in theaters showing

soft-core and hardcore heterosexual movies, such a charged context increased the likelihood that the men in the audience, whatever sort of film was being screened, might have sexual encounters with one another. In such a situation even a "straight" man in the audience may engage in mutual masturbation with another man or allow a man to suck his penis. The screening of hardcore gay pornographic movies tended to reinforce the level of sexual activity going on in the theater.

In the twenty-some years between the Park's first gay program and the early 1980s, there were always a handful of porn theaters in L.A. showing gay hardcore movies, and men went to them to have sex with each other; the Paris on Santa Monica at Crescent Heights, Las Palmas on Las Palmas near Hollywood Boulevard, the Century on Hollywood Boulevard near Normandie, and the Vista on Sunset Boulevard were among the most notable.

In the early seventies, patrons of the Paris and the Century were divided between those who came to see the film and those who came for the sexual activity. As Bruce Lovern, the Paris' manager, observed: "Some have come just for the fantasy of the film and others to cruise. They could care less what is on the screen." [Siebenand, 242] The movies most favored tended not to have a strong story line. Instead they mostly showed sex.

Lovern noted, "We have a very active balcony. The Century doesn't and that is why their business is not as good as ours here. We had an active balcony even when they showed Walt Disney movies here. Our balcony is known to be a very hot place. 'You pays your money and takes your chances.' But many, especially if they sit by themselves, just come for the fantasy. Frustration brings them here, I guess."

Porn critic Harold Fairbanks observed:

> "Most patrons hope to be physically aroused by what they see on the screen. But after you have seen so many of the films, they become less and less stimulating.... Some people do masturbate

in the theaters, but they are mostly the older
patrons. In the East they are called the 'overcoat
trade' because they wear an overcoat so they can
do it without being seen." [Siebenand, 36]

In *The Sexual Outlaw*, John Rechy's "documentary" about
the sexual subculture of Los Angeles during the 1970s, he portrays the experience of entering a porn theater:

He enters a darkness so dense that not even an
outline can be seen. But he's aware of presences
in the roiling blackness. On the screen, a movie
with unsynchronized sound and bleeding unreal
colors is flickering; orange bodies grind on a
green bed. Jim waits until his eyes adjust.
Slowly, outlines emerge. Then forms. Now he
sees men leaning against the back wall or idling
in the space behind the back row, at least eight
hunters in the small area. Perhaps a dozen more
sit in the rows farthest back. Now definite bodies and faces emerge like flotsam from a black
sea. Throughout the cavernous mouth which
almost devours the screen, there is only a scat-
tering of permanently occupied seats, mainly
older men watching the screen raptly. Others
shift constantly from row to row. The concentration of hunters is now in the back—those who
have come to make it, not to see the cheap movie.
[Rechy, 236]

In 1974 gay porn historian Paul Alcuin Siebenand conducted a small unscientific survey of patrons at the Paris Theater. Most of the patrons who answered his questionnaire were
regular attendees—18 percent attended at least once a week,
and 59 percent attended at least once a month. Over 60 percent masturbated while viewing the movie and over half
cruised for sexual partners.

Bruce Lovern reported that while the LAPD's vice squad

visited the Paris routinely, they very rarely arrested any of the patrons. But they frequently confiscated prints of the films. Nor was there any advance warning of a raid. The officers came with a warrant that described a specific print, and the theater typically replaced it in about twenty-four hours.

At the Century, managers tended to ignore any sex that took place except when the police were present. There were warning signs on the theater's front door and a warning was played on the screen. But police harassment was a constant problem. Police officers frequently came in drunk and beat up the theater's patrons. When police officers arrived for an inspection, the cashier in the box office outside buzzed the projectionist, who turned up the lights in the auditorium as a warning to the patrons. Vice cops would arrest anyone masturbating in the theater's back rows. Harassment worsened over the years—until finally in 1988 the LAPD forced the Century to close permanently. The theater stood vacant for years until it burned down in a five-alarm fire in 1992. [Douglas, *Manshots,* 8/96, 12–13, 72]

Porn theaters, in part because of the sexual activity that went on in them, created a communal sense among their patrons. Samuel Delany suggests in his book *Times Square Red, Times Square Blue* (1999) that the encounters taking place in porn theaters encouraged the development of social relationships crossing lines of class, race, and sexual orientation and conveyed a sense of community. In the same light, French director Jacques Nolot's independent feature *Porn Theatre* (2003) offered homage to the porn theater and the sexual diversity and solidarity that often emerged among its patrons from the 1960s through the early 1980s.

Gay hardcore films, like all pornography, offer a fantasy of sex without the ordinary obstacles of time, physical availability, and psychological inhibitions. They also serve as a kind of documentary record of actual gay sex. "Gay films, like gay novels, even the cheapest of them," observed reviewer Jim Kepner, "always tend to be an apology, an explanation, and an exploration of gay life.

"This is a factor which isn't present in heterosexual porno, because the matter is taken for granted. Now you might explore unknown aspects of heterosexual life, the question of having to justify it isn't there. Gay pornography, on the other hand, is a mixture—part sociology, part teaching, part hard-on. I have seen quite a few films though where the first two weren't in for more than a quarter of second flat." [Siebenand, 24]

REFERENCES

Kenneth Anger, *Hollywood Babylon* (New York: Bell Publishing, 1975).

Georges Bataille, *Erotism, Death and Sensuality* (San Francisco: City Lights, 1986).

Leo Bersani, *The Freudian Body: Psychoanalysis and Art* (New York: Columbia University Press, 1986).

Leo Braudy, *The World in a Frame: What We See in Films* (Garden City: Doubleday Anchor, 1977).

Elizabeth Cowie, "Pornography and Fantasy: Psychoanalytic Perspectives," Lynne Segal and Mary McIntosh, *Sex Exposed: Sexuality and the Pornography Debate* (New Brunswick: Rutgers University Press, 1993).

Amy Dawes, *Sunset Boulevard: Cruising the Heart of Los Angeles* (Los Angeles: Los Angeles Times Books, 2002).

Richard deCordova, *Picture Personalities: The Emergence of the Star System in America* (Urbana: University of Illinois Press, 1990).

Tom De Simone, Behind the Camera: Interview by Jerry Douglas, *Manshots*, June 1993.

Jerry Douglas, "The Making of *Song of the Loon:* Interview with Scott Hanson," *Manshots*, Part I, October 1994; Part II, December 1994.

Jerry Douglas, "Jaguar Productions: Interview with Barry Knight and Russell Moore," *Manshots*, Part I, June 1996; Part II, August 1996.

Richard Dyer, *Stars*, new edition (London: British Film Institute, 1998).

Jeffrey Escoffier, "Gay-for-Pay: Straight Men and the Making of Gay Pornography," *Qualitative Sociology*, Vol. 26, No. 4, Winter 2003.

Lillian Faderman and Stuart Timmons, *Gay L.A.: A History of Sexual Outlaws, Power Politics, and Lipstick Lesbians* (New York: Basic Books, 2006).

Hollis Alpert and Arthur Knight, "The Stag Film," *Playboy*, Nov 1967.

Patrick Moore, "The Life and Films of Fred Halsted," in *Beyond Shame: Reclaiming the Abandoned History of Radical Gay Sexuality* (Boston: Beacon, 2004).

John Rechy, *Sexual Outlaw: A Documentary* (New York: Grove, 1977).

Eric Schaefer, *Bold! Daring! Shocking! True!: A History of Exploitation Films, 1919–1959* (Durham: Duke University Press, 1999).

Paul Alcuin Siebenand, *The Beginnings of Gay Cinema in Los Angeles: The Industry and the Audience*. PhD dissertation, University of Southern California, June 1975.

Linda Williams, "Film Bodies: Gender, Genre and Excess," in Barry Keith Grand, ed. *Film Genre Reader III* (Austin: Texas University Press, 2003)

Joseph Slade, *Pornography in America* (Santa Barbara: ABC-CLIO, 2000).

Mark Thompson, ed., *Long Road to Freedom: The Advocate History of the Gay and Lesbian Movement* (New York: St. Martin's, 1994).

Turan and Zito, *Sinema*.

CHAPTER THREE

Paradise and the City of Orgies

"The city of orgies, walks and joys,

.....as I pass O Manhattan, your frequent and

swift flash of eyes offering me love."

—WALT WHITMAN, *LEAVES OF GRASS*

"... he had found Paradise on his first visit to Fire Island."

—ANDREW HOLLERAN,
DANCER FROM THE DANCE

On the night of April 14, 1968, when Mart Crowley's *Boys in the Band* opened at an off-Broadway theater, there was almost no one in the audience. Taxes were due the next day; perhaps most theatergoers were home preparing their tax returns. Surprisingly, by the next evening, there was a line around the block.

Boys in the Band portrayed gay male life in the early 1960s as nights of heavy drinking, vicious repartee, campy one-liners, Broadway musicals, and maudlin self-pity. Crowley was an unemployed screenwriter whose agent had declared the script unsaleable—"I don't know anyone I can send this to. This is like some weekend on Fire Island," he told Crowley. [Crespy, 157]

After it opened, the reviews, however, were mostly favorable. Critic Harold Clurman wrote, "No such overt depiction of a homosexual milieu has ever been presented on our stage…. It aims to show the guilt and self-loathing … from which many homosexuals, like members of all minorities, suffer." [Crespy, 157–58; Bottoms, 291] For many gay men, however, the play was hopelessly outdated.

Shortly after it opened, *Esquire* magazine assigned a writer to do a piece about "the new homosexual." "[T]here used to be this syndrome of drink, guilt and camp," he concluded. "Now it's dope, freedom and well, rock and soul." The new homosexual of the seventies, Burke wrote, was "an unfettered, guiltless male child of the new morality in a Zapata moustache and an outlaw hat, who couldn't care less for Establishment approval, would as soon sleep with boys as girls, and thinks that 'Over the Rainbow' is a place to fly on 200 micrograms of lysergic acid diethylamide [LSD]." He wondered "how the writer of a serious play … about modern homosexuals could have missed all this." [Burke, 77, 84]

More than a year after *Boys in the Band* opened, on a hot June night in 1969, police raided the Stonewall Inn, a bar in Greenwich Village. For once, instead of meekly lining up to file into a paddy wagon, the bar's patrons and the crowd that gathered outside fought the police, setting off five days of rioting. Drag queens, street hustlers, lesbians, and gay men, many politicized by the movement against the war in Vietnam, rioted and taunted the police, throwing bottles and rocks at them. The riots crystallized a broad grassroots mobilization across the country—Stonewall became the central symbol of a gay and lesbian political movement that dramatically changed the public image of homosexuals.

SEX IN THE CITY

Sexual liberation had not waited for gay liberation; gay male sexuality was changing. By the mid-sixties, nights of wild sex had already begun to compete with the more sedate pleasures of bitchy gossip and drinking. Poet Kenneth Pitchford recalled weekly orgies at a friend's apartment in Greenwich Village: "Every Thursday we would go to his place. He would spread sheets out on the floor and provide plenty of Vaseline. We would fuck like dogs." [Allyn,150] By the time of the Stonewall riots, sex in New York City was already available twenty-four hours a day. After Stonewall, the new sense of gay pride and self-respect was contagious.

In New York City plenty of that sex took place in public—out on the decaying Christopher Street piers, in the trucks parked under the elevated West Side Highway, in the Rambles in Central Park, in the showers at the YMCAs, in the public toilets of department stores and libraries, and in the back rows of movie houses on 42nd Street.

These places defined a new gay sexual culture. Participation in the sexual scene gave gay men a chance to learn about sex and about other gay men in a public setting rather than in more furtive personal encounters. Gay men would cruise someone on the way to work, pass a phone number to him, and meet him for sex in the office during lunch time. Men would dart off into doorways for quick blow jobs and orgasms. New York's raunchy sexual landscape generated a rich body of personal stories and in later years achieved a mythological status—marked iconic references such as "the trucks," "the piers," and "the tubs."

As the port of New York declined throughout the 1950s, the shipping industry gradually abandoned piers along the elevated West Side Highway (a nearby section collapsed in 1973) near Greenwich Village. The docks and buildings that had once served ferries, ocean liners, and cargo ships were empty and had begun to decay. Christopher Street, lined with bustling gay bars, was only a few blocks away. During daytime, gay men wandered down to the piers to sunbathe, wearing underwear or jockstraps or often nude; during nighttime, men stalked each other inside the rotting structures. "There were thousands of people fucking in the dark," one participant recalled. "Every day of the week—no matter what the weather." [Rodger McFarlane in *Gay Sex in the 70s*, (Dir. Lovett)]

But the piers were also dangerous. They were not locked, maintained, or inspected—and occasionally, in the dark, men fell through holes in the floor or rotting wood. The men lounging around the piers during the daytime periodically saw floating corpses nearby in the Hudson River.

Under the elevated West Side Highway, near the piers at the foot of Christopher Street, stood "the trucks." After unloading their cargo, commercial trucks that brought produce and other goods to the city were routinely parked under the highway overnight, with the backs unlocked. Like the piers, every night the empty trucks were filled with hundreds and hundreds of men having sex in the dark; the stale smell of sex, sweat, and poppers emanated from the trucks. At one point, a street vendor parked a cart there selling food, soda, water, and even lubricant. They, too, were dangerous. Pickpockets, police, and gay bashers occasionally raided them.

In 1966, more than two dozen peepshows were installed in bookstores around the Times Square area, and by mid-1970 there were more than a thousand. The introduction of curtains and doors, which offered a degree of privacy to allow the customer to masturbate, spurred their popularity. In the beginning they were soft-core and of course mostly heterosexual, but almost overnight the bookstores began to stock explicit magazines and film loops.

"Don't ask me where they came from, but they came: doctors, lawyers, tourists, kids, fags," Martin Hodas, who controlled almost a third of the machines in the area, told a reporter. "Everybody. And they were fighting to get to those peep machines." Profits from the peep shows financed the incredible growth of the pornography business in the Times Square area. [Bianco, 169]

Starting in the late sixties, writer Samuel Delany went regularly to the porn theaters in the Times Square area. He cruised in them and frequently had sex with the men who attended them, despite the fact that the vast majority of the theaters showed straight porn and that most of the men there were also straight.

The men who hung out in the theaters saw thousands of hours of porn films and videos. Those movies, Delany suggested,

> "(I)mproved our vision of sex ... making it friendlier, more relaxed, and more playful— qualities of sex.... For the first year or two the theaters operated, the entire working-class audience would break out laughing at everything save male-superior fucking. (I mean, that's *what* sex is, isn't it?) At the fellatio, at the cunnilingus even more, and at the final kiss, among the groans and chuckles you'd always hear a couple of '*Yuccchs*' and '*Uhgggs*.'

> "By the seventies' end, though, only a few chuckles sounded out now—at the cunnilingus passages. And in the first year or two of the eighties, even those had stopped.... Indeed, I think, under pressure of those films, many guys simply found themselves changing what turned them on. And if one part or another didn't happen to be your thing, you still saw it enough times to realize that maybe *you* were the strange one..." [Delany, 78]

During the same period, gay bathhouses also flourished. There were at least a dozen or so in New York City operating before Stonewall: the infamous Everard, which opened in 1928 as a public bathhouse, in the neighborhood now known as Chelsea; the St. Marks and the Club Baths downtown in the East Village, the Sauna up on 57th Street, and the Continental Baths on the upper West Side where Bette Midler later made her debut in 1969.

The Everard, rumored to be one of Rock Hudson's favorites, was perhaps the most notorious of them all—it was known as the Black Foot Club because the floors were so dirty that the bottoms of its patrons' feet turned black. Nevertheless, as Gore Vidal has said, at the Everard "sex was at its rawest and most exciting, and a revelation to me. I felt the way the Reverend Jerry Falwell must feel when he visits the Holy Land." [Hinds, 92]

Most of the patrons at the baths spent the nights walking along the narrow halls, peering into the small rooms looking for an inviting guest. If you rented one of the small rooms, you could leave your door open and invite any attractive man pacing the halls in for sex. The etiquette was simple—if you liked what you saw you need only smile invitingly. If you were not interested you only needed to walk on by, or if you had a room you could say, "No thank you" or "I'm tired." The men in the rooms might signal their predilections by lying on their backs playing with themselves or on their stomachs with their asses in the air. Some men found rejection at the baths easier to take than after all the jockeying and cruising that took place in the bars. It was more up front.

The seventies were an era of unparalleled sexual freedom for gay men, and that posed an unusual challenge to those who wanted to make gay hardcore films. As one gay man recalled,

> "Pornography couldn't compete with real life.... Anything that was in pornography you could have in abundance on the street any day, walk in any gym—more beautiful men, more dick, more available dick—right out the door into their

apartment, the party starts in an hour, you can
go in the backroom right now. It was like life *was*
a pornographic film." [Rodger McFarlane in *Gay
Sex in the 1970s* (dir. Lovett)]

Late one night in 1970, after a rehearsal for a new show, director and choreographer Wakefield Poole, Poole's boyfriend, the show's composer, and its lyricist decided to go the Park-Miller Theatre to see an all-male porn film. The Park-Miller was the New York outpost of Shan Sayles's chain of porn theaters—where some of the hardcore movies produced in Los Angeles were shown.

"It was one of those Friday nights in New York City," Poole recalled, "where seeing anything decent demands standing in lines that refuse to end."

It turned out to be a disappointing evening and for Poole a somewhat jarring experience. Unlike the dark and cruisey theaters that screened straight porn, the lights inside the Park-Miller were bright enough that the theater's customers could actually read; indeed one patron, Poole reported, was reading *The New York Times*. According to Poole, there was no sex going on between the patrons because the police repeatedly patrolled it. *Highway Hustler* was the main feature that night. It portrayed a young man hitchhiking, who is picked up and taken to a motel where he is fucked while being held at knifepoint.

Poole's companions reacted to the dreary, unerotic plot by laughing or falling asleep. The soundtrack blared out an orchestrated rendition of "June is Busting Out all Over" from the musical *Carousel*.

Afterward they wondered aloud whether it was possible to make a hardcore film that was more erotic and that wasn't degrading.

"Hell," Poole exclaimed, "I've got the camera Peter gave me. Maybe I should try. Just for the fun of it. Who wants to be in it?"

No one volunteered, but Poole wouldn't forget about it.

SEX ON THE BEACH

Like many other gay men, Wakefield Poole had come to New York "in search of something." He was a "settler," to use *New Yorker* writer E. B. White's term: "It was the settlers who gave New York its passion."

Poole grew up in the South, but moved to New York City as soon as he could to pursue a career as a dancer. For a number of years he toured with the Ballets Russes, the American-based successor to Serge Diaghilev's famous Paris-based original. In New York's highly competitive theatrical and dance world, Poole achieved middling success performing in and choreographing Broadway musicals. He had worked with Noel Coward, Marlene Dietrich, Liza Minelli, Bob Fosse, and Stephen Sondheim.

When his lover Peter gave Poole a 16mm movie camera as a gift, almost immediately he began to experiment with it. Inspired by several amateur movies made by Stephen Sondheim shown at parties and other social occasions, Poole created a series of multimedia dance events using light projections and film in addition to more traditional stage elements. He had also shot a short film in homage to Andy Warhol after finding a painting of himself in one of Warhol's shows.

Several months after their outing to the Park Miller, Poole and his lover Peter were invited out to Fire Island Pines to stay with friends. A narrow strip of sand and shrubbery along the southern coast of Long Island, Fire Island was in the process of becoming a mythic landscape. "Fire Island was for madness," wrote Andrew Holleran in his novel *Dancer from the Dance*, "for hot nights, kisses, and herds of stunning men: a national game preserve annually replenished by men each summer arrived from every state in the Union..." [206–7] In *Faggots*, Larry Kramer's portrait of gay life in New York City during the early seventies, his protagonist is overwhelmed by Fire Island Pines: "He wasn't ready for such beauty, such potential, such unlimited choice. The place scared him half to death." [Kramer, 224]

Outdoor cruising and *al fresco* sex were endemic.

Cherry Grove on Fire Island, the tiny neighboring community to the south of the Pines, had been a well-known holiday destination of homosexual actors, writers, and artists since the 1930s and a predominantly gay community, making it "America's first gay and lesbian town." The poet W. H. Auden and his partner Chester Kallman regularly came out to the Grove in the early forties. They were joined by an array of famous gay and lesbian artists and writers, among them Carson McCullers, Janet Flanner, Benjamin Britten and his partner Peter Pears, Christopher Isherwood, Lincoln Kirstein, Patricia Highsmith, Jane Bowles, Tennessee Williams, and Truman Capote. [Newton]

Poole and his partner made plans to spend several months on Fire Island, and it was during this time that he decided he would make his erotic movie that summer. The acute sexual tension on the island and its stunning beauty provided Poole with the germinal idea. "A young man walks down the boardwalk, turns into the woods, and comes out on the bayside of the island. He spreads a blanket, takes off his clothes, and sits and waits, looking over the water. A vision appears like Venus from the sea: a beautiful nude man who seems to walk on water and he approaches the waiting man. They immediately explore each other and eventually go into the woods. When they've finished fucking, the waiting man gets up, kisses the other, leaves, and disappears running into the bay. The man left on the blanket gets up, looks over the water, puts on the clothes left by the other man, picks up the blanket, and walks down the shore as the scene fades." [Poole, 150]

Once he had formulated his idea and begun to script it in his mind, he also thought about the casting for it. At first he asked Tom and Michael, the friends with whom Poole was staying, if they would play the two men in the first scene. They agreed, but almost immediately had second thoughts. Hours later Poole ran into a man named Dino who worked in a little gift shop at the hotel in the Pines.

"The three of us had been flirting for weeks," Poole recalled. "I suddenly turned to him and asked if he'd like to be in a film with Peter. They both looked a bit startled, but moments later we agreed to shoot the next day at 6 a.m. I spent the rest of the afternoon thinking about what I was going to do the following day. I rolled a few joints, loaded my camera and I was ready." [Poole, 150]

The next morning the three of them set off for the little beach on the bayside of the island. Their props were few; besides the camera, they had only a blanket, marijuana, poppers, and some bottles of soda. To his surprise, Poole felt extremely uncomfortable filming his lover having sex with Dino. With the heat, the sand, and the gnats, the two performers also found it a challenge keeping their erections. There was no top, no bottom—indeed, those rigid distinctions had not yet evolved among gay men—and Poole found himself increasingly drawn into the role of voyeur. At the end of the scene, all three were exhausted by the strain of focusing on the sexual performance.

Over the next few months, Poole edited the scene into a fifteen-minute movie. When he showed it to a group of friends, they claimed that it was the best porn movie they'd seen. Marvin Shulman, his business manager, offered to invest into expanding it into a feature-length movie. As he began to sketch two new scenes, Dino decided that he wanted to be paid $2,000 for his participation. Poole chose to recast the scene and reshoot it.

An old friend was present when the casting was being discussed and said to Poole, "I've got the perfect person for you. He's blond, six feet tall, and handsome. He's got a nice dick, a beautiful ass, and he does everything."

A few days later, Cal Culver showed up at Poole's door. He was perfect, Poole thought, "the type you see in magazine ads, not porno movies." [Poole, 154] Culver was a former high school teacher, unemployed actor, waiter, hustler, and man about town.

After seeing the scene with Peter and Dino, Culver was adamant. "I want to do it!" he insisted. "You just tell me what to do and I'll do it. It's really great. When do we start?"

They reshot the scene the following weekend. "After the first few minutes of shooting," Poole remembered, "I knew Cal was going to be terrific. The camera loved him." [Poole, 154]

Culver entered wholeheartedly into the entire project. When they were done shooting, he went back to the house to discuss the other parts of the film. He mentioned Tommy Moore, a longtime fuck buddy who he thought would be good for the last scene, which was set inside a house. Moore was a bartender in Cherry Grove. Culver also suggested his costar for the other scene—Danny DiCioccio, a local builder, whom Culver did not know but whom he had eyed all that summer. In fact, DiCioccio had made a few soft-core short films for Jim French of Colt Studios, so he readily agreed. Culver also found the two locations where the other scenes would be shot—the pool and the house used in the last section. Both were owned by friends of his.

Each of the other sex scenes was shot quickly, before the actors could find any faults in their sex partners. Poole's friend Ed Parente, who later designed the titles and the poster, came along to shoot stills. Shooting the sex scene for "Poolside," the second section, took only two hours. It was an energetic and athletic sex scene. Danny DiCioccio's experience making soft-core porn had proved useful, but he had been so frenetic in his scene that later it was difficult to edit as a coherent scene. Filming the third scene went very smoothly.

"Cal and Tommy were evenly matched," Poole remembers, "both liking everything. They also had no preferences with one another, so there's no top. No bottom in the segment... it's one of the best sex scenes I ever filmed."

Each of the scenes evokes some mythical or magical element: in the first scene, a beautiful man rises from the sea like Botticelli's

Venus. It is a scene deeply indebted to Poole's dance experience with the Ballets Russes—its Debussy soundtrack calling to mind Vaslav Nijinsky's famous ballet *Afternoon of a Faun*. The ballet provoked a huge furor at its premier in 1912 when the faun, danced by Nijinsky himself, relieved his sexual frustration by lying on a nymph's scarf and rubbing against it to the point of orgasm. In the second scene in the film, a man responds to an ad in a gay newspaper for a magic pill to create a beautiful man. He tosses the pill into the pool and, like a genie from a magic lantern, a beautiful man emerges for a passionate sexual encounter. And in the third, a torrid sexual encounter is created in the imaginations of two gay men as they openly cruise one another—one black, the other white, like the mythical homoerotic male bonding in American literature.

When Poole had finished editing the movie, which he named *Boys in the Sand*—the title a deliberate rebuke to *Boys in the Band*—it was necessary to find some way to distribute it. There was no commercial infrastructure to arrange for bookings or collecting the fees.

Poole flew out to Los Angeles to meet with Shan Sayles, "the porno king of the West Coast."

> "Hello, I'm Shan Sayles," the tall, heavyset man said. "I understand you've made a boy-boy picture you want me to look at. I like the title, so that's a good start. There's not much more to talk about until I view the picture. Come back tomorrow at ten and we'll see if we can do some business."
>
> Poole was taken aback that Sayles wanted to take the film overnight.
>
> "I'm not sure I should let it out of my hands." Poole responded. "I really don't know you, and I've heard such wild stories about getting ripped off." But he reluctantly agreed to let Sayles have the print.

Poole was back at Sayles's office first thing in the morning.

"Well, I think your picture is one of the best boy-boy films I've ever seen. How much did it cost you?"

"About four thousand dollars," Poole replied without much thought.

"Well, I'll give you eight thousand for the film outright."

"If it's the best gay film you've ever seen, it should be worth more than eight thousand dollars," Poole rejoined.

"Oh, it's worth more, but that's all I'm willing to pay for it." [Poole, 163]

Poole told Sayles he would to discuss the offer with his business partner, Marvin Shulman. They decided to show it themselves at the 55th Street Playhouse, the ramshackle old theater in New York, where Andy Warhol had screened *My Hustler* and *Lonesome Cowboys*.

Boys in the Sand was a huge hit with audiences and critics. In spite of being a gay hardcore film, it was previewed by *Variety* and was the first gay hardcore film advertised in the *New York Times*. It was on *Variety*'s list of the fifty top-grossing films for almost three months. The gay press was enthusiastic.

THE FIRST GAY PORN SUPERSTAR

Boys in the Sand owes a large degree of its success to Casey Donovan *(Culver's nom de porn)*—not only because of his outstanding sexual performances; in the opinion of many viewers at the time, his physical charm, poise, and acting ability contributed to the movie's success. His performance and stage presence on top of his role behind the scenes—his engagement with the whole project, his casting suggestions, and the support he gave to the other performers were decisive.

Poole of course knew what Donovan had contributed to the movie.

> "He was so natural, he never rushed anything. I could tell him something to do and it was done very slowly and deliberately. He had a sort of magic that made it all work. He was genuine and real, and he had a wonderful quality about him. He loved sex—there's no doubt about that when you see the film. He loved doing it on screen." [Edmonson, 79]

Boys in the Sand catapulted Casey Donovan into a unique position as the first gay porn star. Characterized as a "gay-liberated Robert Redford, the all-American male," he resembled and aptly symbolized the newly liberated gay man living in New York City during the 1970s. Blond and blue-eyed, with a well-toned body and absolutely radiant smile, Donovan exuded sex appeal and communicated an almost irresistible charisma. Once the film opened in other cities across the country, he quickly became a national celebrity. No other performer, in gay soft-core or hardcore films, had succeeded or even approached the renown that he had so quickly achieved.

Donovan grew up in upstate western New York. His family ran a trailer park near the town of Canandaigua, not far from Rochester. Since his freshman year in high school, he had been sexually precocious. He once told of an incident that had taken place while he was in high school. Attracted to one of the football players, who was quite shy and who used to wait until most of the other players had left before taking a shower, Culver noticed that the young man had started to get aroused. Culver stooped down as though he was going to wash his feet, but instead licked the young man's penis. The young man gasped, but stood still as Culver began to suck his dick. [Edmonson, 21]

After high school, Culver attended the teachers college in nearby Genesco. He graduated from college in 1965 and took a contract to teach sixth grade in Peekskill, New York, only forty-eight miles from New York City. He voraciously explored New York's sexual underground and spent much of his time at gay cruising scenes—public restrooms, movie theaters, and the parks.

After a year teaching in Peekskill, Culver took a teaching position at the exclusive Fieldston School in New York City, which was attended by the children of professionals, intellectuals, and celebrities. However, very soon after starting, he was fired for excessively disciplining a student (she was the daughter of actor Eli Wallach) and took up escorting to help meet his living expenses.

Always impeccably dressed and a lively conversationalist, Culver rapidly succeeded as a high-class male escort in New York's wealthy gay circles. He also began to dabble in the theater, which had long held a strong appeal to him; he had participated in theatrical productions throughout high school and college. He found nonpaying opportunities behind the stage and eventually on it, both in summer stock and then in low-budget off-Broadway productions. He often traded sexual favors for the chance to advance. Throughout much of this period, he supported himself through escorting. Eventually he was employed by an escort service. [Edmonson, 36–44] By 1970 he worked full-time as a fashion model for the well-known Wilhelmina Agency, supplementing his income with escort work.

Culver had appeared in a porn movie before *Boys in the Sand*. He found that it was more difficult than he had expected; he "had to produce a hard-on and perform, really fuck for my supper. One kid turned out to be married and was very straight. I don't think he'd ever been involved with a guy and was obviously doing it for the money ... and there was another guy who very uptight and the problem was my having to make them look good." [Edmonson, 55–57]

• • •

After Dark was a cross between a dance magazine and a fashion magazine. Founded in 1968 to give "an exciting and sexy look at the arts," it nevertheless appeared to be an elegant vehicle for soft-core eroticism. It promoted a sense of male beauty in a discreet way that reflected the cautionary ethos of the fifties and early sixties—it offered a peculiar hybrid of beefcake images of dancers in tights with bulging baskets and voluptuous buttocks with glamorous photographs of the leading male and female stars of the day. Initially, it was considered quite a provocative publication. While ostensibly covering Broadway, the arts, and all aspects of show business, it was viewed by many as a soft-core porn magazine for gay men. By the late seventies, most readers thought it a dishonest and somewhat closety gay magazine, especially compared to the explicitly pornographic magazines that had started publishing around that time.

Soon after *Boys* opened, in February 1972, *After Dark* published a headshot of Donovan and brief mention of his appearance in *Boys in the Sand*; then in March it offered an upper body shot of Donovan while referring to a recent theatrical appearance; finally in July, Donovan appeared on the cover with a spread inside. "It was the talk of New York," Donovan told friends. [Edmonson, 108] *After Dark* was an essential bridge that allowed Casey Donovan to cross over from the pornographic fantasy world of *Boys in the Sand* to that of fashionable show-biz glamour—and back again.

Donovan experienced the full force of *After Dark's* role in promoting what the *New York Times* later called "porn chic" when he returned from a short stint making a soft-core bisexual movie in Yugoslavia for noted director Radley Metzger. He both loved the celebrity and dreaded it. As he put it, it was "kind of fun, to be up there on the screen. You ... become a fantasy figure for a lot of people. I … get off on that." [Edmonson, 87] In other respects it was also a burden.

> "In a way it was like being a new face, but not exactly a new face. But it was really incredible that first weekend back—everybody knew who I was. It was really frightening. I went through the whole recognition trip, people doing numbers, and people sort of stopping and doing double takes. And I thought, 'Wow now I realize why people in Hollywood want their privacy and why they don't go out in public, and why they don't like to sign autographs, and why they don't like to be recognized, and why they want to be left alone.'" [108]

Although the persona of Casey Donovan was created expressly for pornographic movies, it was derived from Cal Culver's psychological and physical characteristics. As a porn star, he enacted a fantasy that any gay man could have sex with any other man, that no sex act was too outrageous, and that no man was too unattractive. He lived up to the fantasy of sexual accessibility that marked the age: "So many men, so little time." It was, as novelist Brad Gooch aptly named it, the "golden age of promiscuity."

HARD-CORE CITY

Within weeks of *Boys in the Sand*'s premier, Jerry Douglas, a young playwright and off-Broadway director who had directed a couple of nude plays (a somewhat unique 1960s specialty), was approached by a director of TV commercials to make a gay pornographic film. Producing a hardcore film was still considered such a taboo project that the film's backers asked Douglas to not reveal the production company's name to anyone, to memorize the firm's address and telephone number, and to never put anything in writing. Though Douglas went on to shoot the movie, the contract he requested was repeatedly promised but never delivered.

Like Wakefield Poole, Jerry Douglas had not come to New York to make hardcore skin flicks. He was born in Des Moines, Iowa, and had what he called "a very Norman Rockwell childhood, classically so with one notable exception: my parents were divorced when I was ten years old, and my father left home. I was raised by a single mother—*not* a single mother, she'd die if she heard me say that!—a divorced mother and two younger brothers. Sleigh rides and pup tents and county fairs—all very traditionally American." [interview, 2001]

Douglas became aware of his homosexual desires in high school and began to masturbate to fantasies of James Dean, Farley Granger, and Montgomery Clift in a basement room dedicated to and papered with images of his favorite movie stars—a scene he later recreated in his 1999 film *Dream Team*.

While attending Drake University in Des Moines, he had his first homosexual encounter.

> "I was hitchhiking from the campus to my home late at night after play rehearsal. Some dirty old man stopped and went down on me. That was basically the extent of my homosexual activity until my junior year in college. ... I got married just before my senior year at Drake. I got a Danforth Fellowship to Yale, for graduate study, which covers everything—the works—and wife. So, Barbara and I went off to New Haven. By then I had a pretty good idea that my interests did not lie in my wife's body." [Douglas, unpublished interview, 10/1/2001]

From 1957 until June 1960 Douglas attended Yale Drama School. During his last year there he met the man who became his first lover. When he graduated from Yale, he and his lover moved to New York. He spent much of the next five years working on *Rondelay*, a musical version of Arthur Schnitzler's

La Ronde, which dramatizes the impact of a series of inter-locking sexual encounters.

Rondelay opened on November 6, 1969. The *New York Times* drama critic, Clive Barnes, gave it very harsh review and the play closed soon after it opened. Douglas was devastated. He'd spent five years of his life on it. "This is what I've come to New York to do with my life," he thought to himself, "and they're not gonna let me do it." Many years later he made a gay porn version of Schnitzler's play, his 1993 film *Jock-A-Holics*.

Douglas went on to produce and direct the off-Broadway production of his play *Score*. He was then approached to doctor a gay sexploitational play called *Circle in the Water* that had some nudity in it. "By then," he recalled, "I'd gotten something of a reputation of how to handle nudity on-stage, and obviously, was preoccupied with things sexual. So it was only a hop, skip, and a jump to hardcore pornography." [Douglas, 9/98, 19]

When Douglas was approached to make a gay porn film, he agreed to write and direct the film—and to cast *Boys'* star in it. While Douglas had worked for the previous five years in the New York theater world, he had never made a movie, much less a pornographic one. *The Back Row*, the movie Douglas decided to make, was a sexually explicit takeoff of *Midnight Cowboy*, the X-rated movie that had recently won an Academy Award. Like *Midnight Cowboy*, *The Back Row*'s hero was a naïve young cowboy just off the bus from the West who takes a walk on the wild side of New York's gay sexual subculture. Douglas thought of the movie as an act of homage to the world of sex in the back row of the porno movie theaters.

Donovan was an old friend and had appeared in a play Douglas had directed. Since Donovan was available only for a brief time before going on a national tour for a play he was in, casting and production had to be scheduled almost immediately. Just as he had during the production of *Boys in the Sand*, Donovan constantly made useful contributions to production of *The Back Row*. During the auditions, Donovan brought a young fireman he had picked up: George Payne had just flown in from Ohio, where he'd left his wife to come to New York to do some bathing suit modeling. Douglas hired him on the spot to play "the cowboy." Donovan was constantly thinking of things to help make the sex more exciting and the scene run more smoothly. For instance, he brought props and lube for the three-way in the men's room at the theater.

• • •

It was 5 a.m. on a Sunday morning in February 1972 at the Times Square IRT station. Jerry Douglas stood alone on the platform. "Where were the others?" he wondered. Then reassuring himself, he thought, "It's much too early ... for anyone to have been arrested yet."

When Douglas's cast and crew had finally assembled, they boarded the last car on the first downtown train that came along. The six men boarded an empty car—exactly what they were hoping for. It wasn't easy to find an empty subway car on most days, which is why they decided to try very early on a Sunday morning on a downtown train to Wall Street. They were planning to shoot a scene for a pornographic movie.

Douglas positioned the two young actors opposite one another in the center of the car. He explained what he wanted them to do. Douglas called "Action" and the young men groped each other in the crotch and unzipped their flies just as they arrived at the next station. A drunk staggered into the car, stared into the camera, went to the far end of the car, plopped himself down, and passed out. The Eastern European cameraman never stopped filming and they were finished by noon without any further incidents. They had film in the can, Douglas thought; "Now, they could be arrested." Making a porn movie in 1972 was an illegal act—not to mention shooting it "in public" on the subway. [Douglas, *Manshots*, 9/89, 21–22]

The movie follows the sexual adventures of a young, innocent "cowboy" who arrives in New York at the Port Authority Bus Terminal and unwittingly falls into the clutches of the sex-driven Casey Donovan. Payne and Donovan play a cat-and-mouse game that takes them into a sex scene with a hard hat, smoking a joint together in a movie audience, down to the Pleasure Chest (then a funky little Greenwich Village sex shop before it became a national chain), on to a couple of scenes at a porno theater—the last one a three-way sleaze fest on the dirty floor of the theater's men's room.

Like all early hardcore directors, Douglas faced technical challenges—how to portray sex on film, how to shoot penetration scenes, how to encourage the performers to get erections and have orgasms. He had observed that in many "skin flicks … the photographing of the sex act is never very flexible or revealing." He wanted to "find new and interesting camera angles which are at once unobtrusive to the actors, yet provide a better vantage point for what people will be paying to see." One solution was to shoot sex on a glass-topped coffee table from below. [Douglas, *Manshots*, 9/89, 58]

The cameramen positioned themselves on the floor, flat on their backs. The performers, both with erections, lay down on the table, ready to begin fucking. Douglas called "Action" and as the performers began to move, suddenly, not even ten seconds in, a terrifying crack sounded. Splintering glass flew everywhere. Both performers fell into the metal frame of the coffee table, covered in tiny pieces of glass.

Donovan's panicked thought was "Please, God, if I have to die, that's okay—but don't castrate me." Both performers were unharmed and they completed the scene on a waterbed. [Douglas, *Manshots*, 9/89, 58]

• • •

One year after they started shooting, *The Back Row* opened at the 55th Street Playhouse. For weeks the theater was packed. Collecting the box office receipts was daunting. Every day Douglas went to the theater to make sure that the daily box office statements were relatively accurate. It was far worse in

San Francisco and other cities. Often, the larger theaters with big box office receipts were the most difficult to collect from. When *The Back Row* was playing (at Shan Sayles's Nob Hill Theater) in San Francisco, Douglas asked a lawyer friend to be his "bag man." When Douglas's friend showed up at the theater, the manager was stunned. No one had ever done that before. The owner had always been able to mail a check off whenever he wanted to, but all of sudden here was someone, a lawyer no less, asking for the check immediately and depositing it in a San Francisco account to be sure it cleared.

Because theaters showing sexually explicit films were not quite legitimate, and since making hardcore films for theatrical release was still a new business, there were few established firms without Mafia ties distributing the movies. There was no guarantee that the filmmaker would be paid his share of the box office, and there was no way to prevent the theater owner from duplicating the print, returning the original, and continuing to run the film without the filmmaker's knowledge. Moreover, the wear and tear on the prints meant expensive repairs to them each time they were returned—*if* they were returned. All contributed to the difficulty and high cost of scheduling features theatrically. With no reliable distribution, producers like Poole and Douglas were at a distinct disadvantage compared to theater owners who produced their own hardcore films.

In 1975, Douglas directed another pornographic film, *Both Ways*, a bisexual murder mystery, before deciding to retire from the adult film business. Making movies took an enormous amount of his time—fund-raising, casting, and producing. More important, he hadn't been able to make money. Nor had he gained any recognition from his films that might have advanced his theatrical career. Despite the presence of Wakefield Poole and one or two other independents in New York, the city had not become a center of porn production as Los Angeles and San Francisco had.

SUBWAY TO THE ADONIS

Poole's *Boys in the Sand* and Douglas's *The Back Row* documented the new gay sexual culture that had emerged in the sixties. In *Left-Handed* (1972) and the films that followed, Jack Deveau set out to tell the stories of people who were affected by that culture. Of the gay erotic films that opened in New York at that time, *Left-Handed* had the most elaborate plot and a degree of character development, though it had no dialogue since it was shot without synchronized sound.

Left-Handed was about an antique dealer, his hustler boyfriend, and their pot dealer: a typical story of the sixties and early seventies. It recounted the story of a gay man (the hustler) seducing a straight man (the pot dealer), the gay man eventually topping the straight man, who becomes emotionally involved and begins to explore homosexuality, even participating in a gay orgy. At that point, the gay man loses interest in the sexually curious "straight" man.

But unlike the films of Poole, Halsted, or Douglas, the lead character of *Left-Handed* is not a symbol of the sexually liberated gay man but rather a cynical young man who seduces a sexually curious straight man, fucks him, and then abandons him. The hustler moves from the typical role of being a bottom to a straight man to that of topping him. However, once the straight man is emotionally and sexually hooked, the hustler loses interest in him. The film also includes a scene of heterosexual sex between the drug dealer and his girlfriend. Deveau and his parter Robert shot it in about three weeks, mostly on weekends. Then editing it took another eight weeks.

• • •

Deveau was born in January 1935 and grew up in Manhattan. He attended Cornell University for one semester before moving back to Manhattan where he became a partner in an architectural and design firm. Once he started making pornographic films, he thought of it as a business. He sold some stocks in order to make *Left-Handed*. Widely considered the master of narrative gay porn, Deveau made a series of heavily plotted erotic films during the seventies: *Drive* (1972); *Strictly Forbidden* (1972), which was shot in France; *Ballet Down the Highway* (1975); *Wanted Billy the Kid* (1976); *Hot House* (1977); *Sex Magic* (1977); *A Night at the Adonis* (1978), set at the famous porn theater; and two movies set on Fire Island, *Dune Buddies* (1978) and *Fire Island Fever* (1979).

At the same time, he and Alvarez set up Hand in Hand Films to produce and distribute gay erotic films. They had decided that they would sell final prints of their films, but would try to control the process of printing and leasing the prints. As soon as *Left-Handed* was done, they traveled across the country and visited theater owners in all the major cities. Getting enough product was always a problem for theater owners, as Shan Sayles and Monroe Beehler had realized when they started showing porn in their theaters.

"We're in the movie business," Deveau and Alvarez told exhibitors, "and we're going to be making a lot of movies. Rent from us. We will have product. You'll get better prints. You'll get better services from us."

Like Sayles and Beehler before them, Deveau and Alvarez sought out films made by others to distribute. One of the first projects after *Left-Handed* was releasing a collection of Peter DeRome's 8mm shorts in a 16mm format. In 1972, Deveau and Alvarez also acquired the Lincoln Art Theatre on West 57th Street as a showcase for the films they made and distributed through Hand in Hand. However, before they even started showing gay porn, they booked *The Devil in Miss Jones*, the acclaimed straight adult film of 1972 that Alvarez, like many others, considered one of "the best pornographic films" ever made. But it ran for years, and by the time it closed, a local theater to showcase their own films had become superfluous, Hand in Hand had become a national distributor. [*Stallion,* 23–25, 46–47]

After *Left-Handed*, Deveau and Alvarez decided to make *Drive* (1974), a movie with a transvestite/transsexual role, which became their second film. It is an extravagant and flamboyant film, with a script written by Christopher Rage (later to become a director as well), who also played in drag the role of villainess Arachne. The large cast comprised more than fifty people. The "drive" of the title refers to the male sex drive, which Arachne is determined to eradicate, and to the movie's hero driving around Manhattan in a Lamborghini.

In the following year Deveau made *Ballet Down the Highway*, the story of a love affair between a dancer and a truck driver and the disruption it causes in the dancer's life. The film starred Gary Hunt as the truck driver. It was probably the first of Deveau's films to be built around a particular actor—who was a charismatic sexual performer.

In 1977, Deveau began production on *A Night at the Adonis*, set in the theater where most of their films were shown in New York. In part it was a tribute to the great role that porn theaters played in the 1970s, showing porn and creating a sexual environment for gay men, and in part a tribute to Jerry Douglas's 1972 film *The Back Row*.

A Night at the Adonis is one of Deveau's best movies. Each of the film's characters ends up at the Adonis because some sexual or emotional disappointment leads him there as a distraction—for example, Jack Wrangler, who goes to the Adonis when he fails to have sex with his boss, or like the "kept man" whose lover isn't spending enough time with him. And in a nod to *The Back Row*, the final scene is a grand orgy in the bathroom.

Founded as a legitimate theater, the Tivoli on Eighth Avenue had a long and honorable career as a vaudeville theater before showing soft-core nudies. Its name was changed to the Adonis in March 1975 when it starting running hardcore all-male films. Deveau's film was actually shot at the theater. In order to maintain its regular schedule, the set was lit up after the theater closed at 1:00 a.m. Shooting went through the night until noon, when everything had to be packed up until that night. What is

remarkable is that the movie showed sex taking place throughout the theater. It's unclear whether or not Deveau or the theater's owner was concerned about alerting the police to the
activities that took place daily.

"Around 1975 there was a general downward trend in theatrical distribution," noted Deveau and Alvarez's business
partner Case Chapman in 1983. "Jack began to realize that you
couldn't spend the kind of money we had spent on, say, a picture like *Drive.*" Deveau frequently considered his work to be
"no matter what—this is recorded literature or a piece of literature. You can be sure when you're dead that that piece of
literature will be around." [*Stallion,* 47]

The commercial success of the early gay hardcore films that
showed in mainstream movie theaters proved that there was a
market for gay pornographic movies. Theaters in Boston, Washington, D.C., Chicago, San Francisco, and other mid-sized cities
showing "all-male" films flourished. The new gay porn movies
promulgated the erotic promise of the sexual revolution: sex
without apology, without restraint, and without distinction.

REFERENCES

Allyn, *Make Love, Not War.*

Anthony Bianco, *Ghosts of 42nd Street: A History of America's
Most Infamous Block* (New York: Harper Perennial, 2004).

Stephen J. Bottoms, *Playing Underground: A Critical History
of the 1960s Off-Off-Broadway Movement* (Ann Arbor: University of Michigan Press, 2004).

Tom Burke, "The New Homosexuality," *Esquire,* December 1969.

Cowie, "Pornography and Fantasy" in Segal and McIntosh,
Sex Exposed.

David Crespy, *Off-Off-Broadway Explosion: How Provocative
Playwrights of the 1960s Ignited a New American Theater*

(New York: Back Stage Books, 2003).

Michael DeAngelis, *Gay Fandom and Crossover Stardom: James Dean, Mel Gibson and Keanu Reeves* (Durham: Duke University Press, 2001).

Samuel Delany, *Times Square Red, Times Square Blue* (New York: New York University Press, 1999).

Jerry Douglas (as Doug Richards), "The Gay Film Heritage: Filming 'Back Row,'" *Manshots*, September 1989.

Jerry Douglas, "The Legacy of Jack Deveau," *Stallion*, April 1983. [Stallion]

Roger Edmonson, *Boy in the Sand: All-American Sex Star* (Los Angeles: Alyson, 1998).

Andrew Holleran, *Dancer from the Dance* (New York: Harper, 1978).

Patrick Hinds, *The Q Guide to NYC Pride* (New York: Alyson, 2007).

Larry Kramer, *Faggots* (New York: Grove, 1978).

Jonathan Mahler, *Ladies and Gentlemen, The Bronx is Burning: 1977, Baseball, Politics, and The Battle for the Soul of a City* (New York: Farrar, Straus and Giroux, 2005).

Esther Newton, *Cherry Grove, Fire Island: Sixty Years in America's First Gay and Lesbian Town* (Boston: Beacon, 1993).

Wakefield Poole, *Dirty Poole: The Autobiography of a Gay Porn Pioneer* (Los Angeles: Alyson, 2000).

Turan and Zito, *Sinema.*

Michael Warner, *The Trouble with Normal: Sex, Politics, and the Ethics of Queer Life* (New York: Free Press, 1999).

CHAPTER FOUR

Porn Capital
of America

San Francisco today is indeed the porn capital of the country.... This exalted status hasn't been achieved simply on the basis of the quantity of pure porn being hustled. New York and Los Angeles, for instance, have just as many dirty movies, book stores, nude dancers, live sex shows, model studios, message parlors, swap clubs, underground publications and prostitutes. Probably more, even when counted on a per capita basis.

What distinguishes San Francisco from any place else is the style with which porn is marketed, its practitioners' attitude towards it and the tolerance most square citizens display concerning the whole questions. The basic assumption, it would seem ... is that a "mature adult" is entitled to get his kicks any way he can, provided decent citizens don't have to witness the process and nobody gets hurt.

—WILLIAM MURRAY,
NEW YORK TIMES MAGAZINE, JANUARY 3, 1971

San Francisco is where gay fantasies come true,
and the problem the city presents is whether,
after all, we wanted these particular dreams to
be fulfilled—or would we have preferred others?
Did we know what price these dreams would
exact?

—EDMUND WHITE, *STATES OF DESIRE*

The Condor Club, a go-go bar in San Francisco's North
Beach, struggled financially throughout the spring of 1964.
Then in May, clothing designer Rudi Gernich, who, inciden-
tally, belonged to a circle of politically conscious gay men,
launched the "monokini" bathing suit. In contrast to the
bikini, which consisted of a top and a bottom, the monokini
had no top. That gave the Condor's rather desperate promoter
the idea of having the club's go-go dancers wear the monokini
to spice up the show. So on June 23, the club's lead dancer,
Carol Doda, initiated the new routine and danced that evening
wearing Gernich's topless swimsuit. One of the first women in
the country to have silicone injections to increase the size of
her breasts, she went from a size 34B to a 44D. The newspapers picked up on Doda's topless performance and soon there
were lines of men around the block waiting to get in. The Condor did very well after that. When the police department
decided not to press charges, the other go-go clubs in North
Beach soon followed in its footsteps.

Topless dancing was a major break from traditional bur-
lesque performances—strippers like Gypsy Rose Lee had long
worked the delicate line between dancing and showing flesh,
between sex and the tease. Topless changed all that. Soon topless bars proliferated up and down the West Coast, but Carol
Doda and the topless club symbolized San Francisco's long

history as a wide-open town, dating back to the Gold Rush.

That summer, *Life* magazine published a special feature on "Homosexuality in America." The magazine noted that "Homosexuality—and the problem it poses—exists all over the U.S., but is most evident in New York, Chicago, Los Angeles, San Francisco, New Orleans and Miami." [Boyd, 200] Not only did large cities offer more tolerance, relative anonymity, and employment opportunities, but the magazine expounded, "homosexual men also had greater opportunities to meet other homosexuals in the cities' parks, bathhouses, and bars." [Haveman, 68; Boyd, 200] The article portrayed San Francisco as a city with a rich and vigorous gay community and went on to identify it as "the gay capital" of America. It noted that there were "more than 30 bars that catered exclusively to a homosexual clientele." [Haveman, 68] With the publication of that article, the city became the desired location for many young men coming to terms with their homosexuality.

Once a blue-collar industrial city and a bustling port, San Francisco started changing almost imperceptibly in the sixties. The port gradually declined and the manufacturing industries moved to the outlying suburbs. Blue-collar workers followed the industrial jobs. Gradually San Francisco emerged as a regional financial center—but tourism increasingly became the mainstay of the city's economic life. In fact, early in the sixties the city's tourist industry depended on perpetuating its reputation for sexual license. At the end of the decade, sociologist Howard Becker noted that San Francisco was "more tolerant of odd behavior, of dope smoking and freaky sex, of alternate life styles, than most big cities." [Becker, 1971, 2]

Starting as a trickle in the late sixties and swelling during the seventies, soon thousands of young gay men and lesbians left the suburbs, small towns, and modest cities to move to the cosmopolitan cities of New York, Los Angeles, Chicago, Boston, New Orleans, and San Francisco.

In the late 1960s the first gay bar opened on Castro Street in the cozy blue-collar Irish neighborhood of longshoremen, stevedores, factory workers, and policemen nestled in a little valley between Twin Peaks, Noe Valley, and the Mission. Slowly, businesses serving the gay population opened along the two blocks of Castro Street from Market and Seventeenth and Nineteenth streets. Within five years, many of the Irish families had sold their Victorian homes to gay men moving into the neighborhood.

By the early seventies, gay men were pouring into the Castro district. Gay businesses opened in abandoned storefronts. In 1972, two former gay activists opened Paperback Traffic. Their business more than tripled over the next four years. In 1973, just up the street from the bookstore, Harvey Milk, a New York businessman turned hippy, opened the Castro Camera store with his lover. Founder of the Castro Village Business Association and the city's first openly gay member of the Board of Supervisors, Milk, who first ran for office in 1973, dominated San Francisco gay politics until his assassination in 1978. Almost a dozen gay bars attracted gay men from all over the city; All American Boy, a clothing retailer, sold Levis and jockstraps; Leather Forever took over the old florist shop; restaurants were filled with young gay men dressed in work shirt and jeans, the dress code uniform of the "Castro clone," the new masculine gay male stereotype that replaced the campy queen of the days before Stonewall. [Shilts, 81–83, 111–113]

GOLDEN BOYS

Even before the massive influx of gay men in the late sixties and seventies, a small group of young gay men in San Francisco had become involved with the publication of physique magazines and the production of 8mm erotic movies. In March 1965, local businessman Bob Damron and partners Jack Trollop, Jack Tennyson, and Hal Call opened the Adonis Bookstore. The Adonis sold beefcake magazines, nude photographs, and 8mm hardcore loops. [Sears, 519]

The year before, Damron had started publishing a small

book listing all of the gay bars that he encountered on his extensive travels in the United States. More than thirty-five years later the company Damron founded is still operating and now publishes men's and women's travel guides, maps, and city guide books. Damron's partner Hal Call had been one of the founders of the Mattachine Society, the first modern gay rights organization, in the 1950s. In a sidebar *Life* published a photograph of Hal Call preparing the *Mattachine Review* for press. However, by the mid-sixties, he had given up on gay politics and became involved in the production of porn.

A couple of years after opening the Adonis Bookstore, Bob Damron founded Calafran Enterprises with local photographer J. Brian. Calafran published *Golden Boys*, a five-by-seven-inch color publication that was one of the first physique magazines to print nude photos of models with no jockstraps—and one of the first to publish photos of young men with partial erections— as beefcake publications slowly moved toward publishing images with full erections. [Masters, *Manshots*, 11/97, 10]

In 1965, the twenty-two-year-old John Travis got a job developing prints for a "dirty old man" who ran a studio called HIM selling photographs of young men in posing straps. Travis started taking photographs himself and sending them to Herman Lynn Womack's Guild Press in Washington, D.C.

Womack, the publisher of physique magazines *MANual*, *Trim*, and *Grecian Guild Pictorial*, was a pioneer in the fight to free homoerotic images from censorship. The U.S. Post Office seized three of his publications in 1960 for appealing to "prurient interests" as defined by William Brennan in the *Roth* decision. Womack sued and took the case to the Supreme Court. In 1962, the majority opinion found that the physique magazine photographs "of the male nude cannot fairly be regarded as more objectionable than many portrayals of the female nude that society tolerates. Of course not every portrayal of male or female nudity is obscene.... [The material was] dismally unpleasant, uncouth and tawdry ... [but] lacked patent offensiveness." [Waugh, 275–80] The 1962 Supreme

Court decision was an important step, freeing physique publishers from harassment by the Post Office.

After two years of working in the HIM darkroom and shooting photos on his own, John Travis went to work at J. Brian's Calafrans publishing company, where he shot stills for *Golden Boys*.

In 1966, Scott Masters, after driving his parents out west from Chicago, visited San Francisco. There, he discovered that the adult bookstores were selling more "titillating" male physique magazines and photographs than anything he had seen back home. When he returned to Chicago he persuaded local bookstore owners to let him buy gay material for their stores. He developed strong ties to photographers in San Francisco and Los Angeles and soon began to publish soft-core—and later hardcore—porn magazines himself. Masters started his own business.

> "...(At) about the time the *Golden Boys* magazines came out, which were the first gay-oriented publications of male nudes. Prior to that, there had been a couple court cases won in which nudity, in and of itself, was not obscene, so the next step was to push it from more innocent nudity to less innocent nudity, and from totally soft cocks to tumescence. *Golden Boys* began this process at the same time that I began buying photo sets from various photographers who also had nudes of their models." [Masters, *Manshots,* 11/97, 10]

When Masters made the move to California, he chose not to settle in San Francisco but in Los Angeles, where his magazines were printed. [Masters, *Manshots,* 11/97, 11]

"Golden Boys"—lightly built and handsome young men, often blond—became synonymous with J. Brian's vision of porn. Born Jeremiah Brian Donahue in Alameda County, just across the bay from San Francisco, he was noted for his models: he carefully selected them for their youth, their wholesome good looks, and especially, their large penises. [*Update,* May 29, 1985, 2] Brian enrolled many of the young men he photographed as call boys in the "boy brothels" he ran with John Summers—both Tennessee Williams and Truman Capote were said to have patronized them. [Sears, 527]

"Brian ... was like God in San Francisco," reported filmmaker Toby Ross, who had moved to San Francisco to make porn movies; "his [model] agency and also his *Golden Boys* magazines had established an incredible mystique. He was a legend. There's no doubt about it ..." [Douglas, *Manshots,* 3/97, 11]

Brian had no trouble finding young men. Tony Ross recalled:

> "In those days, you did not have to advertise."
> "The atmosphere in San Francisco was so party-like that you used to walk up to somebody in a donut store and say, 'Hey, would you like be interested in being in a movie?' ... If you went to the baths and you saw somebody walking around with the biggest dick, you just went to him and said, 'I have a great offer.'" [Douglas, *Manshots,* 3/97, 10–11]

One performer Brian attempted to enroll in his agency was Jim Cassidy, who was based in Los Angeles. It didn't work out very well. "He got busted," Cassidy recounted.

> "And it couldn't have happened to a finer guy.... Up there in San Francisco he was running those male whorehouses. He invited me one time. He said, 'Come up for a weekend, Cassidy, I'll advertise you're coming and you can do some hustling around and line up some $100 numbers.' Anyway, I was a day late getting there, and he was mortified. All his super people that were waiting to see me had to be put off and this and that. He didn't even want to talk to me.... He was the guy that was calling me every week to come up there." [Siebenand, 187]

In 1973, after producing half a dozen hardcore movies and a couple of nonsexual features, Brian, exhausted by his legal hassles with the San Francisco police over his escort service, moved to Hawaii. He remained there for a little more than a year before returning to San Francisco. However, once back in California, he resumed making 8mm films for his mail-order business, though on a smaller scale than before. [*Manshots,* 3/89, 4]

HARD-CORE AMERICA

In 1969 San Francisco became the first American city where hardcore movies played in theaters throughout the city. More than twenty-eight theaters offered films—many were hardly more than loops—showing fellatio, cunnilingus, mutual masturbation, group sex, and mild S/M, as well as vaginal and anal sexual intercourse. The minimal plots, almost all built around the search for and achievement of sexual climax, were simple stories of housewives seducing delivery boys or of thieves forcing their victims to perform sex acts.

These developments were a culmination of the economic pressures and cultural experimentation experienced by theaters across the country. The Roxie Theater on Sixteenth Street near Valencia in San Francisco's Mission District first showed foreign films to bring in the audiences swept away by television—then during the sixties it switched its format and began to show "nudies" and, according to its manager, "business picked up" again.

But by the mid-sixties, even the "nudies" weren't bringing them in anymore. Early in 1967 the *San Francisco Examiner* advertised a bill at the Roxie called "Naughty Nymphs and Eager Beavers at Their Busy Best." Calling itself "Home of the Eager Beaver Films," the Roxie offered shorts that had previously sold in 8mm formats via mail-order; converted to 16mm for theaters, beaver films showed full female nudity and focused primarily on female genitalia. Very quickly the beaver film evolved into the split beaver (with the labia spread), the action beaver (with masturbation or digital manipulation), and hardcore action (with sexual intercourse). [Hubner, 50–51; Schaefer, 375–77]

"We could make a nudie or two ourselves," San Francisco State film student Jim Mitchell recalls saying to his classmate Earl Shagley. "Maybe not right away. We could start with stills. You know, take some pictures of girls with their tops off and try to sell them to bookstores on Market Street.... We find a hippie chick and ask her if she'll take her top off and let us take her picture." [Hubner, 50–51]

"In a nudie, you get tit shots," Jim's brother Artie explained. "They're old hat. Nobody would see a nudie today. Beavers are the happening thing. In a beaver you get muff shots." Soon they were making short (ten- to twelve-minute) loops that they sold to the Roxie for $100 a loop. [Hubner, 77]

• • •

The other major force on the San Francisco hardcore scene was Alex de Renzy, who had originally come to San Francisco to work as a cinematographer on industrial films. He had originally come to San Francisco in the 1960s to work for the Gordon News Service as a photographer. [Hubner, 78] Soon after arriving in San Francisco he began to moonlight on stag films. In 1968 he leased the Screening Room, a fifty-seat storefront theater in the Tenderloin, San Francisco's Skid Row district, and renovated it. After the theater opened, weekly box office grosses went from $100 to an average of $8,000 by the end of the summer in 1970.

Like theater owners showing porn in Los Angeles and New York, de Renzy shot a new ninety-minute film each month to bring back repeat viewers. In the beginning he cast prostitutes as the stars of his films, but soon after he began to cast amateurs—mostly hippies—whom he recruited through ads in the local underground newspapers like the *Berkeley Barb*. For many years, the theater also offered a "Copenhagen-Style Live Show."

In 1967, Denmark had abolished all laws restricting pornography—the first nation to do so. When in the following year Denmark reported that sex crimes had dramatically declined, de Renzy decided to go to Copenhagen to attend Sex 69, the country's first porn trade show. While there, he made a documentary about Denmark's porn industry, which was released as *Pornography in Demark* in 1970. De Renzy and his partner spent $15,000 to produce the film, and eventually went on to gross more than $2 million. The first week alone at the Screening Room, de Renzy took in $25,000. Following very much in the footsteps of Scandinavian documentaries like 1967's *I Am Curious (Yellow)*, which had been very lucrative for Grove Press (a book publisher and its U.S. distributor), *Censorship in Denmark* was able to dodge censorship in the United States because it was passsed off as a documentary, despite the fact that it included sexually explicit scenes of "lesbianism, fellatio, cunnilingus and every detail of conventional sexual intercourse." [Turan and Zito, 80–82]

De Renzy exemplified the emerging lifestyle heralded by the sexual revolution. He lived with his secretary and one of his former actresses in a palatial hilltop estate in Marin County—along with children by each of the women and his children from a previous marriage. A handsome man, he had long blond hair and a Fu Manchu mustache. But De Renzy also considered himself a serious filmmaker. "I just want to make movies," he told Murray. "You have to show something people haven't seen before and sex is what people want to see now. I'd never make a movie that didn't have sex in it. It's got more punch than the chase scene." [Murray, 22] Writing in *The New York Times Magazine*, William Murray christened de Renzy "the Jean-Luc Godard of the *nouvelle vague* in porn."

When Jim Mitchell told his brother Artie, "To make any real money in porn, you have to have your own theater," Artie replied, "We got to do what de Renzy's done." [Hubner, 78]

In 1969, the Mitchell brothers bought a vacant building that had once housed a Pontiac dealership at the corner of Polk and

O'Farrell. On July 4, 1969, the O'Farrell Theater opened. The brothers continued to make nudies and beavers to show at their theater. By 1972, when they released their classic hardcore film *Behind the Green Door*, they had produced more than two hundred movies to show at the O'Farrell. [Hubner, 64–100]

Five years after the Roxie started showing beaver films, San Francisco was designated the "porn capital of America" in a *New York Times Magazine* article.

> Prostitution was flourishing, with open solicitation taking place on street corners in the heart of town.... There are 30 movie houses scattered all over that screen only hardcore films. Several places put on live sex shows. Dozens of book stores deal exclusively in porn and others maintain porn sections for the prurient browser. The underground press churns out newspapers, comic books, posters and postcards to delight the dirty-minded. And in the North Beach and Tenderloin districts naked girls dance continuously for the exclusive delectation of the imbibing voyeur. Just walking around the city can give the casual visitor the impression that porn, not tourism, is San Francisco's leading industry. [Murray, 8–9]

Despite the booming hardcore theatrical scene of the times, few gay films were screened. One of the few films with homosexual content shown in theaters was *Meat Rack*. Directed, photographed, and edited by Michael Thomas, a twenty-one-year-old theater manager, *Meat Rack* portrayed a series of sexual encounters between a bisexual San Francisco-based-hustler called J. C. and his male clients and girl friends. Released in 1970 and with no hardcore sexual scenes, it nevertheless offered a gritty portrait of gay life in San Francisco at the time. [Turan & Zito, 190]

Another was J. Brian's hardcore pastoral *Seven in a Barn*, one of the first gay hardcore movies made for theatrical release. It was shot almost entirely in a single setting, a straw-filled barn in which seven suntanned all-American young men sit in a circle playing strip poker. While much of the sexual action was oral, it included several penetration shots of anal intercourse—and nearly every round of sexual action concluded with a cum shot. Brian originated a style of gay pornography, along with a type of casting, that eventually dominated the gay porn industry in the 1970s and 1980s—the all-American young man in search of sexual fulfillment, sun-tanned and usually blond, and often set outdoors, in idyllic surroundings that were increasingly exemplified as California. "Brian's films," wrote critic and filmmaker Jerry Douglas, were "characterized, first and foremost, by the breathtaking golden boys.... All seem to be fresh, young, healthy, versatile, creatively kinky and apparently insatiable." [Douglas, *Stallion*, 18]

The third significant theatrical opening was *Nights in Black Leather* in 1972. Directed by Ignatio Rutkowski, a student at the San Francisco Art Institute, and starring Peter Burian—who later changed his stage name to Peter Berlin when a Hollywood actor also named Peter Burian threatened to sue—it follows the sexual adventures of a young German visitor to San Francisco. Beautifully shot, the movie included very little sexual action—mostly fellatio, in soft focus or in shadows, with simulated fucking. Most of the film lingered on Berlin's lean and muscular body. [Turan & Zito, 196]

In addition to playing in San Francisco, *Seven in a Barn* (1971) followed *Boys in the Sand* at the 55th Street Playhouse in New York and theaters in Los Angeles. Brian's other films, *Five in Hand* (1970), *Four More Than Money* (1971), *Chapter Three* (1971), and *First Time Around* (1972), were all distributed by Monroe Wheeler's Los Angeles-based company, Jaguar Productions.[Turan & Zito, 195–96]

THE MAILING LIST

Porn theaters thrived in San Francisco, but only six out of the twenty-eight theaters operating in 1970 showed any hardcore gay movies. [Nawy, 168] Shan Sayles's Nob Hill Theater was probably the preeminent venue for gay porn. A number of local gay hardcore filmmakers chose not to make movies for theatrical distribution. Instead, most of them seemed to have started their businesses based on a single mailing list.

While working at J. Brian's magazine *Golden Boys,* John Travis met John Summers, a heavy-set African-American man later known as "the Black Buddha," who ran a series of boy brothels in partnership with and sometimes in competition with Brian. Summers was interested in the gay film pornography business and encouraged Travis to shoot 8mm hardcore loops to be sold through mail order. [Adam Video Guide/AVG, 89]

Travis set up a small company called Telstar and built up a small catalogue of 8mm loops—including two with the legendary straight porn star, John Holmes. Once he started making the 8mm shorts, Travis decided he wanted to meet his customers in person and find out what they were interested in seeing in the future. "I'd get a hotel room in various cities, invite these guys over and give them a glimpse of the films that I had." [AVG, 89]

At one point in the early seventies, when J. Brian had a falling out with one of his partners, presumably Travis, John Summers and Brian broke into his former partner's office one night to get Brian's films back. On the way out, according to Summers, Brian yelled to him, "Grab that mailing list. And make a copy of it. You'll need it some day." [Travis, *Manshots,* 3/89, 4, AVG, 89–90]

Only a couple of years after starting Telstar, Travis decided to get out of the mail-order business. Not only had his mailing list "disappeared"—apparently sold by Summers to two other businessmen starting porn companies—there were the legal and financial burdens of continuing to do business. Matt

Sterling was one of the businessmen who obtained the list and used it to start Dimension. Under that name he made almost twenty short films. Among them were *A Matter of Size* and *Inch by Inch,* as well as *Hurts So Good* and *Out of Control.* These early shorts involved two or three young men in sexual scenes that did not require elaborate setups, merely showing them engaging in sex in a bedroom or an outdoor setting. Often the sequence did not follow what later became standardized genre convention of oral-anal-and-orgasm, but moved back and forth between oral and anal. And many times performers might have an orgasm in the middle of the scene, before the final session of anal intercourse, though orgasms usually concluded the scene.

After a year Sterling changed the company's name to Brentwood Studios. Soon after the name change, Sterling hired John Travis as the cameraman for Brentwood films. At the time, Travis was also working for Chuck Holmes's Falcon Studios, another small San Francisco-based company. However, Sterling and Holmes made very different kinds of movies. The Brentwood loops were like one-act plays, while the Falcon films were more purely sexual action. According to Travis, Sterling wanted to make "Pepsodent-smile, mainstream pretty-boy movies," while Holmes liked "leather and hard, more forceful sex." But Travis felt that he had more creative input at Brentwood and decided to leave Falcon.

While the tug-of-war between Sterling and Holmes over Travis went on, Summers continued to be involved in the productions of both Sterling and Holmes. Throughout the early seventies, all four of the men engaged in a sometimes acrimonious, sometimes friendly rivalry.

One of the most notable of early Brentwood loops shot and directed by Travis was *The Paperboy and Mr. Egan,* which as the title suggests portrayed a sexual scene between an older man and boy who delivered the newspaper. Travis believed that it was "a fantasy that many people ... have thought of as the newsboy throws the paper at the door everyday. Small

Town, U.S.A." [Travis, *Manshots*, 3/90, 8]

Travis told Jerry Douglas in a *Manshots* interview,

> "I never script sex. Ever. And I always try to put the camera where the customer would like to be. Where I want to be and what I want to be looking at if I was seeing these two people. You kind of give your actors an idea of what you are trying to capture, and they go to it. And you in turn photograph whatever you can." [Travis, *Manshots,* 3/90, 8]

FALCON TAKES FLIGHT

Chuck Holmes moved to San Francisco from Indiana when he was promoted to the position of western sales manager for a company that manufactured prefabricated homes. During the recession of the early 1970s the market for prefabricated houses experienced a downturn and when the company closed its San Francisco office in 1972, he was out of a job. John Summers, whom he had met through J. Brian, suggested that he start a mail-order business selling gay hardcore films.

"Well," Holmes thought, "maybe I should do this for a year or two, until I can get back into the corporate world." [*Unzipped*, 19]

He borrowed $4,200 and purchased a handful of already-made films from John Travis (mostly his Telstar shorts)—one of which was a gay short with legendary straight hardcore performer John Holmes—and launched Falcon Studios in April 1972. To give Holmes a customer base, Summers sold him a copy of John Travis's mailing list. [*Manshots*, Summers 3/89, 4] Chuck Holmes, as it turned out, had been one of the customers Travis had met on his road trips. When they met in Cincinnati, Holmes was selling prefabricated houses.

Holmes decided to call to call his company Falcon Studios.

"I wanted ... something that had an image of fierceness and power and grace and was natural.... I thought a falcon represented that. It was a bird of prey. With sexual acts—at least the way we make 'em here at Falcon—there is generally someone who is is the predator and someone who's the prey. Now I don't mean that in a harmful way, but by the end of a Falcon film, somebody has snatched someone and given it to 'em good." [Douglas, *Manshots*, 1/89, 22]

Business was slow at first—in part because the supply of new product was limited. He relied on the loops other companies and producers made. But soon he was producing his own 8mm shorts. After Travis closed down his own business, Holmes, who called Travis "one of the best natural gay sex videographers born onto this earth," offered him a job shooting the 8mm hardcore loops for Falcon. [Douglas, *Manshots*, 1/89]

Travis shot the first movie Falcon made—a two-part loop called *Muscle, Sweat and Brawn* (Falcon 508, reissued as FVP010), which featured one of the early stars of gay porn, Dean Chasson. As someone who'd grown up in the Midwest, Holmes wanted to recreate his own fantasy by shooting a scene of sexual action outdoors in California. Holmes shot the stills while Travis handled the 16mm camera. In Holmes's words, "I was a baby in this business. I kept my mouth shut and my ears open." [Douglas, *Manshots*, 1/89, 19]

Along with Chassen, *Muscle, Sweat and Brawn* starred Ray Todd, who also went on to become a first-generation gay porn star. Chasson (sometimes spelled Chasen or Chassen) had appeared in Brian's *Seven in a Barn* (1972) as well as numerous loops for Matt Sterling's Dimension. He also made many low-budget "all-male beaver films." Holmes also hired him for two other early Falcon loops: *Fourgy* (FVP 012), *Taste My Love, Parts 1 and 2* (Falcon 504 and 505), and *Ace in the Hole* (FVP 055). He was one of few models of the period to do well for himself financially, saving money from his appearances in porn and escort work and investing in real estate. By the end of the eighties, he owned a vineyard in southern California and rental property. [Douglas, *Manshots,* 1/89, 19]

Ray Todd appeared in Jaguar's epic dramatic feature film *The Light from the Second Story Window,* which also featured gay porn star Jim Cassidy. In addition to stars like Dean Chasson and Ray Todd, Holmes also hired Jimmy Hughes before the latter's arrest and prison sentence, as well as big-dicked straight porn star John Holmes (no relation to Chuck) for several of his rare all-male hardcore scenes. Most of Falcon's loops starred handsome and sexually energetic young men who went by nondescript names like Tom, Dan, Gary, Dave, Kenny, Rod, Phillip, Michael, Bill, and Pete. Since there were few publications that reviewed 8mm loops, most of the young men who became porn stars in the early seventies achieved their fame through theatrical releases, not via 8mm mail-order purchases. Theatrical shows of gay hardcore movies were much more likely to be reviewed in the new gay newspapers that emerged in the early seventies.

Falcon followed the erotic formulas developed by J. Brian, John Travis, and Matt Sterling—perhaps stressing sexual action even more than Travis or Sterling. Most of the Falcon loops portrayed sex scenes in a straightforward manner with simple production values. Lighting, always the most difficult-to-manage production factor, varied greatly from film to film; there were almost never expensive or exotic locations; and the loops rarely showed dramatic or sexual action that extended over a long period of time. These were, after all, only short movies, consisting of one scene no more than fifteen or twenty minutes long. For the most part, they were built around an anecdote, never a full-fledged story. They merely provided a setup that created a charged atmosphere in which the sexual action could unroll. The sex almost always involved fellatio and anal penetration. The cum shots were not yet formalized as the ending of a scene, nor did they always take place after fucking—but sometimes the performers might have several orgasms at different points in the film.

Travis worked as director/cinematographer for Falcon until 1982. While there he shot almost 40 percent of Falcon's movies—not counting the Telstar and Brentwood shorts that they acquired and distributed as part of the Falcon Video Packs. His contributions, however, were unknown to the public because Travis's work for Falcon was uncredited. In fact, for many years, Falcon films did not list any credits. That reflected the need in the early years for anonymity, but also Holmes's philosophy:

> "Everyone [at Falcon] contributes their maximum effort.... If the art director, the still photographer, the production manager, or even the gaffer who's lugging the lights wants to make a suggestion, if it sounds reasonable to me, I'll call time out and we'll have a production huddle. We're a real team here." [Douglas, *Manshots*, 1/89, 22]

From the beginning, Holmes clearly envisioned the Falcon brand of sexual action to be "fast, urgent, desperate sexual contact between two or more persons, as desperate as we can capture on film or video." And that remained his goal: "The basic formula at Falcon has not changed ... and I do not foresee it ever changing." [Douglas, *Manshots*, 1/89, 19] Casting and the performers' grooming were also important to him:

> "Nobody could have dirty feet in a Falcon movie. Because I come from the Midwest, and they'd have these VFW stags where they'd have these porno movies and all the men and all the women would always have dirty feet. And I always thought, 'Those lazy bastards, why don't they wash those people's feet? It's distracting.'"

Holmes wanted to see the boy next door "who looked like they wouldn't ever do anything but be the best little fellows—

the little businessmen, the good members of their community—and all of a sudden they'd just kiss each other, and all hell would break loose, and they'd just try to fuck one another to death." [*Unzipped*, 21]

• • •

Holmes adopted a business model built on aggressive pricing and marketing policies. Falcon set its prices considerably above those for other companies' 8mm loops. The high prices Falcon charged for films, and later for its videos, went far beyond what was necessary to support its costs of production.

From the beginning, Falcon operated strictly as a mail-order business. Though hardcore theatrical releases garnered publicity and prestige, theatrical distribution was both more expensive and riskier than the production of loops for mail-order distribution. "We didn't want to let sixteen millimeter prints out of our hands," he explained, "that's all you needed to make an inter-negative and make all the eight millimeter and Super 8 copies you ever wanted. And back then, there were a lot of people in this business who did a lot of illegal duping." [*Manshots*, 2/93, 72]

Falcon's policy stressing its mail-order business catered to customers who were older and wealthier than the audiences who attended theater showings—more closeted as well. They were also more likely to live outside the metropolitan areas that had large and growing gay communities.

THE CASTRO CLONE

Ever since the late sixties, the gay sexual scene in San Francisco had been exceptionally lively. In 1970, only a year after the Stonewall riots, researchers from the Kinsey Institute found that 40 percent of the white men and a third of the black men had had over five hundred sexual partners, while 28 percent of white males had had over a thousand. A decade later, the Castro had become the hub of gay sexual activity in San Francisco—"the most active cruising strip in the city—perhaps the country," ventured Frances FitzGerald in *Cities on a Hill*.

> "Even in the daytime there were hundreds of young men out cruising in the bars, the bookshops, the restaurants, and the stores—even in the vast supermarket some distance down Market Street. At night the bars were jammed—there were lines out on the sidewalks—and cars had trouble getting through the crowds of men. The scene was mind-boggling to newcomers: the openness of it and the sheer turnover." [55]

Over the course of the seventies a new masculine style evolved. Rejecting the traditional idea that male homosexual desire implied the desire to be female, gay men turned to a traditionally masculine or working-class style of acting out sexually. Camp as an effeminized gay sensibility was out. The new style of gay men was almost macho—but macho with a twist. Macho and sexually provocative, the new style included denim pants, black combat boots, a tight t-shirt (if it was warm), covered by a plaid flannel shirt (if it was not), pierced ears or nipples, tattoos, and beard or moustache. The men who dressed this way were known as clones or, especially in San Francisco, as "Castro clones." The Marlboro man, a cowboy, was the iconic masculine model for the clone look—ironically, the man who popularized the masculine style for Marlboro cigarettes was gay.

The clone look was sexually coded style. "[C]lothes emphasize, eroticize, fetishize the vague animal reality underneath and mold our way of seeing it," wrote Edmund White in *States of Desire*.

> "The V-shaped torso by metonymy from the open V of the half-buttoned shirt above the sweaty chest; the rounded buttocks squeezed in jeans, swelling out from the cinched-in waist, further

emphasized by the erotic insignia of colored hand-
kerchiefs and keys; a crotch instantly accessible
through the buttons (bottom one already undone)
and enlarged by being pressed, along the scrotum,
to one side; legs molded in perfect, powerful detail;
the feet simplified, brutalized and magnified by
the boots." [White, 45–46]

Moreover, the clone style codified, very precisely, the new
sexual norms of gay male life. "For gay men," White explained,
"there are three erotic zones—mouth, penis, and anus—and all
three are vividly dramatized by this costume, the ass the most
insistently so, since its status as an object of desire is historically the newest and therefore the most in need of re-defini-
tion." [White, 46]

The clones, both sartorially and sexually, thrived most fully
in San Francisco and New York. Castro Street in San Francisco and Christopher Street in New York were the pylons that
anchored the gay male sexual culture of the seventies—which,
as many people have claimed, far exceeded in intensity and
excitement anything portrayed in gay porn films.

If the intensity of everyday sexual encounters often exceeded
that of sex scenes in porn films, the sexual experiences of the late
seventies eventually did make their way into video pornography.
As just one example, in his book, *Gay Macho: The Life and Death
of the Homosexual Clone*, Martin Levine recorded an overheard
real-life bathhouse encounter in the late seventies that has come
to resemble the dialogue in dozens of porn films:

"Yeah take a good look at that big fucking dick.
Uh huh. Look at how big, long, and hard that
fucker is. Yeah. That fucker is going to go up
your fucking asshole. Uh huh. That big fucking
cock is going to be plowing your ass, ramming
and ramming your manhole. Shit you're going to
be begging for more. Yeah. You want dick,
fucker, you want it?"

> At this point, a second voice chimed in, rasping hungrily, "Give me that dick, man. Yea. Give it to me. Give me all of that man meat. Shove it down my hot throat. Yeah. Gag me with that huge tool." [77–78]

The sex experienced by gay men in the seventies converged with the sex portrayed in porn. Ultimately, almost exactly parallel to the action in many porn movies, a fairly standard sequence of sexual acts evolved. "To get a guy hot, I like to first play with his dick while I'm kissing him. Then I suck his cock while squeezing his tits and playing with his ass. After rimming him a while, when his hole is nice and loose, I then fuck him until I come in his ass. I like them to come by jerking themselves off while I'm fucking them." [Levine, 94] Except for the required withdrawal from fucking in order to come for the money shot, the scene Levine overheard satisfied the formula for almost any porn scene.

Cruising for sex and "tricking" were the mainstay of the Castro clones' erotic style. Their code stressed the pursuit of sexual gratification over the achievement of emotional intimacy; and it assumed a detached and impersonal objectification of their sexual partners. As one man told Martin Levine, "Familiarity for me kills desire. Knowing someone is a turn off because their personality ruins the fantasy I have of them. Besides sucking the same dick and fucking the same ass is a drag. Variety, after all, is the spice of life." [Levine, 93]

BLOCKBUSTER

Throughout the seventies John Travis, Matt Sterling, Falcon Studios, and numerous other producers of gay male porn incorporated a great deal of San Francisco's gay sexual culture. The scale and intensity of the city's sexual scene had created a distinctive world of shared experience. Anonymous sex in a communal setting—in a sex club or a bathhouse or at an orgy—led to a community based on pleasure rather than politics.

Performing in porn was merely an extension of the communal sex in which so many men took part. The city's pornographers often took their scenarios and images from the city's gay sex life. They recruited performers from the community and they translated their own sexual experiences to the screen.

In the fall of 1977, Chuck Holmes met with his production and marketing staff to discuss upcoming projects. Falcon's cameraman of the moment, Colin Meyer, a recent graduate of the film program at San Francisco State University, suggested that they make a series of short loops putting "all the biggest porn icons at that time into one movie"—three "generations" of the top gay porn stars.

Very quickly the Falcon team decided that Al Parker, who had been a huge hit as a Colt model and whom they had already used in *Weekend Lock-up* (Falcon Nos. 610–11, FVP 004) and *Rocks and Hard Places* (*Help Wanted*, FVP 019), should be one of the three. They also chose Dick Fisk, a young performer who had recently also made a number of loops for them: *Steam Heat, One to One: The Runner* (Falcon Nos. 621–22, *Steam Heat*, FV018), and *Help Wanted* (FVP 019). Finally, the third choice was obvious to Holmes: "We knew we'd have to have Casey Donovan, because of *Boys in the Sand*. He was the original first gay porn icon."

Donovan had made a handful of gay erotic films since *Boys in the Sand* and *The Back Row* but had never appeared in a Falcon movie. Holmes was fairly certain he could secure him for the movie.

> "I had met Casey at Fire Island, and become personally acquainted with him.... [H]e had so much energy and so much personality, and such a strong sexual presence. He was 'the linchpin of the movie.' Donovan looked at the whole cast and told Holmes that 'he couldn't wait to fuck with

every single one of them.' ... He was really hot for all those boys ... they were [all] just like crazed dogs in heat." [Douglas, *Manshots*, 2/93 29]

Once the cast was secured, the Falcon team came up with a "script." According to Holmes,

"Somebody said, 'Maybe we could make a movie in snow.' And I thought, 'Hmm, nobody's done that.' And besides I wanted to go skiing and I had a couple of friends, a couple of gay guys who were a lot of fun and who had a cabin outside Lake Tahoe. I called one of them and said, 'We'd like to make a movie up at Tahoe in the snow. Can we use your place?'" [Douglas, *Manshots*, 2/93, 28]

The story of *The Other Side of Aspen* (FVP 001, 1978) was developed around the casting concept and location. "In those days, the script was in your head," Holmes explained.

"We had it planned out, but—basically, what we had was a scenario. And the scenario was about this ski instructor. Actually we tied the movie together after we got back to San Francisco, because we'd gone up there and shot all this fabulous footage of fast sex scenes, but the movie really needed a framework to web it together. So we came back here and shot the footage of Jeff Turk [the sky instructor] jogging and remembering what had happened the winter before. And we did a voice-over." [Douglas, *Manshots*, 2/93, 28]

If Casey Donovan was the linchpin, Al Parker was the top dog. Donovan and Parker had never met, but Donovan considered Parker one of his "porno dream men." Almost ten years younger than Donovan, Parker was born Andrew Okun in 1952. Parker seemed destined for porn since the day when as a fifteen-year-old he stumbled across a tattered magazine that included beefcake photos from the legendary Colt Studios. Around the same time, Parker attended the famous concert at Woodstock, where he spent practically the entire weekend in the back of a hearse having sex with a hairy Hells Angels biker—and though barely in attendance at the concert itself, he managed to show up on the poster for the movie.

He moved to California where he worked as a butler at the Playboy Mansion in Los Angeles and was eventually introduced to the photographer Rip Colt. The standard Colt model was very muscular, with well-defined features. The photographer actually hesitated to shoot Parker and even published his pictures with a disclaimer because Parker was not as muscular or well defined as the typical Colt model. But Parker's slender hirsute masculinity had become popular almost instantaneously, and he went on to be one of gay porn's most enduring icons. His "look" soon came to epitomize the new gay masculine style—the man with a beard wearing a work shirt.

Soon after posing for Colt's nude stills, he made his first sexually explicit movie for Brentwood Studios, directed by Matt Sterling (though he had not yet begun to use that name). Like Casey Donovan, Parker's performances and style conveyed a fantasy of unrestrained availability, but Parker also created a persona that represented something new: a gay man with a traditional masculine, even macho, style—a muscle-bound, sexually aggressive, hard-living "Marlboro" man—one that included both the active and the passive roles in anal intercourse. Though Parker was primarily a top, he was a versatile top and was comfortable as a butch bottom. The macho style he created became known as "the clone" in part because it became the norm in San Francisco, the "Castro clone."

Writer Robert Richards believed that Parker's riveting screen presence was also due to the photographic reflection of his remarkable skin tones. "I'm convinced that [Parker's] stardom was attributable, at least in part to his skin. I've talked to cameramen and others in the know, and they attribute much of his success to the way he photographed. There was an inner glow when you see him on the screen. It is a very rare quality." In fact, many aspects of Parker's persona made him one of the most popular stars ever among gay men—certainly, the photographic representation of his flesh and skin tones, also his portrayal of masculine homosexuality, but above all, the sheer energy and demonstrable pleasure of his sexual performances cemented his popularity and status.

In *The Other Side of Aspen*, Donovan and Parker, in fact both sexually versatile, each adopted only one sexual position—Donovan played the bottom in three scenes (and for the three other performers in those scenes) while Parker topped Donovan in all three of those scenes. Their first scene was electrifying. It had started off as a still photography shoot, but with the actors unable to restrain themselves, the cameraman jumped in and started filming. It quickly escalated into a full-fledged sex scene that culminated with Parker fisting Donovan.

Donovan and Parker had never met until the afternoon they flew from San Francisco to Lake Tahoe, which Donovan considered a plus. "I think it's easier because then you can perform on a strictly chemical level. ... I like the spontaneity of anonymous encounters.... A couple of hours later we did our first scene together and he wound up fisting me. *Quite an experience!*" Donovan exclaimed after it was all over. *The Other Side of Aspen* put Donovan back into the spotlight and confirmed Parker's celestial status.

The film also crystallized Chuck Holmes's vision of the erotic movie, that all that was necessary was to shoot liberated gay men having sex.

> "[I]f you get the sexual energy going, the only thing that's holding you up is putting the film in the camera. ... You don't have to plan it, you hardly have to direct it, you merely have to capture it, because it's happening right before your eyes as a natural sequence of sexual events. It doesn't always happen like that. But in this movie we had it, because

we had a 100% gay cast, 100% hot, and 100% hot
for one another.... There was nobody who said, 'I'm
a top only' or 'Gee, I don't do this or I don't do that.'
... [A]t this point in time, there were really no constraints. This movie was made at the height of the
sexual revolution, and Gay America was on the
move. People were free, and we had rights for the
first time, and this movie was kind of a ... celebration ... of that freedom and the idea that sex
wasn't dirty and it didn't have to be dark and it
didn't have to be hidden. And this was the thing—
I wanted to present sex in a really wholesome, athletic atmosphere. [Douglas, *Manshots*, 2/93, 30]

The Other Side of Aspen had started out as a series of loops,
but once Holmes decided to create a framework linking the
scenes it quickly morphed into Falcon's first feature film. It
resembled *Boys in the Sand* in some ways—four sexual scenes
with no plot set in a vacation setting. And ironically, once
again Casey Donovan played the same role linking the scenes
together by his sexual presence and energy.

Falcon ramped up its marketing strategy by sending out a
"pre-mailing" with reservation cards to its best customers.
Reservations poured back in. Then a brochure was mailed; the
response to the brochure was also phenomenal, producing the
highest revenues in the history of the company up to that point—
five to seven times greater than ever before. By 1993, 45,000
copies of *The Other Side of Aspen* video cassette had been sold—
making it the best-selling gay porn film up to that time.

The Other Side of Aspen was Falcon's first blockbuster, and
like all blockbusters it accounted for the lion's share of Falcon's earnings. Its explosive impact marked a turning point for
a company selling its films only through mail-order transac-
tions—unwittingly preparing it for the coming age of the VCR.
The success of *Aspen* transformed Falcon into a different sort
of company—one that began to increase its production values

and adopt other policies such as signing performers as exclusives—that made it into the powerhouse of gay porn companies. With *Aspen*, Falcon discovered the Midas formula; it went on to produce four sequels in its Aspen series—often starring the most popular performers of the day.

In the late eighties, the studio established a policy of having "exclusive" contracts with half a dozen or more performers whose careers they strictly regulated by controlling their access to the gay press, their repertoires of sex acts, and the roles and characters they play in their films. Falcon "exclusives" were unable to appear in productions by other companies as long as they were under contract. Holmes explained,

> "When we do that with a model, we agree to a
> minimum amount of work and minimum amount
> of money, and they agree to work only for us. So
> that allows us to spend the money to really pro-
> mote them, to really take the time and blanket
> the country with them and create a demand for
> that model. And then the only place you can get
> that model is from us." [*Unzipped*, 22]

Falcon Studios was built on the gay macho fantasy in the shorts and feature length films it made in the 1970s. The studio eschewed anything that appeared campy or less than rigorously masculine. But *The Other Side of Aspen* was a milestone for the gay porn film industry as well. It signaled the culmination of the gay macho sexual ethos, the confirmation of the ideal gay male body—young, a swimmer's build, no tattoos, and little hair—and the codification of gay porn movies as a genre.

REFERENCES

· Adam Video Guide: *The Films of John Travis* (Los Angeles: Knight, 2000).

Howard S. Becker, "Introduction," Howard S. Becker, ed. *Culture and Civility in San Francisco* (New York: Transaction Books, 1971).

Nan Alamilla Boyd, *Wide Open Town: A History of Queer San Francisco to 1965* (Berkeley: University of California Press, 2003).

Jerry Douglas, "Seven in a Barn," "Stallion 50 Best: All-Time Best Male Films and Videos 1970–1985," *Stallion*, Special Issue #4, 1985.

Jerry Douglas, "Inside Falcon Studios," *Manshots*, January 1989.

Jerry Douglas, "The Gay Film Heritage: The Making of *The Other Side of Aspen*," *Manshots*, February 1993.

Roger Edmonson, *Clone: The Life and Legacy of Al Parker, Gay Superstar* (Los Angeles: Alyson, 2000).

Frances Fitzgerald, *Cities on a Hill: A Journey Through Contemporary American Cultures* (New York: Simon & Schuster, 1986).

Ernest Havemann, "Homosexuality in America," *Life*, June 26, 1964.

John Hubner, *Bottom Feeders: From Free Love to Hard Core—the Rise of the Counterculture Heroes Jim and Artie Mitchell* (New York: Doubleday, 1993).

Martin Levine, *Gay Macho: The Life and Death of the Homosexual Clone* (New York: New York University, 1998).

Scott Masters, interview by Jerry Douglas, *Manshots*, 11/97.

William Murray, "The Porn Capital of America," *New York Times Magazine*, January 3, 1971.

Harold Nawy, "The San Francisco Erotic Marketplace," *Technical Report of the Commission of Obscenity and Pornography, Volume IV: The Marketplace: Empirical Studies* (Washington, D.C.: Government Printing Office, 1970).

Toby Ross, interview by Jerry Douglas, *Manshots,* March 1997.

Gayle Rubin, "The Mirace Mile: South of Market and Gay Male Leather," James Brooks, Chris Carlsson, and Nancy Peters, eds., *Reclaiming San Francisco: History, Politics, Culture* (San Francisco: City Lights Books, 1998).

Eric Schaefer, "Gauging a Revolution: 16mm Film and the Rise of the Pornographic Feature," Linda Williams, ed., *Porn Studies* (Durham: Duke University Press, 2004).

Paul Alcuin Siebenand, *The Beginnings of Gay Cinema in Los Angeles: The Industry and the Audience,* Ph.D. dissertation, USC, June 1975.

Mick Sinclair, *San Francisco: A Cultural and Literary History* (New York: Interlink Books, 2004).

James T. Sears, *Behind the Mask of the Mattachine: The Hal Call Chronicles and the Early Movement for Homosexual Emancipation* (New York: Harrington Park Press, 2006).

Randy Shilts, *The Mayor of Castro Street: The Life and Times of Harvey Milk* (New York: St. Martin's, 1982).

Turan and Zito, *Sinema.*

John Travis, interview by Jerry Douglas, *Manshots*, March 1990.

"John Summers, Behind the Camera:" Interview by Jerry Douglas, *Manshots,* March 1989.

"Gay Porn Pioneer Dead at 53?" *Update*, May 29, 1985.

"Falcon: The Bird's-Eye View, How Founder Chuck Holmes Built a Sex-Video Giant," *Unzipped*, April 13, 1999.

Thomas Waugh, *Hard to Imagine: Gay Male Eroticism in Photography and Film from their Beginnings to Stonewall* (New York: Columbia University Press, 1996.)

Edmund White, *States of Desire: Travels in Gay America* (New York: Plume, 1980).

CHAPTER FIVE

The Real and the Fantastic

There are two levels where we can lead our lives. The real and the fantastic. We have to disco and do drugs and fuck if we want to live fantastic!

—THE DEVINE BELLA IN
LARRY KRAMER, *FAGGOTS*

Pornography couldn't compete with real life.... Anything that was in pornography you could have in abundance—on the street any day, walk in any gym, more beautiful men, more dick, more available dick, right out the door into their apartment, the party starts in an hour, you can go in the backroom right now. It was like life was a pornographic film.

—RODGER MCFARLANE IN
GAY SEX IN THE 70S

Fantasy is clearly a separate realm from reality, but it also exists only in so far as reality circumscribes it.

—ELIZABETH COWIE

In October 1976 a sex club opened on the second floor at 835 Washington Street, near Little West 12th Street in New York's meatpacking district. There was no sign over the door; its habitués knew it by its address only. Widely rumored to be a Mafia-controlled bar, the Mineshaft soon became one of the city's most notorious and charged arenas for the playing out of S/M sexual fantasies. Its founder and grand maestro was Wally Wallace. "He taught us all what it is to act like a man," said Arnie Kantrowitz. "He was the set designer for exposing the beautiful darker side of our sexuality." [Hoffman, *New York Blade*, 9/17/99]

Entry to the Mineshaft was up a flight of stairs. At the top was a guard who collected the admission fee and passed on the dress and appearance of the patrons. There was a dress code posted that stipulated:

> "[C]ycle & western gear, Levis, T-shirts, uniforms, jock straps, plaid or plain shirts, cut offs, club patches, overlays & sweat. No cologne or perfumes or designer sweaters. No suits, ties, dress pants or jackets. No rugby styled shirts or disco drag. No coats in the Playground." [Gooch, 171]

The first room appeared to be a well-lit gay bar with long wooden bar, pool table, and benches. People stood around, drinking and talking. From that room, a doorway with a leather curtain led to another room that was dark and lit by dim red light bulbs; the room was lined with props and equipment—in the center was a leather sling suspended from the ceiling by chains. There a man might climb into the sling and put his feet into stirrups to expose his anus for sexual play. In the next room there was usually a crowd of men kneeling and sucking men standing. Everyone took turns sucking and getting sucked. The soft sound of moans underlay the music, pierced by the biting sound of whips on soft flesh.

Another stairway led down to the street-level rooms, which had an intense smell of leather, urine, and sweat. The center room was the Mineshaft's grand theater. Spotlights throughout the room lit up the equipment, but the central feature was an ancient bathtub where whoever chose to could climb in and be urinated on. This room had stocks and chains hung from the ceiling with manacles for wrists and ankles. Cubicles set up on the sides allowed for more private activities.

The Mineshaft was a theater of sexual fantasies and pleasures. Many of the players were, like the performers in porn, professionals, hired by Wallace to help set the tone of the activities that took place there. These players, observed writer John Preston, "still live in the imagination of many of the people who paid to make their own appearances."

> "These players were paid to present themselves and the public personas they had developed to the rest of the clientele. They had the well-designed attire, the muscularly powerful bodies, and the carefully cultivated attitudes. They were not there just to be the stars, they were there to enable others to enter into the mood. They were coaches, paid to show the novices the ropes, to let them see how the right kind of roles should be played." [Preston, 57]

Throughout the seventies, sex was explored in places like New York and San Francisco with tremendous originality and freedom. The Mineshaft, like pornography itself, was a portal into an erotic fantasy world—a place set off from the "real world," the everyday world that people live in, go to work in, or raise families in. To participate in a sexual encounter at the Mineshaft or view an encounter there was akin to watching a theatrical performance. "The key word to understand S/M is fantasy," Pat Califia explains. "The roles, dialogue, fetish costumes, and sexual activity are part of a drama or ritual. The participants are enhancing their sexual pleasure, not damaging or imprisoning one another." [Califia, 31]

The Mineshaft was an entertainment complex, and like a theme park, it allowed its patrons to live out some of their fantasies. "What it offers," Edmund White concluded, "are the props of passion, an arena of experiment, a stimulating dimness."

> "Many of the dramas enacted there are mild enough, some are creative. Sex therapists ascribe most sexual dysfunctions (impotence, delayed or premature ejaculation in men) to, among other causes, an inability to generate erotic fantasies; for that reason pornography of all sorts is often used to restore function. People have seen things at the Mine Shaft they would not dream of performing themselves, but the spectacle of such varied sexual scenarios can awaken their imaginations." [White, *States of Desire*, 284]

HIGHWAY FANTASIES

The late 1970s were a moment of "virilization" for homosexual men. "[T]hey embraced a new vision of themselves as hypermasculine—the famous 'clone' look. Soldier, cop, construction worker—these were the new gay images, rather than dancer, decorator or ribbon clerk." [White, *Arts and Letters*, 299] The rise of the clone look and of bars like the Mineshaft in New York and the Slot in San Francisco helped to promulgate the new gay masculinity, but porn took it to the rest of the country—and the man who bridged the old world of the closeted straight man and the new gay masculine sexuality was filmmaker Joe Gage.

In 1975, Tim Kincaid, a TV commercial and film actor, shopped around a script for a gay hardcore road picture called *Highway Fantasies*. One person who saw it was a producer/theater owner who turned it down and remarked that he thought the title was "too soft." Eventually Kincaid and a friend, under the names Joe and Sam Gage, raised the money to produce it themselves—that movie became *Kansas City Trucking Company*. "I started off making it a journey," Gage said. "It was supposed to go from one place to another, and as I was writing, creating events that would illuminate character and would also be 'money events'—sexual episodes—I discovered that it was not only a journey, it was a journey of self-discovery." [Gage, *Manshots*, 6/92, 13]

Kansas City Trucking Co. was released on Christmas 1976 and proved extremely successful with audiences as well as highly profitable for Gage and his partners. It had been almost ten years since Gage had read an article by Vincent Canby, the daily film critic for the *New York Times,* that had started him thinking about making sex films. Canby's article was about the proliferation of theaters showing "sexploitation" movies—low budget, sensationalistic, feature-length movies made with plenty of violence, sex, and nudity. The article stressed the movies' profitability. [New York Times, 1/24/68]. Kincaid was intrigued by the possibility, and whenever he was on set making a TV commercial, he began to pay attention to the production process. With a friend, Gage began making straight soft-core films and soon turned to hardcore films. He began to think about making a gay hardcore film and performed in a gay hardcore movie called *Morning, Noon and Night* in order to see what was it like to perform sex before cameras. Gage loved B-movies—Roger Corman's horror movies and biker flicks like *The Wild Angels*. "At the time, Wakefield [Poole] was bringing a very artistic, cultural sensibility" to the making of gay hardcore movies "and I thought it would be great to have a sort of B-movie-Tom of Finland-Li'l Abner-balls-out-cartoon kind of moviemaking." [Gage, *Manshots*, 6/92, 13]

• • •

From the beginning, Gage had decided that "trucking company" was to be in the title.

> "[W]e looked for the right town, the right place to come from to make the journey proper. ... when French or Italian filmmakers come to the United States, they always see the U.S. as New York and Los Angeles, and everything in between is a desert with cactus and cowboys ... and that was a great image to me." [Gage, *Manshots*, 6/92, 13]

Once the script was complete and the money raised, the first person Gage cast in the film was Richard Locke. Gage had seen him in a poster for a hardcore feature called *Pool Party* at the Adonis Theater. Locating the actor was difficult, however. He eventually found Locke living in a shack in the desert, with no running water and a generator for electricity, where he was building a geodesic dome—"A real wild child ... the last of the true live-and-let-live hippies." [Morris] Locke had moved to the desert because he believed cities were centers of disease due to overpopulation. Gage was surprised to find the clean-shaven Locke now had a full thick beard with gray on both sides. Locke offered to shave his beard before starting the movie, but Gage told him: "Don't touch it. It's a great look!" [Gage, *Manshots*, 6/92, 14]

When Gage started to make *Kansas City Trucking Co.*, there were few professional performers. Richard Locke was born in 1941, in Oakland, California. Though his mother was the daughter of a preacher, he never hid his homosexuality from his family. As a performer Locke always felt he had an obligation to the men living in small cities far from the major gay centers like New York, San Francisco, or Los Angeles. "The sexual revolution was well underway," Gage remembered. "The majority of men who applied wanted to appear in the films for political reasons as much as anything else." [Morris]

• • •

Kansas City Trucking Co. follows a trucker named Hank (played by Locke) on a long haul to Los Angeles with a newly hired man riding shotgun, played by newcomer Steve Boyd. Another early porn star, Jack Wrangler, plays the dispatcher— he and Locke have a quickie before Locke goes on the road. Then the ostensibly straight man—he has been dropped off by his girlfriend—has sexual fantasies about Wrangler as they drive to Los Angeles. Along the way, Locke and Boyd fantasize, experience flashbacks of sexual fantasies, or pass by a number of sexual encounters on the side of the road. At the end of the journey they both join in an orgy at the truckers' bunkhouse in L.A.

In spite of its seemingly rough style, it was "completely scripted," Gage told the *Bright Lights Film Journal*, "down to the last detail, including all sexual situations and dialogue." In the sexual scenes, Gage told the actors,

> "This is what I'm going to want from you ... I'm going to want you here ... I'm going to want you there ... We'll shoot four or five minutes on this, four or five minutes on that, and then I want you to come ... And I want you to come this way or that way or whatever. And how do you feel about it?... Which way is most comfortable for you?" [Morris]

Gage never built sex scenes around specific sex acts; instead, he choreographed the sex as a confrontation between two characters. Masturbation is the most common sex act in Gage's films and anal sex the least common. In contrast to many other gay porn filmmakers, Gage thought that "anal sex is not very cinematic."

> "The whole idea of making homosexual pornography ... [if] you strip it down to its absolute basics, [is] the worship of the phallus, the worship of the penis. If you're going to make homosexual pornography, you'd better light the dick. So masturbation and oral sex are ... the best way to photograph. You're highlighting the penis—that's what it's about." [Gage, 6/92, 17]

Throughout his career, Gage never portrayed or identified anyone as gay in his films. "They're never 'straight,' though," he swore.

> "That's the point. People constantly say, 'Oh here's another Joe Gage movie, he's going to have straight guys going gay or straight guys having sex.' But no, that's not it at all. My stuff is always about guys who get up in the morning, go to work, do their job and then see what happens ..." [Rodriguez, 19]

Since *Kansas City Trucking Co.* was so financially successful, Joe and Sam Gage immediately began to plan a sequel. *El Paso Wrecking Corp.* launched almost exactly a year later. Again, it starred Richard Locke. Fred Halsted, the acclaimed director of *LA Plays Itself, Sex Garage,* and *Sex Tool,* who had appeared in some of his own movies, shared equal billing with Locke. Even more than *Kansas City Trucking Co., El Paso Wrecking Corp.* was the classic road movie/buddy film. When Locke and Halsted are fired from Kansas City Trucking, they head to El Paso. Along the way, they stop at busy bars, public restrooms, and just on the side of the road to watch sex or to have it themselves.

Like all of the men in Gage's movies, their characters are not gay or straight, but up for any sexual adventure. After Halsted has sex with a guy in the back room of a bar while the guy's girlfriend watches, a homophobic patron starts a fight with them. Locke cautions Halsted, "You've got to learn to keep your hands to yourself."

"Awh, shit I couldn't help it. Those two [the man and his girlfriend] were too much. Listen, Hank, no more guys. This time I mean it."

"Yeah, I've heard that before." Locke replies. "Your dick gets you into more trouble than anyone I ever met."

The third picture, *L.A. Tool and Die*, was released a year after *El Paso Wrecking Corp.* Locke stars with hunky moustachioed brunette Will Seagers, who plays Locke's love interest. Casey Donovan also appears in the movie—in a scene where he is fucked in the woods by stalwart early performers Terri Hannon and Derek Stanton.

L.A. Tool and Die is more romantic than the other films in Gage's trilogy. The character played by Seagers is reluctant to commit himself to Locke, and has a vivid memory of the death of the buddy he loved in Vietnam. Locke almost misses his fateful get-together with Seagers when he gets caught up in an orgy in a restroom near where they are supposed to meet—but true to the spirit of the seventies, Seagers checks out the men's room and joins in himself. Locke invites Seagers to live with him on the desert plot that he bought with his life savings, but it is disappointingly bleak. They have decided to leave when they accidently discover water on the land—a figurative "money shot," it gushes like an ejaculating penis. The film ends with Locke and Seagers making love in the candlelight.

The last scene was uncharacteristic for Gage. Unlike so many other gay hardcore filmmakers, he had no interest in gay identity or gay relationships. "I never made relationship pictures, except in the widest definition of the term. Even so I wanted to create this thing at the end of *L.A.* where Hank finds this guy who is grieving, and the two of them make a life together." [Gage, *Manshots*, 13]

Gage's three films—sometimes referred to as "the Kansas City trilogy"—had an enormous impact on the gay men who saw them. As critic and historian Jerry Douglas notes,

> "Joe Gage's first three films introduced a new sort of hero to the gay film, and celebrated the freedom of the sexual revolution that had spread across America during the years that they were being made. Today, in retrospect, the trio stand together as the definitive cinematic statement on the emergence of the macho homosexual whose sexual transiency and voracity influenced larger and larger numbers of gay men—until the advent of AIDS." [*Stallion*, 49]

In 2006, *Unzipped* magazine listed Gage's three movies—*Kansas City Trucking Co.*, *El Paso Wrecking Corp.*, and *L.A. Tool and Die*—among the hundred greatest gay porn films made since 1968.

The world Gage created in his films was a masculine twilight zone between the closet and a man's acknowledgment of homosexual desire as masculine. The ambivalence and reticence about sexual identity resonated with a great many men at the time. Gage himself inhabited that twilight zone. He never identified as a gay man; for him, sex was always more significant than identity—"I think it's so confining, so diminishing to say, 'I am a gay man.'" [Rodriguez, 18] In fact, in the eighties, he married and then raised two sons with his wife. Unlike some of the characters in his films, Gage abstained from having sex with men after he married. "I was one hundred percent faithful to my wife," he explained, "during my years as a full-time husband." [Rodriguez, 18-19] Gage's films portray, as Jerry Douglas points out, "men's initiation into pansexuality. These films are rife with women, sexual women whose men (while not explicitly bisexual) are, or *become*, firm believers in the Sixties adage: 'If it feels good, do it.'" [*Stallion*, 49]

The fantasy world created by Gage closely resembled the one drawn by erotic artist Tom of Finland. It was, as Alan Hollinghurst observed,

> "A fantasy-world of uncomplicated and exaggerated male sexuality....[He] created a whole type of men, square-jawed, thick-lipped, with powerful muscular bodies, packed jutting asses and huge cocks.... [He] was always rendering explicit the sexuality of certain male stereotypes—lumberjacks, cowboys, hitch-hikers." [Hollinghurst, 11]

In Gage's world, much like that of Tom of Finland, "The best homosexual sex is anonymous, impersonal, promiscuous and public."

THE ROAD TO CATALINA

Gay porn production on the West Coast was divided between San Francisco, where Matt Sterling, John Travis, and Falcon Studios were based, and Los Angeles, where Shan Sayles, Monroe Beehler, and Tom DeSimone were making gay erotic movies that resembled full-length Hollywood features.

In 1977 Scott Masters (who at that time worked under the name Robert Walters) launched Nova Studios with photographer Jim Randall. Like so many of the early filmmakers, Masters had come to hardcore filmmaking from producing soft-core—and later hardcore—porn magazines. He cast, staged and photographed "sex narratives" for more than five hundred magazines between 1970 and 1977. During the course of working on the magazines, he had developed an entire "visual vocabulary" for erotic storytelling.

Based in Los Angeles, Masters wanted to move from magazine publishing into filmmaking. He approached Monroe Beehler with an idea for a hardcore feature film inspired by the mainstream Hollywood blockbuster *The French Connection*. "I had wanted to call it *The Greek Connection*. It was a thriller. The key to the mystery was a tattoo on some guy's ass. But someone else came out with a film called *The Greek Connection* just before I did, so we changed it to *Greek Lightning*." Rising porn star Jimmy Hughes was the lead. [Masters, *Manshots*, 11/97, 14]

Masters launched Nova Studios in direct competition with Falcon. Drawing upon Masters's expertise as a publisher, Nova produced glossy full-color brochures to market its short films. Each sixteen-page brochure was illustrated with photographs of the film's action. Rather than the standard ten-minute loops, Masters made loops of fifteen to twenty minutes. The longer loops offered a more polished and glamorous product than the handheld efforts shot at that time in seedy motel rooms. The longer loops also allowed Masters to tell "slightly more complex stories" in his films. [Masters, *Manshots*, 11/97, 14]

Most Nova releases had a story to tell, with clear transitions and dramatic conflict. Masters transferred the editorial approach he had developed as a magazine editor: "I had become very adept at telling a story visually and using sex to tell the story.... In those days, it was a little trick to set up a story situation whereby sex told the story. It's like a good song in a musical forwards the plot." [Masters, *Manshots*, 11/97, 12]

The typical Nova film showed men having sex with other men in settings not typically considered "gay" locations: a factory, garage, football locker room, or stable. The fantasy created was that "jocks, hardhats, wranglers all segued into sex right there in the workplace. But by his accurate settings, props, and garb, Walters helped his viewers 'suspend belief.' The point was above all to show 'hot guys having gay sex,' not '*gay* guys having hot sex.'" [Hardesty, *Manshots*, 7/97, 12]

By the mid-eighties the new video technologies were dramatically changing how porn was made and how the industry was organized. The changes affected Nova on an economic level: "Nova never made enough money. One of the terrible things that video brought into the business," Masters bemoaned, "is [that] it brought in the riffraff. It brought in the idea that anyone who could hold a camera, could make a movie.... there was no commitment to a craft ..." [Masters, *Manshots*, 11/97, 14]

Masters decided to close the studio in 1986 when Jim Randall, his business partner, disappeared with the stills and film master of their latest release. [Masters, *Manshots*, 11/97, 14] By that time, Los Angeles had numerous small companies using video technology to make gay male porn movies.

• • •

William Higgins was a late bloomer. He was approaching thirty-five and had never had sex with either a man or a woman. He was running a stained glass business in Houston where he taught housewives how to make stained glass decorations for their homes. He explored his sexuality by going to theaters to watch gay porn, but he thought the movies were so bad that he decided he wanted go to California and try to make better ones. To prepare himself, he bought a copy of Stephen Ziplow's recently published *The Filmmaker's Guide to Pornography* (New York: Drake, 1977), which provided a checklist of the various sexual acts that should be included in a "straight" porn film (masturbation, penis-to-vagina sex, lesbianism, oral sex, three-ways, orgies, and anal sex) along with instructions on how best to film them. He also purchased a secondhand 16mm movie camera. But before going he also thought he should start having sex, so he started cruising the gay clubs. He especially liked the Midtowne Spa, a popular bathhouse in Houston.

In early 1978, Higgins set out for San Francisco, though he only got as far as Los Angeles. There, he headed for Hollywood because someone had told him that that was the gay area of town. As he drove down Santa Monica Boulevard, lined with hustlers "hitchhiking," he knew he was in the right place. Finally he touched down at the French Market, long one of the most popular restaurants for gay men in the West Hollywood area.

At the restaurant, Higgins met a man and told him he'd specifically come out to California make a gay porn movie. The man encouraged him: "Well, okay, let's go do it." The man helped Higgins to find a cast, and they shot the film in his apartment. They also brought in Steve Scott, who'd made some straight and gay hardcore films, to edit it—in the credits Scott was listed as the director. The film was called *A Married Man*. It starred Jack Wrangler—one of the leading stars at that time.

The filming went badly in many ways. None of the three principals got along. They disagreed about shooting, performance, and editing. Higgins had virtually no previous experience with photography or filming. The film had been loaded backwards in the camera; it was also underexposed and shot with a red filter to simulate a gaudy set that was not available. Nor did he have enough sexual experience—he had never seen two men fucking close up until he directed *A Married Man*. Though Monroe Beehler's Century Theater booked the film, the owner of New York's Adonis Theater declined because he thought Jack Wrangler was "overexposed."

It was such an unpleasant experience that Higgins decided to call it quits. He then took a job as a clerk at a bathhouse in the San Fernando Valley and settled down in Venice Beach with a young man he'd met. Venice Beach, with its scantily dressed surfers and shirtless young men roller skating, proved to be too titillating a sexual scene for Higgins to ignore: "I was walking around Venice Beach and I said, 'Oh, this would really be an interesting movie.'... And I started shooting some footage with film we had left over from making *A Married Man*." [Higgins, *Manshots*, 12/90, 8]

The footage shot sat on the shelf until Monroe Beehler called.

"Wow! We really liked *A Married Man*, and I'm looking for a picture as my big Christmas feature which is, you know, an important thing. Why don't you make another film?" [Higgins, *Manshots*, 12/90, 8]

Higgins quickly agreed and put together a film he called *The Boys of Venice* (1979), the film that launched him as a director. Set along the beach in Venice, the movie was built around the youth culture that had emerged there during the sixties. Higgins incorporated the roller-skating fad into the movie. The opening scene of the film takes place in a small bathroom with two performers having sex and fucking with roller skates on—a virtuoso performance.

The Boys of Venice already displayed many of the trademark characteristics of Higgins's films—the use of an everyday public ambience to set the stage, shooting outdoors, the use of multiple cameras, shots from below and between the legs, and filming the cum shot in slow motion with a wide-angle lens. In *Boys* Higgins eschewed the feature film approach with a strong narrative. Instead, the film is made up of short scenes loosely held together by a theme. He rarely used a "script."

> "I found that it never works out that way. I think that pornography is like shooting a sporting event ... they run the big touchdown past you, and you can't say, 'Okay, back up, let's do this over again.' You better have your camera going and you better use your experience to be in the right place.... you have to roll with the punches. I don't know of anybody that doesn't do it that way.... Now, people have come in very rigidly scripted, [but] it's not like a Hollywood movie where the sex is fake. It's the real thing." [Higgins, *Manshots*, 12/90, 9]

The Boys of Venice was a tremendous box office success and decisively launched Higgins on his career. He set up his own companies to handle production (Laguna Pacific) and distribution (Catalina), and went on to become the most prolific gay porn filmmaker in the United States. Over the next five years, he made twenty movies—most of them major moneymakers. He set new production standards for gay pornography. His films codified the California aesthetic—called "the William Higgins tradition" in promotional copy on box covers—of slender, generally blond young men in the outdoors, hiking, surfing, at rodeos, or on the beach: the look that J. Brian had initiated with his publication of *Golden Boys*. And he launched the careers of a whole new generation of major porn stars in the 1980s—among them Kip Noll, Leo Ford, Lance, J. W. King, Jon King, Derrick Stanton, John Davenport, Jeff Quinn, and Kevin Williams.

Though *Boys of Venice* was filmed without a lead, Kip Noll emerged as the star of the movie. He was the first major "twink" porn star. In fact he personified the twink—an attractive young gay man with a slender build and little or no body hair.

Originally recommended to Higgins by Monroe Beehler, Noll was not new to gay porn. He had performed before in a series of loops for director Mark Reynolds. Generally assumed to be straight, Noll actually seduced Reynolds on their first meeting.

"When Kip Noll got off the plane, he really didn't look that good. He had a look about him that was kind of butch, but not that attractive. Part of it was his having a little moustache that just didn't work.... Overall, he just didn't look like he would photograph that well."

Reynolds was about to send him back home,

> "But ... [I thought] I ought to at least interview him.... The first thing he did was say, 'Let me show you what I look like.' And he dropped his pants, which made me take a second look at him.... He had one of the prettiest cocks I've ever seen. Really. He wasn't hard, but was hanging about six or seven inches soft. At that point, he said, 'Why don't you take your clothes off?' Now I try to keep these things very aboveboard and businesslike—but he insisted, mainly I think because he wanted to show me how he could perform. So reluctantly, I took my clothes off. Now,

I've been around—but he proceeded to do things to me that were erotically exciting.... And of course he had the right equipment. It was an incredibly hot scene that to this day has not been topped." [Reynolds, *Manshots*, 11/88, 7]

Like Reynolds, Higgins was not immediately taken with Noll.

"I didn't like him at first, he was a very street-wise boy. And I didn't like that quality in him at first. But as I got to know him ... I liked him a lot more. I certainly liked him as much as any-body after we got to know each other.... [H]e is one of those persons that looks incredibly better in photographs then he does in person. The cam-era loves him. He's got kind of blotchy skin, but it doesn't show up on camera." [Higgins, *Man-shots*, 12/90, 10]

As a sexual performer, Noll, who both routinely topped and bottomed, claimed he was motivated by his "enjoyment" and "drive for sex."

For many, Kip Noll was the iconic William Higgins star. Over the next three years they made five other films together: *Kip Noll and the Westside Boys* (1979), *Pacific Coast Highway* (1981), *Class of 84, Part 2* (1981), *Brothers Should Do It* (1981), and *Kip Noll, Superstar*, a compilation of scenes from the first five movies that included a new scene with butch power bot-tom Jon King, one of Higgins's latest discoveries. Over the course of these movies, Noll's appearance ranged from the twink at the disco club to the somewhat rougher and scruffy wild boy of *West Coast Highway*. One of his most famous scenes in the film finds him hiking along a dirt road in the wilds of California. Jeremy Scott and Jack Burke drive by in a jeep. They stop to invite him to join them for a joint and some sex. Scott and Noll take turns fucking Burke on the front of the jeep. Burke comes all over the windshield, which he then cleans off by turning on the windshield wipers.

On top of the Kip Noll movies, Higgins went on to make a series of films in 1981, 1982, and 1983 that became instants classics—*These Bases are Loaded* (1981), *Members Only* (1982), *Best Little Warehouse in LA* (1982), *Sailor in the Wild* (1983), *Leo and Lance* (1983), *Cousins* (1983), and *Class Reunion* (1983)—many of them starring two new discoveries, Jon King and Leo Ford.

Jon King was the next Higgins discovery to emerge as a major porn star. Brought to Higgins's office by performer Jamie Wingo, Higgins immediately saw King's potential.

> "You know, when you're in the business you're always talking about the one that got away. You want to get somebody before he becomes a big star, build him into a big star and make as much money as possible. There are so many that have come along, and you didn't have the right situation.... I realized that [Jon King] is a star. And he said, 'Well when can I make a movie.' And I said, 'It's one-thirty now—why don't you show up at five o'clock and you'll make a movie.' I'd had so many of them slip through my fingers, and I said, 'This is a star.' That's the fastest I've ever organized a shoot in my life." [Higgins, *Manshots*, 12/90, 78]

Born in Florida in 1963, King had been fascinated by pornography ever since finding his father's *Playboy* magazine when he was twelve. Later, he attempted to contact gay pornographic filmmaker Jack Deveau, but Deveau turned King down. In 1980, he and his boyfriend visited Los Angeles on their summer vacation, planning to go back to school in Florida in the fall. However, soon after settling in L.A., King met Higgins and launched his career in porn films. His incipient career was stalled when he stole and wrecked a car in 1982 and then spent eleven months in prison. He appeared in more than twenty-five movies during the eighties. [King, Onpedia]

Higgins's first movie with King was *Brothers Should Do It*, in which he starred with J. W. King, whom he resembled and who was billed as his "brother." "[I]n my whole career in pornography up to that point, that was the first time—and one of the few times—I just turned the camera on and let it run ... just unbelievable." [Higgins, 12/90, 78]

Starting with *Sailor in the Wild*, Higgins cast Leo Ford in a number of what became several of his most famous films. Paired with Brian Thompson in *Sailor in the Wild*, Ford also appeared with the popular blond bad boy performer, who went by the name Lance in *Leo and Lance*.

Blond and self-possessed, Leo Ford's first appearance in gay porn was in J. Brian's 1981 movie *Flashbacks*. He appeared in a scene with his then boyfriend Jamie Wingo. Jerry Douglas considered their scene "the high point of the picture" and said that "their enthusiasm, rapacity, and versatility make the scene as scorcher. Finally, the cum shots—especially Ford's— are sensational." [*Stallion*, 24] Ford was born in Dayton, Ohio, in 1957. He attended less than a year of college before going to India to study meditation. He later settled in Fort Myers, Florida, where he started his own business, before moving on to San Francisco and then to Los Angeles to pursue his career in porn. He was an energetic performer, sexually versatile, and he effectively communicated the pleasure he took in sex. He made two extremely popular movies, *Leo and Lance* (1983, Dir. William Higgins) and *Blonds Do It Best* (1985, Dir. Richard Morgan) with Lance, a blond drifter and troublemaker with whom he had an electric sexual rapport.

In 1983, Higgins released *Class Reunion*. Modeled on J. Brian's *Pool Party* (1972), Higgins's favorite porn movie, he decided to use "all the stars from the past that happen to be around" and capped it off by giving away a motorcycle in a raffle. Invitations were sent out, but Higgins had no idea how many performers might eventually show up for the shoot.

> "We shot on a Saturday afternoon at this big mansion out in Glendale. We hired buses and

everything. And actually there were some people in there who snuck in that I'd never shot before or seen since. We had three cameramen. Well you didn't wait for a hard-on. Everybody paired up with someone else. They sort of found their own element and they went off and did their own thing. So when you got enough footage on someone, or his dick went down, then you just looked over: 'Oh well, that's interesting,' and you turned the camera over there.... [W]e shot the whole thing in six hours.... [I]t was a real party, fun atmosphere. It was the funnest film I ever shot. And also, I had the most criticism of any film I've ever done, because right after that the AIDS crisis hit. It didn't hit during the film, it hit after the film came out and they said, 'He's promoting AIDS by having these big orgies.'" [Higgins, *Manshots*, 2/91, 32]

The sheer joy and sexual abundance of *Class Reunion* perfectly summed up the era of sexual exuberance that existed before AIDS struck. Orgies are communal events. The social conventions and distinctions that normally constrain the sexual free-for-all disappear. Potentially, everyone present is sexually available. *Class Reunion* celebrated a special moment in American gay life, though with tragic irony it was one that was about to end. In early 2006, *Unzipped* magazine commemorated *Class Reunion* in its list of the "Unzipped 100: The Greatest Gay Porn Films" as "one of the greatest all-male orgies in skin flick memory." [*Unzipped*, 25]

BIGGER AND BETTER

While gay porn as a "business" was founded in San Francisco, the center of gravity began to move south to Los Angeles with

William Higgins's rise to prominence. During a business slump in 1980, Matt Sterling closed the clothing store he had run in the Castro after "retiring" from making porn, and moved to Los Angeles. However, within a year he had decided to direct hardcore movies again; Chuck Holmes of Falcon Studios had offered to finance a couple of low-budget films. John Travis had already moved from San Francisco to southern California early in 1980 and settled in Tustin in Orange County. There, he began to develop new talent—among them, "a bevy" of young men from a nearby Marine base.

Travis and Sterling had similar erotic tastes, and they both kept a lookout for men who had, as Travis put it, "The Look, The Face, The Body and The Merchandise." Travis believed that "the Merchandise" was not always the most important factor; being an exhibitionist was just as important.

> "The first thing to look for is the face and the body, and if they have it, or close to it, you send them off to the gym for a month. Their sincerity in wanting to do it is important. Many young people have a fantasy to make a film, and some of them work for a few weeks, and there are others who want to make a career out of it, because they enjoy the exhibitionistic aspect of it and the money." [Travis, *Manshots*, 3/90, 8]

Travis cast many of the Marines he had cultivated in a series of movies he made with Matt Sterling (*Huge, Huge 2*) and for Falcon: *The Other Side of Aspen 2*, *The New Breed*, *Spring Training*, and *Splash Shots*, Falcon's first video production.

Sterling's first two movies produced in southern California, *Huge* and *Huge 2*, were basically a set of loops, but they were the first gay porn movies released under the name "Matt Sterling"—most of his previous work was uncredited—and they quickly became bestsellers. The success of the *Huge* videos made Sterling's reputation. From there he went on to make a series of feature-length movies over the next three years that set new standards in gay porn, featuring spectacular casts of stylish and glamorous young men with a high coefficient of sexual chemistry. Sterling decided to make his first feature-length movie, but as in his loops, he focused on the performers and the sex. "[W]hen I decided I was going to make my own films, I got together with some friends of mine and we talked about what they'd like to see as sexual fantasy—what fantasies were left to cover—and then take a little more depth and in a slightly more sophisticated manner." [Sterling, *Manshots*, 9/88, 6]

A Matter of Size (1983) was the first of the four. It was also the first feature-length gay porn movie shot directly on video. The new technology encouraged them to use natural background sounds through the film, and cum shots were shot in natural time rather than in slow-motion as was common then. Released in video format, it was a bestseller. Sterling's second feature-length entry was *Like a Horse*. Less successful than its predecessor, it is nonetheless a first-class video that included decent acting and good sex. [Parrish, *Stallion* 37]

Sterling followed up *Like a Horse* with *The Bigger the Better*. Two scenes featured performer Matt Ramsey. In one scene he plays a teacher who is fucked by student Rick Donovan. Under the name Peter North, Ramsay became one of the most popular and respected performers in straight porn. It quickly became a best seller and was very favorably reviewed. Jerry Douglas wrote in *Stallion*:

> "[The movie is] flawlessly cast, professionally photographed, and evocatively scored, though familiarly conceived and carelessly edited. Still, these are minor quibbles in terms of Matt Sterling's monumental achievement, for *The Bigger the Better* is one of the two or three hottest films of all time." [Douglas, *Stallion*, 7]

Sizing Up was the fourth in Sterling's series of feature-length movies. Inspired by the 1984 Olympics, it was built around the locker room exploits of a decathlon team.

> "The episodes are woven so tightly into this tale, that the story line never intrudes on the sex, and the emotional impact of sex is enhanced by the strong narrative. Credible acting by the entire cast adds the finishing touch. This kind of superb blending is rarely achieved in gay porn, but Sterling has accomplished it with seeming ease." [Troy McKenzie, *Stallion*, 59]

Sterling and Travis worked on these films together, except for *A Matter of Size*. At the same time, they also collaborated on a series of videos for Falcon—the sequel to *The Other Side of Aspen* as well as two new videos that spawned two other popular Falcon franchises, *Splash Shots* and *Spokes*.

Travis had also begun working with William Higgins, and in 1985 he left Falcon and became director of production for Higgins's Catalina Studios. As early as 1978, Higgins had set up Laguna Pacific as his production unit, while Catalina was the distribution arm that also handled sales for Scott Masters's Nova Studios and some of the videos that Travis and Sterling went on to make starring Jeff Stryker. The regrouping of three of the industry's founding fathers from San Francisco—John Travis, Matt Sterling, and John Summers—in southern California, where Scott Masters was based and running Nova and where William Higgins had successfully established Catalina, consolidated a major shift of the industry. Catalina had become the hub of gay porn filmmaking and distribution in Southern California, while Chuck Holmes's Falcon Studios was increasingly the hub in northern California.

PORN AS HOME ENTERTAINMENT

In the early seventies, commercial pornographic films achieved public visibility and became harbingers of the sexual revolution by playing in movie theaters. The big porn hits of the early seventies—*Boys in the Sand, Deep Throat, Behind the Green Door*, and *The Devil in Miss Jones*—all released in theaters, helped move sexually explicit motion picture imagery away from the crude 8mm loops and the closed world of stag movies shown at bachelor parties and the local VFW, or the exclusive preserve of the affluent men who purchased the 8mm films for their private viewing, to a broad public. San Francisco was the first city to show hardcore sex films in theaters. A year later, theaters in cities like Indianapolis, Dallas, Houston, Chicago, and of course, Los Angeles and New York, were also showing hardcore pornographic movies.

After years of research, Sony launched its videocassette recorder in 1975. Commercial porn producers quickly saw its economic advantages—in contrast to the portrayal in the 1997 film *Boogie Nights* that many of the earlier directors and producers resisted the change. It also made it much cheaper to produce movies and offered new channels of distribution. Sexually explicit movies could be produced on videotape at a fraction of the cost of shooting the same feature on film. The porn industry was quicker to respond to the development of video than the mainstream film industry—and it soon flooded the market with adult movies in the less expensive VHS format.

It was possible to transfer very easily and cheaply the images from the hardcore films produced in the late sixties and early seventies onto video tapes. The potential market was huge. It was also a much larger market than the one for theatrical-release hardcore films. Few theaters in any city ever showed gay hardcore movies, and if they did, the theaters were typically in red light districts or rundown areas.

The demand for VCRs grew throughout the eighties—prices dropped dramatically and the number of households with video players grew correspondingly. In 1979 only 1 percent of all Americans owned a videocassette recorder, but by 1988 nearly 60 percent owned them, and by 1997, 87 percent.

The consumption of porn greatly increased because the VCR

made adult content available in the privacy of one's home; it reduced the embarrassment factor that discouraged many potential customers from going to the local porn theater. While many gay men took advantage of the porn theaters to engage in sex, there was an even larger audience of gay men more comfortable with viewing hardcore movies at home without risk of either police harassment or arrest. And since it could be viewed in the privacy of one's home, one did not need to see it in theaters or view it in peep show booths—both locations facilitating a significant amount of live sexual activity. Porn videos could also be sold discreetly or rented along with mainstream movies.

REFERENCES

Pat Califia, "Feminism and Sado-Masochism," *Heresies*, Nos. 3/4 (1981).

Vincent Canby, "Films Exploiting Interest in Sex and Violence Find Growing Audience Here," *New York Times*, January 24, 1968.

Elizabeth Cowie, "Pornography and Fantasy," in Segal and McIntosh, *Sex Exposed.*

Arthur C. Danto, *Playing with the Edge: The Photographic Achievement of Robert Mapplethorpe* (Berkeley: University of California Press, 1995).

Joe Gage, "Interview with a Legend," by Jerry Douglas, *Manshots*, Part I, June 1992; Part II, August 1992.

Brad Gooch, *The Golden Age of Promiscuity: A Novel* (New York: Knopf, 1996).

Rolf Hardesty, "Gay film Heritage: Nova Studio," Part I: The Pre-Sound Years, *Manshots*, July 1997; Part II: The Final Years, *Manshots*, August 1997.

William Higgins, Behind the Camera: Interview by Jerry Douglas, *Manshots*, Part I, December 1990; Part II, February 1991.

Wayne Hoffman, "Wally Wallace," *New York Blade,* September 17, 1999.

Alan Hollinghurst, "Robert Mapplethorpe," in *Robert Mapplethorpe, 1970–1983* (London: Institute of Contemporary Art, 1983).

"Jon King" onpedia.com/encyclopedia/jon=king=(porn=star). Retrieved February 20, 2009.

Troy McKenzie, "The Legacy of Kip Noll," *Manshots*, March 1989.

Scott Masters, Behind the Camera: Interview by Jerry Douglas, *Manshots*, November 1997.

Patrick Moore, "Theater of Pleasure: The Mineshaft," in *Beyond Shame: Reclaiming the Abandoned History of Radical Gay Sexuality* (Boston: Beacon, 2004).

Gary Morris, "Keep on Truckin': An Interview with Joe Gage," *Bright Lights Film Journal*, *www.brightlightsfilm/42/gage.htm*. Retrieved 7/19/08.

Patricia Morrisroe, *Robert Mapplethorpe: A Biography* (New York: Random House, 1995).

John Preston, "The Theater of Sexual Initiation," in *My Life as a Pornographer & Other Indecent Acts* (New York: Masquerade Books, 1993).

Mark Reynolds, Behind the Camera: Interview by Jerry Douglas, *Manshots,* November 1988.

Frank Rodriguez, "Joe Gage," *Butt: A Quarterly Magazine*, Spring 2007.

Stallion Editors, "Stallion 50 Best," *Stallion.*

Matt Sterling, Behind the Camera: Interview by Jerry Douglas, *Manshots*, September 1988.

John Travis, Behind the Camera: interview by Jerry Douglas, *Manshots*, March 1990.

Waugh, *Hard to Imagine*.

White, *States of Desire*.

Edmund White, "Robert Mapplethorpe," *Arts and Letters* (San Francisco: Cleis Press, 2004).

"The Unzipped 100 Greatest Gay Porn Films," *Unzipped*, Special Collector's Edition, Winter/Spring 2006.

PART II

DEATH AND DESIRE

CHAPTER SIX

Sex in the Ruins

Safety ran counter to the whole expansive spirit of the seventies, the exhilarating suspicion that we were pioneers in the pursuit of human happiness and no one had found its limits yet. The plague provided limits.

The Mayans left temples in the Yucatan; we seem to have left pornography.

—ANDREW HOLLERAN, *GROUND ZERO*, 1988

For many gay men, the 1970s was the golden age of sexual freedom—especially for those who had grown up during the dark days of the closet in the 1950s and early 1960s. However, by the late 1970s the huge increase in sexual opportunity and freedom was increasingly accompanied by a growing epidemic of sexually transmitted diseases. The diseases spread by sex are numerous and ancient: gonorrhea, syphilis, genital warts, genital herpes. Toward the end of the decade the country was swept by waves of gonorrhea and syphilis. Most men just treated the regular recurrence of sexually transmitted diseases as a minor annoyance, and considered it a small price to pay for the glorious adventure of unrestrained sexuality. They merely went to the STD clinic for medicine that soon rid them of the minor irritation. But along with the standard portfolio of STDs also came intestinal parasites, hepatitis A and B, herpes, and venereal warts, all of which were much more difficult to treat.

The discovery of what eventually became AIDS, a new sexually transmitted disease, a disease that destroyed the very mechanism that normally protected the body from diseases, created a concatenation of crises—medical, social, and political.

The AIDS epidemic also provoked a crisis about sex itself within the gay male community, not only a crisis about sex in general, but also about the kinds of sex gay men in particular engaged in—fellatio, fisting, anal intercourse, casual sex with strangers and with multiple partners. However, even before the identification of the virus that causes AIDS, sexual promiscuity was believed by many both within and outside the gay community to be the most likely aspect of the gay lifestyle responsible. Was the sex gay men engaged in "inherently" dangerous or bad? Could gay men continue to engage in sex at all if they risked death from AIDS? How could gay men have sex in an epidemic of a sexually transmitted disease? The debates both inside and outside the gay community produced fatal displacements—many of those most concerned failed to address either the practical actions one could take to prevent spreading the disease or how best to defend gay male sexuality in the situation. As Leo Bersani pointed out, attention "turned away from the kinds of sex people practice to a moralistic discourse about promiscuity." [Bersani, 220]

The crisis about sex also created a profound sense of paranoia. "Sex is just a completely different thing now," porn star/director Al Parker exclaimed.

> "The entire time you're having sex you're thinking: 'I'm having sex with everybody this person ever had sex with. I wonder what he's done and

where he's been and if he's positive or negative. I wonder if I'm giving him anything,' If you can keep a hardon while all this is going on in your head, you're better than I am." [Fenwick, 36]

NEW YORK: GROUND ZERO

Andrew Holleran had arrived in New York in 1971 just as the exhilaration of gay liberation was beginning to make an impact. His first novel, *Dancer from the Dance,* which portrayed a life of sexual excess of the early seventies, was one of the breakthrough gay novels of the time.

A decade later he found himself at the center of a widening circle of ailing and dying friends. In 1983, Holleran began to write a series of essays about the impact of AIDS on the emotional and sexual lives of gay men. He had begun to see New York as a giant cemetery. "The bars, the discotheques, that are still open seem pointless in a way;" he wrote.

> "...The social contract, the assumptions, that gave them meaning is lost. They turn you serious, if you stay long enough—because every bar, every dance floor, reminds you eventually of a friend. The memory of friends is everywhere. It pervades the city. Buildings, skylines, corners, have holes in them—gaps: missing persons. And if the present is a cemetery, the future is a minefield." [Holleran, 21–22]

The aging, decayed, and somewhat sordid movie houses that showed porn drew Holleran in—the Adonis, the Jewel, and the one closest to where he lived, the Metropolitan. There was, according to Holleran, "something sad, delicious, and infinitely erotic about these movie houses now that in the past seemed merely sordid." [Holleran, 20]

These theaters, these "chambers of seed," were like wombs,

offering a harsh contrast to the brightly lit and antiseptic rooms of hospitals.

> "At the end of a day spent visiting friends in hospital rooms, intelligent, brave, accomplished men breathing oxygen through tubes, staring at a brick wall outside the window, when I get down to the street, my instinct is to run, not walk, straight through this earthly hell to the Metropolitan ... to one of these doorways and obliterate everything in the dark, warm chamber of seed. Nothing else provides the comfort this place does—no other experience." [Holleran, 19–20]

Fire Island offered no escape from the city's grim round of hospital visits and memorials, of sick men wasting away and covered with purple lesions. It was no longer the realm of beautiful men and wild sex parties. The summer of 1982 was "my last summer on Fire Island," film composer Howard Rosenman told Charles Kaiser.

> "There were people coming off the boat with IV things plugged into their arms, walking down the boulevard with those metal stands on which you hung the IV bag. And it was deathly, and people were dying, fucking getting sick left and right by eighty-two, I definitely think that the combination of gay liberation and the gay sexuality, the freedom of it, bred the matrix in which the epidemic could form—the way gays sanctioned promiscuity innocently." [Kaiser, 300]

Yet as one friend remarked wistfully to Andrew Holleran, "I keep thinking there's a beach at the end of this, an island, and we'll be happy again." [Holleran, 26]

• • •

The safe-sex campaigns of the 1980s, as anthropologist Gayle Rubin observed, "worked on the premise that it was not the number of partners a person had, the location where sex acts took place, or the presence or absence of sex toys or fetish gear, that mattered. What mattered was whether the activity provided an opportunity for transmitting a pathogen." [Rubin, 116]

There was some initial resistance from gay men to condoms. Holleran recalled that condoms were "something one was once embarrassed to even suggest...."

> "...At the beginning—for fear one would be considered anal-compulsive, neurotic, germophobic. Rubbers were jokes, the idea of constraints on sex anathema to those who argued that the essence of sex was freedom, and the glory of freedom sex.... There was no romance in rational sex." [Holleran, 24]

Outside the gay community, skepticism about the effectiveness of condoms alone was common. Most critics of "the condom code" believed that it failed to address the most significant factors underlying the AIDS epidemic—promiscuity and anal sex.

Promiscuity, which could mean, to quote Holleran, "having many, many different partners; [or] having no standards for the people with whom one sleeps," was nevertheless one of the cardinal tenets of gay men's sexual freedom. [113] It was a form of orgasm experimentation; it gave perspective on the body's capacity for pleasure.

While many considered advice that proposed that gay men stop engaging in anal intercourse altogether homophobic—no one, for instance, had proposed banning vaginal sex—many gay men also considered anal sex one of the most valued aspects of their sexuality. "The rectum is a sexual organ," argued Joseph Sonnabend, a prominent AIDS physician.

> "...And it deserves the respect a penis gets and a vagina gets. Anal intercourse has been the central activity for gay men and some women for all of history.... We have to recognize what is hazardous, but at the same time, we shouldn't undermine an act that's important to celebrate."
> [Rotello, 101]

SAN FRANCISCO: LIFE IN THE LUST LANE

In September 1981, when Scott O'Hara moved to Hawaii after a "summer of unrestrained sex in San Francisco," he had never heard of AIDS. He had spent four years after graduating from high school moving around the country. The summer after graduation was spent exploring the leather bars on Chicago's Gold Coast—though he was underage at the time. "[That] was my month to make up for four years of frustrated near-abstinence," he recalled. "I got fucked almost every night, sometimes more than once. And I loved it." [O'Hara, 41]

On a short visit to San Francisco during the time he was living in Hawaii, O'Hara saw the obituary in the *Bay Area Reporter* of the last person he had had sex with in San Francisco before moving to Hawaii. In March of 1983, it was estimated that 1 out of every 333 gay men in San Francisco had AIDS. By the following summer, 5,394 cases of AIDS were reported nationally— 634 of those were in San Francisco: that was equivalent to 1 out of every 100 gay men. New York City had a larger number of cases, but San Francisco had by far the highest number of cases per capita. By the time O'Hara moved back to San Francisco, most of his sexual activity consisted of masturbation.

On arriving back in San Francisco, O'Hara lit upon an ad in the *Bay Area Reporter* for Savages, a rundown porn theater in the Tenderloin, San Francisco's red-light district. It advertised live jack-off shows. "I was thrilled beyond words," O'Hara wrote.

> "This was all my fantasies come to life, all those high school circle jerks that had never come true. I hightailed it down there. Yes, it was a sleazy dive: dark, dirty broken seats, the usual ... When that first dancer got up onstage and jerked off, I thought I'd go crazy. I was right up there in the front row—an unpopular position, believe it or not—so the guy onstage played directly to me, and yes I had my dick out, pumping it. I think I stayed until the place closed." [87]

The theater's management also noticed O'Hara's unusually large penis—as well as his energetic masturbating. As he was the leaving the theater, the manager asked if O'Hara would like to work there full time. O'Hara enthusiastically agreed, and he worked at Savages all summer.

Barely a month later, the theater manager approached O'Hara about doing a porn movie. O'Hara accepted the offer quickly. He had often fantasized about becoming a "porn star." [88] Long fascinated by pornography, he believed, "People are born with the inherent desire for porn.... [T]he idea that watching other people have sex, watching people enjoy themselves, is an essential human pleasure. Voyeurism is the most natural of perversions, the most universal." [83]

As a child he had found what he called "porn"—by which he meant material to stimulate his erotic longings—in his mother's magazines such as *Reader's Digest* and *Redbook* as well as other magazines his family subscribed to. Porn was an article of faith to him. He firmly believed, "If we're deprived of the normal dose of pornography that every child deserves, we make up our own." [83]

California Blue, the film the theater manager asked O'Hara to be in, was shot later that summer. But even before it was finished, O'Hara was approached by Dennis Forbes, a talent scout for Falcon Studios. Forbes had been hired by *Playboy* magazine to cover the "Biggest Dick in San Francisco" contest, which O'Hara had won. Over the next two years, O'Hara made a series of scenes, mostly shot in video rather than on film, for Falcon— "Water Sports" (October 1983) and "Hard-Pressed" (February 1984) and then *The Other Side of Aspen II* (shot in April 1985), a sequel to Falcon's breakthrough film of the late seventies. And in June 1985, he appeared in *Sgt Swann's Private Files*, the first military-themed video made by Dirk Yates of San Diego. In none of these films had he used a condom.

• • •

In 1984, when he started having sex with men again—apart from the movies he was in—O'Hara used condoms, although he found safe sex somewhat frustrating. He had an extended affair with one man who had on one occasion fucked him "dry," that is without a condom. At the time O'Hara was convinced that "it didn't matter," but a year later that man got sick and died. O'Hara wrote in his memoir:

> "During this period, late 1984 to early 1985, since I wasn't having a lot of sex with other guys, I began to be meticulous about recording the sex I was having with myself. My sex journal is rather monotonous: myself, myself. I recorded the time, place, what fantasy I was using, what visual or chemical aids I was employing, the intensity of the orgasm, etc.... [And] I regularly visited SF Jacks, or other jackoff parties...." [121]

Even when the HIV test became available, O'Hara did not immediately get tested. He showed no sign of AIDS until 1989—when he suddenly noticed a flock of Kaposi's sarcoma lesions on his legs. In the years before that, he'd have a scare every now and then, usually followed by a long night of panic.

But he laughed about it in the morning, though as he later remarked, "it's no laughing matter when it's happening." Yet as he eventually conceded, "Death was sitting my shoulder, grinning at me." [124]

SAFETY RATIO

Since the AIDS epidemic had begun in 1981, the public debate about gay men's sexual activities had grown increasingly virulent—their sexual promiscuity was often targeted as a public menace: in particular, the danger posed by men engaging in anal intercourse and the possibility of multiple orgasms with many partners who spread the disease by switching roles in anal sex from the man penetrated to the one who penetrates—the sexually "versatile" man who was, erotically, the ideal man of the seventies

Since the late seventies, anal sex had become the narrative focal point of gay porn. While it is difficult to document, the shift away from oral sex as the normative activity to anal sex was one of the major changes that accompanied the sexual revolution of the sixties and seventies. And one of the most notable developments of gay male sexuality since the Stonewall riots was the dramatic increase of sexual versatility—of moving from being the one penetrating to the one penetrated, from top to bottom.

By 1985, the growing furor over gay men's sexuality—explicitly promiscuity and more implicitly their sexual versatility—caused many producers of gay porn to re-examine how sex between men should be represented in erotic videos. AIDS activists and gay leaders argued that porn should help "eroticize" safer sex. Porn stars could serve as role models for condom use.

Directors and producers of porn videos hesitated to use condoms because they believed that showing performers taking precautions and using condoms would inhibit the sexual arousal porn films were meant to provoke. Of course, the debate over whether oral sex without a condom was risky or not also made the companies hesitant to portray safe sex extensively. Nevertheless, they paid some lip service to these concerns. In 1988, Chris Mann, the vice president of Catalina Videos, announced that "AIDS became a factor about three years ago. We've really taken a hard look at the situation. We've had to. This is something that drastically affects the entire nature of our business." [Fenwick, 36]

For activists and community leaders, the importance of porn stars acting as role models for safer sex blended with concerns that sexual activities on the set posed risks to the performers. Most people in the industry believed that the sex that took place on porn sets was relatively safe. Since performers must pull their dicks out for the obligatory cum shot, there was no need for performers to come inside someone's ass or mouth. Nonoxynol-9— then widely believed to be an effective safety precaution—was widely utilized whenever anal sex was performed. Industry insiders frequently argued that most performers understood the risk and willingly chose to take it in order to create fantasies that would encourage many viewers to stay home rather than engage in high-risk sex with another person.

As Mann explained,

> "What we would like to do is have the erotic industry be a positive influence ... not a negative one. The public knows there's a health crisis. We show them how [to have sex safely] and still make it a fun, joyous experience. But part of the celebration of being gay is the celebration of your sexuality. If we did *only* safe-sex films, the erotic value would truly be gone. After all, when you watch a regular film you don't go out and drive your car the way those people do in the street chases: It's a *fantasy*, not real life. I would not want to create videos that depict truly unsafe sex—the exchange of bodily fluids. And we do

employ safe-sex techniques in the production of our videos. We just don't depict it as such." [Fenwick, 37]

For twelve or thirteen years, sex among gay men—as well as the sex, both portrayed and actually engaged in, in gay hardcore porn movies—had experienced only the limits set by a sexually repressive society. There were no "natural" limits that threatened anyone's life; it almost seemed that in sex, everything was possible. AIDS suddenly put on limits. Now sex, especially anal sex, had potentially fatal consequences. Porn producers seemed loath to accept those limits; to portray safer sex in pornographic movies was to accept those limits. Did risking death make sex without a condom more sexually exciting? So producers of porn seemed to think.

Various studios countered with claims that they screened the actors who appeared in their movies and used only "healthy" performers. "We use healthy people," Mann said.

> "We do not use prostitutes, we do not use street hustlers—and the fact that we have stopped depicting certain activities has brought us a much higher safety ratio.... [Y]ou won't find bodily fluids being exchanged. There are no oral come shots, and nobody ejaculates inside bodily orifices. Before an actor appears in an anal scene, he has douched and used a spermicide. But in a long shot you're not going to see the use of nonoxynol-9 and a rubber. We have very good editors and they edit out a lot of safe-sex techniques. We don't want to detract from the fantasy." [Fenwick, 37]

In an effort to avoid losing their audience with performances that only consisted of safer sex, studios first tried a more didactic approach. Starting in 1987, both Catalina and Falcon Studios put a three-minute instructional trailer produced by Gay Men's Health Crisis (GMHC) on their video tapes. Catalina also included a note that stated: "Laboratory studies have shown that using a lubricant with a concentration of 4–5% or higher on nonoxynol-9 can kill many viruses and greatly reduce the chance of infection from sexually transmitted diseases." Even as late as 1988, condoms are evident in only a minority of the gay pornographic movies released. Most producers of hardcore videos relied on nonoxynol-9 for protection from HIV and other STDs. [Douglas, R.W. Richards, *Manshots*, 9/88, 23]

Many producers and studios left safe sex up to the performers themselves. Director J. D. Slater, who adopted the laissez-faire approach, said,

> "As far as safe sex in my work is concerned, I will not preach or morally judge. I am simply a documentarian of sexual incidents. What an actor does is completely his own decision. I let an actor do exactly what he wants any way he wants to do it. Some directors think it's their job to instruct the public on safe sex, and for them, that's great, but that's not my responsibility." [Burger, 79]

After shooting *In Your Wildest Dreams* for Falcon in 1987, Scott O'Hara told the film's producer, "Look, you know I like working for you, but I really wish you would let us use condoms." According to O'Hara, the producer responded: "Well, you should've said something! I had condoms and lube in the bag, right there!" [112]

Later that year, O'Hara made *New Recruits* for Le Salon, a local San Francisco-based studio, in which condoms were used by all the performers. After that, condoms were used in all the remaining films in which he performed. "Prior to that, the prevailing wisdom had been 'no one will buy a video with condoms.' .... The industry standard seemed to have suddenly changed overnight," he wrote. [116–117]

O'Hara never quite reconciled himself to safe sex. In 1997 he wrote that "I still don't believe it's possible to make a porn-flick with condoms and make it look like the actors are enjoying themselves." [123]

When Al Parker was asked if he thought performers would insist on using condoms, he replied, "I don't think so. There are always new people coming up, and there are moments during sex when practically everyone is susceptible to almost anything." [Richards, *Manshots,* 11/88, 49]

But Parker also thought there was less risk during a shoot than during a real-life sexual encounter outside the porn set. "When you're making a movie, it's much safer sex than it is if you're doing it in a room with just two people because you're doing it for a camera." [Richards, 37]

Chris Mann of Catalina believed that "explicit videos create an alternative, a surrogate ... to going out and having sex." But Mann also warned,

> "You can't expect people who for years have been leading a somewhat promiscuous life-style to just stop. If they have to resort to masturbation, they need something to help it along. Video is the perfect tool for that. Lovers who once would have picked up a third partner might still do that but might also take home a video and engage in safe sex. The video helps their fantasy." [Fenwick, 65]

There had always been a group of gay men who were ambivalent about porn. They believed that porn promoted certain stereotypes of masculinity and represented commodified forms of physical desirability—but with porn increasingly considered a safe alternative to casual sexual encounters, they had come to believe that the AIDS epidemic had to some extent legitimized porn. Porn became another form of "safe sex."

Scott O'Hara didn't think there was any need to legitimize porn. "It already serves an excellent and valuable function. It arouses people. But it shouldn't replace the desire to fuck." [Richards, *Manshots,* 3/89, 45] O'Hara's concern was not misplaced. For many men, porn replaced the desire to go out and fuck. In his eyes, porn didn't need legitimization; he thought it should be valued for itself. But on the other hand, it was no substitute for sex or physical intimacy between real people. It was a fantasy world; sex between real people was a different kind of pleasure.

• • •

Ironically, while discussions among gay porn producers were taking place, a fierce debate raged in Congress over funding for "AIDS education, information, or prevention materials." [Crimp, 259]

On October 11, 1987, over half a million lesbians, gay men, and their supporters, one of largest demonstrations ever to take place in Washington, D.C., marched both for their civil rights and to protest the Reagan Administration's failure to act promptly to address the AIDS epidemic. The Names Project presented its memorial quilt on the Washington Mall, in which the names of people who had died of AIDS were inscribed in over two thousand panels. It covered the equivalent of two football fields.

Days later, in his introduction to the debate, Senator Jesse Helms from North Carolina dismissed the demonstration as "this mob over here this weekend." He then proceeded to introduce legislation guaranteeing that no AIDS prevention literature or efforts would go to gay communities. The amendment he proposed adding to a Labor, Health and Human Services and Education bill allocating a billion dollars for AIDS research and education sought "[t]o prohibit the use of any funds provided under this Act to the Centers for Disease Control from being used to provide AIDS education, information, or prevention materials and activities that promote, encourage, or condone homosexual sexual activities or the intravenous use of illegal drugs." [Crimp, 259]

What had provoked Helms to introduce the amendment was his encounter with a sexually explicit safer-sex comic book—

Safer Sex Comix—published by GMHC, a recipient of federal funding ($674,679) for AIDS education. Helms objected to the fact that the comic book illustrated in explicit detail the sexual encounter of two young gay men—with bulging baskets, big erections, and bubble butts!—using condoms. Helms believed that the comic book promoted "sodomy and the homosexual lifestyle as an acceptable alternative in American society." [Crimp, 260]

These debates about AIDS prevention and condom use raised fundamental issues about the importance and meaning of sex—and most crucially about particular acts or kinds of sex: anal sex and fisting, accompanied by drugs or toys or according to the protocols of sadomasochism. But it also challenged how sex—whether in commercial pornography or in HIV educational materials—was portrayed. Despite the fact that the condom code was fairly well established by 1985-86, neither the gay porn industry nor the federal government acknowledged it.

Was sex without condoms hotter and more exciting than sex with condoms? Does the sex portrayed in pornographic movies need to be transgressive? Or should porn aim for "the education of desire"?—thus helping gay men to eroticize sex with a condom. No questions were ever conclusively answered, except perhaps in theory, but condoms became the centerpiece of HIV prevention and a vast majority of gay porn producers chose to make movies using condoms—whereas the straight industry choose not to and instead adopted a rigorous policy of HIV and STD testing. One result was that the straight industry chose to employ only healthy performers, while the gay industry chose to portray "safer sex" in order to "educate desire" but employed performers who could be HIV positive.

• • •

SAFER FOR SODOMY

Nevertheless, some insiders were critical of the porn industry's stance. Terry le Grand of Marathon Films declared,

> "Producers are very wrong when they say 'We must produce a fantasy for the viewer.' I say 'Bullshit! Fantasy time is *over*. Fantasy has to stop.' I think the biggest message we can give to people is through videotapes, as long as it's subtly done.... If they see enough movies where people are getting screwed with condoms, then maybe it will become part of their own lives." [Fenwick, 37]

After 1985, commercial producers attempting to be "responsible" and activists and public health educators wanting to be effective adopted similar approaches—they produced explicit safe-sex videos.

One of the first performers to take up the cause of safe sex was porn actor Glenn Swann. Discovered by San Diego-based Dirk Yates, who owned several gay sexually oriented businesses (including a bookstore, a bathhouse, and a photography mail order business) that served a clientele that, like himself, was sexually interested in soldiers, sailors, and marines, Swann made his first hardcore sex video in 1985. Swann and Yates met through a mutual friend soon after Swann got out of the Marines in the mid-eighties. They hit it off immediately and Swann moved in with Yates and stayed for almost a year and a half.

When Swann entered the Mr. Nude San Diego contest, he won the chance to perform in a gay video. However, Yates, not wanting to lose Swann to the fast life of Los Angeles, quickly put together his own video, *Sgt. Swann's Private Files*, starring Swann. As it happened, Yates lost Swann almost immediately. After finishing the video, Swann moved to Miami—where he moved in with Bob Campbell, owner of the

Club Baths, at that time a national chain.

Inspired by the AIDS epidemic, Swann began to travel around the country promoting himself as Mr. Safe Sex. He gave performances that were part solo jerk-off show and part safe-sex lecture/demonstration. Eventually the performances were videotaped. They included his safe-sex talk, the jerk-off show, and a discussion of some of his offstage sexual adventures. He demonstrated his masturbation techniques, but his basic advice was "don't fuck your buddy without a rubber." [Richards, *Manshots*, 9/88, 22] His adamant stand on safe sex was way ahead of anyone else in the adult film business.

Life Guard (HIS Video, 1985) was the first commercial production of a safe sex video. Produced by HIS, the gay line released by straight adult megafirm VCA, it starred some of the period's most popular performers. Sandwiched in between the first two scenes, Robert Bolan, the president of the S.F. AIDS Foundation, spoke about playing safely. The video's promotional copy announced that "Safe sex doesn't have to be dull—and this hot flick shows you why! Dr. Robert Bolan ... warns against high-risk behavior, he identifies all the activities that are safe. And then, in a scorching series of in-depth demonstrations, top male stars like Rick Donovan and Leo Ford show just how much fun playing safe can truly be! Now you can have it all—good health and good sex." *Life Guard* was the most explicit demonstration of the compatibility of safe sex and sexually arousing pornography.

Other safe-sex videos were made by groups outside the commercial porn industry. GMHC, New York's leading AIDS service organization, made *Chance of a Lifetime* (1985). Casey Donovan was in the cast, and it consisted of three loops of men showering, hugging, caressing, fondling each other's genitals, and practicing frottage. Acknowledging the level of fear current at the time, the actors say things like: "I haven't done it with anything but my VCR in the last twelve months," or "Remember when sex was fun?"

A group of clinical psychologists funded *Inevitable Love*

(1985), a romantic narrative about two college friends who lose touch with one another after they leave school. Casey Donovan was again in the cast. Both friends discover their homosexuality, and after coming out are reunited in a happy ending. It was probably the most cautious of the early safe sex videos; there is no penetrative sex in the film. The range of safe sex activities shown include wrestling, sucking a cock through gym shorts, frottage, embracing, kissing, fucking and sucking with condoms, playing with handcuffs, ice cubes and whipped cream as sex toys, toe sucking, circle jerks, and of course, masturbation in many varieties. The depth of the uncertainty and fear at the time is demonstrated by an opening statement that announced, "Some authorities believe there could be some risk from open-mouthed kissing or intercourse with condoms, through accidental exposure to blood and semen. Check the latest information with an AIDS hotline or current gay publications." [D. Richards, *Manshots*, 11/88, 22]

Except perhaps for *Life Guard*, all of these movies were used as educational videos to promote safe sex through the use of condoms and alternative sexual techniques.

• • •

In the late eighties, Al Parker, a popular performer and director of more than a dozen films, decided to leave the business. He closed Surge Studios when Richard Taylor, his longtime lover and business partner, died from AIDS in 1987. "I was having a wonderful time until this disease came along," he told *The Advocate*'s Henry Fenwick. "I was truly expressing myself and making movies and making money, and I truly liked my job. Now, with this disease, I don't like my job anymore, and I won't do it." [Fenwick, 36]

He decided to adopt a new role in the porn business.

> "Why am I different than all the other men who
> made films and were sexually active from the

late 70s to the mid 80s? My experience has been the same as theirs—no better, no worse. We're all exposed to the same things. As a matter of fact, I think that, used properly, my exposure and experience could now make me a powerful voice for safe sex." [Edmonson, *Clone*, 179]

He began to work on *Turbo Charge* (Le Salon, 1988), a short safe-sex video that could be attached to all gay porn films. The short consisted of a scene in which Parker had sex with Justin Cade—performing oral and anal sex with condoms, and using Saran wrap with various sex toys. He later expanded it into a full-length movie called *Better than Ever* (also released under the title *Turbo Charge*). As Parker told Robert Richards, "[I]t *is* a safe sex film, but nowhere in it do I say that it is. What I tried to do was a *hot* film that was also a *safe* film.... There is a little oral sex, but not involving bodily fluids." [R.W. Richards, *Manshots*, 11/88, 49]

Like many other films of the period, *Better than Ever* (Surge Studios, 1988) started off with the standard disclaimer that the performers engaged in safe sex practices, but for artistic reasons, they would not always be visible. *Better than Ever* was accused of paying lip service to safer sex, although according to some viewers not everything portrayed in the film was strictly "safe." [Patton, 124]

By the late eighties, the biggest companies, Catalina and All Worlds Video among them, regularly included short trailers promoting condom use—without necessarily showing their use explicitly in the videos. All Worlds Video concluded its tapes with a trailer of a sexy young blond in sailor whites holding up a condom and proclaiming: "Hope you enjoyed. It was all in fun and fantasy. But remember, in the real world out there, there's an epidemic going on. So when we play, let's play safely."

Catalina included a trailer on all its videos that showed porn star Michael Henson demonstrating how to put on a condom and proceeding to fuck both Eric Radford and Sheri St. Clair. Why

Catalina gave it the bisexual twist is unclear—perhaps to generalize the idea of using condoms for all kinds if intercourse,

Years later, Chuck Holmes, the founder and owner of Falcon Studios, insisted that Falcon had begun using condoms and nonoxynol-based lubricants in the mid-eighties, several years ahead of other studios. "No responsible gay erotica producers," Holmes insisted, "would ever make a decision [not to use condoms]. They'd be drummed out of the business because the models wouldn't talk to them, not the distributors would touch it." [Andriote, 157] But there was absolutely no consensus in the mid-eighties on the use of condoms in gay pornographic movies—in fact, there was concerted opposition to it, mostly by people on the inside of the industry.

The positive role pornography could play by explicitly showing safe sex in videos was debated throughout the gay community but rarely ever scientifically studied. GMHC did conduct a small study in the late eighties. It gave different kinds of safe-sex educational materials to four different groups. Only one group was shown a sexually explicit film of safe-sex practices. Two months later, the group that saw the explicit film had made the greatest changes in adopting safe-sex behavior. [Kolata, NYT 11/3/87]

Commercial considerations were the main impediment to routinely using condoms in gay hardcore movies. Most producers believed that no one would buy a video in which condoms were used. In part, the appeal of pornography, many presumed, was that it was transgressive, and the problem with safe sex was that using a condom was a responsible act.

In 1989, the Boston AIDS Action Group sought to work with Al Parker on *Better than Ever*, but when it became clear that Parker held to the industry's position about maintaining the "fantasy" and playing down or editing out the explicit safe sex practices, the group withdrew. [Patton, 120-124]

Nevertheless, most of these early educational efforts were relatively modest attempts. By the early nineties, AIDS activists had convinced most producers that hardcore movies must show the application and use of the condom during sexual intercourse to effectively promote safe sex. By not referring to condoms or by editing out the condoms and other safe-sex practices, the producers encouraged viewers to continue fantasizing about, even if not practicing, unsafe sex.

By the early nineties, producers of gay porn began to explicitly show condoms in videos. The most significant change took place between 1987 and 1990. In *Touch Me*, the 1988 winner of the AVN award for Best Gay Video, no condoms were used; however, two years later, the 1990 winner, *More of a Man,* used condoms—and one of the lead characters was an AIDS activist. The underlying rationale was to "educate desire"; many inside and outside the industry believed using condoms in porn movies helped to eroticize safe sex. And at the very least, using condoms protected performers from being infected by other performers who might be HIV positive.

• • •

The AIDS epidemic and the fear of casual sex amplified further the demand for video porn. [Lane, 50–53] Rentals and sales of gay porn videos exploded during the eighties. Many gay men turned to video porn in lieu of live sex with other men. By the late eighties, the gay porn industry had also adopted— almost universally—the leading directors, and the most prestigious production companies regularly showed condoms being used during all scenes of anal sex.

As Dave Kinnick, a gay porn reviewer/videographer noted: "The anti-sex backlash of the '80s" in response to the fear of AIDS "had a devastating effect on the nation's bathhouses and x-rated theaters, but it fueled profits in the video industry. People may have stopped *having* sex, but they certainly hadn't stopped *wanting* sex. Like bathtub gin during Prohibition, the popularity of videos soared…" [Sadownick, 153; Kinnick, 45]

Doug Richards tells of visiting a old fuck buddy in the early eighties—just as VCRs were taking off. When the subject of safe sex came up, his friend proclaimed, "I was into 'safe sex' long before that's what they called it. Back in the Age of Trashing, jerking off was always considered 'baby sex'—a pejorative term, if ever there was one. Now, masturbation has become The Sex Act of the Eighties—very trendy, very chic." Inviting Richards to join him, he stripped down, took out a tube of K-Y, and popped a cassette of J. Brian's *Seven in a Barn* into the VCR. [D. Richards, *Manshots,* 9/88, 20]

Yet viewing the gay porn made in the previous decade sometimes produced an ambivalent reaction—it could be seen either as "fantasy" or as the sign of an imminent disaster. "Most people are having sex with video machines at this point," porn star and director Al Parker noted in 1988, "and they're watching their videos to get away from all of it. And in their fantasy world they don't want to be hit over the head with AIDS." On the other hand, he exclaimed, "there are so many models who are dead now, who died of AIDS. You watch them in these old movies, and they squirt into somebody's mouth, and you're shouting at the screen, 'Don't do that!' It makes you cringe." [Fenwick, 64]

DEATH OF A GAY AMERICAN IDOL

Casey Donovan was actively involved in several of the early attempts to develop safe sex videos, but otherwise, he saw no need to change his way of life. He continued to hustle and perform in porn movies where condoms were not used.

"My whole existence," he told journalist Rob Richards in 1981, "is based to this day on that one movie. I've done thirteen films ... but everything since is predicated on *Boys in the Sand,* including my hustling." [Edmonson, *Boys in the Sand,* 172]

"My sex life is my social life is my business life is my sex life," he once explained. His entire life revolved around his public identity as a gay male porn star and an escort. However, performing in porn movies never provided any kind of significant income. He had worked briefly as a fashion model soon after being featured in *After Dark,* he worked occasionally without much success in the theater in New York and Los Angeles, and for a number of years he lived with and was supported by Tom Tryon, a successful novelist, but mostly he earned his living hustling.

From 1977 on, hustling was his primary source of income. Many of his clients came through the advertisements he regularly placed in *The Advocate*, the national gay newspaper. He exemplified a kind of high-minded professionalism.

> "I'm often asked how I can have sex with so many kinds of people, some of them seemingly turn-offs. I can always get past their bodies, because I'm interested in who they are, what they are, what they think ... of themselves ... of me. My attitude is to give, if not the best, at least the nicest sexual experience they've ever had."
> [Edmonson, 173]

While sex was the basis of Donovan's professional life, it also continued to be one of the most important activities in his personal life. He seemed to be almost insatiable and would frequently engage in casual sex between appointments with his escorting clients.

After an absence of several years, Donovan returned to porn in 1982. The Gage brothers cast him in *Heatstroke* (HIS Video, 1982). Though at the time there was already some concern about the mysterious disease soon to be called AIDS, the film is unrestrained in its exchange of bodily fluids.

Set in a Montana town during a rodeo, the film tells the story of a crew of cooped-up and sexually frustrated ranch hands let loose over a weekend in town. Donovan stars in the orgy scene. He gives a blow-job to a ranch hand, who then ejaculates on Donovan's face and his own hand. Donovan licks the man's hand and laps it up as the man sticks his dick down his throat. Another man ejaculates into Donovan's mouth, and Donovan spits it into the man's mouth and kisses him deeply.

Toward the end of 1984, Donovan and Wakefield Poole decided to return to Fire Island and shoot *Boys in the Sand II*. They both hoped the sequel would revive their sagging fortunes; neither had achieved any great success independently of their first joint venture.

Boys in the Sand II opens with Donovan and another man having sex in the shrubbery. In the second scene, the famous scene from the first version of *Boys in the Sand* is reprised, in which Donovan emerges from the bay—only in this film a young Pat Allen emerges from the bay as Donovan returns to the waves—to disappear, almost forever.

Donovan hoped the sequel might again put him on the covers of magazines and give him national recognition. One friend recalled that "[h]e was more ebullient than ever, and I could clearly see that he was trying to keep in check his fantasies of becoming the man of the moment all over again." [Edmonson, 217–18] But the film wasn't released until two years later—the producer had died of a heart attack on the day Poole started shooting the film, and the ownership of the film stock was the subject of legal battles lasting over two years.

By the time it came out in 1986, there was no buzz or anticipated excitement, no moment of renewed celebrity. The world it came into was quite different from the one the original *Boys in the Sand* had entered—it was more competitive, in a field created by the new technology of video, and it offered a vision of sex that seemed outdated. In the era already dealing with AIDS, it seemed innocent and naïve.

In fact, Donovan's film career seemed to go into hiatus. In 1985, he made two of the first safe-sex films—*Chance of a Lifetime* (1985) and *Inevitable Love* (1985). In 1986, he approached Christopher Rage about making a movie with a "fuck buddy" who physically resembled him. According to Rage, "They wanted to document their sex life by making a movie called *Brothers* or *Cousins* or *Step-Brothers*. ... Casey Donovan was an extraordinary human being. He was a grand old sex machine. [But] he was a drug addict toward the end. And he had no interest in moderation." [Rage, *Manshots,* 11/91, 12]

When Donovan and his friend arrived, Rage thought that "they both looked great." But as the filming progressed Rage was increasingly unhappy with what was going in front of his camera.

> "It was too gross. I couldn't believe I was going to be able to put out a movie with someone behaving like this. I was appalled at Casey's behavior. He turned into the most greedy, uncaring pig. It was all *me, me, me.* After the other actor left, Casey went up to take a shower. When he came back, he wanted to fuck with me, with anybody. I gave him his money and he said he was going to the baths. I told him that was too much money to take to the baths. He tried to have sex with me again. I threw him out."

When Rage edited the footage, he thought, "There's nothing here.... This was an evil, black documentary on drug abuse." [Rage, *Manshots,* 4/91, 13] He called the movie *Fucked-Up.* It was favorably reviewed when it was released, but many of Donovan's friends felt it portrayed an overly negative picture. "What people don't want to acknowledge is that it was a very accurate picture of Casey." Rage recalled, "It was Casey. And yet Casey loved the movie.... I can't watch it."

Donovan died on August 10, 1987. He never openly acknowledged to anyone that he had AIDS. He appeared to function up until a few weeks before he died. [Edmonson, 224–26]

REFERENCES

John-Manuel Andriote, *Victory Deferred: How AIDS Changed Gay Life in America* (Chicago: University of Chicago Press, 1999).

Leo Bersani, "Is the Rectum a Grave?" in Douglas Crimp, ed.,

AIDS: Cultural Analysis, Cultural Activism (Cambridge: MIT Press, 1988).

John R. Burger, *One-Handed Histories: The Eroto-Politics of Gay Male Video Pornography* (New York: Harrington Park, 1995).

Michael Callen, *Surviving AIDS* (New York: Harper Perennial, 1991).

Douglas Crimp, "How to Have Promiscuity in an Epidemic," in Crimp, Douglas, ed., *AIDS: Cultural Analysis, Cultural Activism* (Cambridge: MIT Press, 1988).

Jerry Douglas, "The Legend of Casey Donovan," *Manshots*, April 1992.

Roger Edmonson, *Boy in the Sand: Casey Donovan, All-American Sex Star* (Los Angeles: Alyson, 1998).

Roger Edmonson, *Clone: The Life and Legacy of Al Parker, Gay Superstar* (Los Angeles: Alyson, 2000).

Henry Fenwick, "Changing Times for Gay Erotic Videomakers: Growing Market and New Expectations in the Age of AIDS," *The Advocate*, February 2, 1988.

Frances FitzGerald, "The Castro," in *Cities on a Hill: A Journey Through Contemporary American Cultures* (New York: Simon & Schuster, 1983).

Mirko D. Grmek, *History of AIDS: Emergence and Origin of a Modern Pandemic* (Princeton: Princeton University Press, 1990).

Andrew Holleran, *Ground Zero* (New York: New American Library, 1988).

Charles Kaiser, *The Gay Metropolis, 1940-1996* (San Diego: Harcourt, 1997).

Edward King, *Safety in Numbers: Safer Sex and Gay Men* (New York: Routledge, 1993).

Dave Kinnick "How Safe is Video Sex," *Frontiers*, September 1991.

Gina Kolata, "Erotic Films in AIDS Study Cut Risky Behavior," *New York Times*, November 3, 1987.

Frederick S. Lane III, *Obscene Profits: The Entrepreneurs of Pornography in the Cyber Age* (New York: Routledge, 2001).

Scott O'Hara, *Autopornography: A Memoir of Life in the Lust Lane* (New York: Harrington Park Press, 1997).

Cindy Patton, *Fatal Advice: How Safe-Sex Education Went Wrong* (Durham: Duke University Press, 1996).

Christopher Rage, Behind the Camera: Interview by Jerry Douglas, *Manshots*, April 1991.

Doug Richards, "Safe Sex Videos," *Manshots*, September 1988.

Robert W. Richards, "Al Parker: Still Here!" *Manshots*, November 1988.

Robert W. Richards, "Scott O'Hara: Pleasure Giver," *Manshots*, March 1989.

Gabriel Rotello, *Sexual Ecology: AIDS and the Destiny of Gay Men* (New York: Dutton, 1997).

Gayle Rubin, "Elegy for the Valley of Kings: AIDS and the Leather Community in San Francisco, 1981–1996," in Martin P. Levine, Peter M. Nardi, and John H. Gagnon, eds., *In Changing Times: Gay Men and Lesbians Encounter HIV/AIDS* (Chicago: University of Chicago Press, 1997).

Doug Sadownick, *Sex Between Men: An Intimate History of the Sex Lives of Gay Men Postwar to Present* (San Francisco: Harper San Francisco, 1997).

Safer Sex Comix #4, Artwork by Donelan, Story by Greg (New York: GMHC).

"'Safe Sex' Stops the Spread of AIDS," *New Science*, January 7, 1988.

Joseph Sonnabend, "Looking at AIDS in Totality: A Conversation," *The New York Native*, October 7, 1985.

Edmund White, *The Burning Library* (New York: Knopf, 1994).

CHAPTER SEVEN

Real Men and Superstars

[M]ost people say that to be a successful porn star you have to have two of three characteristics: a beautiful face, a beautiful body, or a big dick. Now, if you have two of those three, you can work. If you have all three of them, you'll be a superstar.

—JERRY DOUGLAS

In 1985, a short young man with brown hair, brown eyes, and a cocky walk arrived at the Los Angeles airport. Twenty-three years old, he had grown up in Carmi, a small town in southern Illinois, and had rarely spent any time in a big city. Though he had been to Chicago and once worked on an oil rig in Texas, he had never been so far away from home. Somewhat leery, he was afraid people in Los Angeles would take advantage of him. Though nervous, he was also excited.

The young man was met at the baggage carousel by a stocky older man in loose-fitting jeans and a sweatshirt. As his baggage came down the ramp, the young man picked his suitcase up energetically. It snapped opened, and his clothes flew out in all directions, strewn on the floor and the moving ramp. Together the young man and the older man gathered the clothes and headed to a car.

The older man was John Travis. He was there to pick up Charles Casper Peyton, who had sent him some bad photographs of a young man with dark, smoldering good looks. Three months later, Peyton took the name Jeff Stryker and went on to appear in a series of porn movies produced and/or directed by Travis.

Charles Peyton was in his early teens when he saw John Holmes in an adult film. One of the most famous male porn stars in the first twenty years of the commercial porn industry, Holmes appeared in almost 2,500 straight porn scenes in the seventies and early eighties as well as a handful of gay loops. At the time, his penis was believed to be the longest in the porn film business. Stryker wasn't impressed by the size of Holmes's penis—all the men in his family were well-endowed—but by Holmes's lack of physical attractiveness. "My God," he thought, "if that's all it takes, I'm there. If this guy can be king, I can go beyond.... [T]here wasn't anything happening in my life. In the city I was in, there was nothing. I didn't really seem to be going anywhere.... I decided this is what I'm gonna do. I'm gonna go away and never come back." [Spencer, *Manshots*, 9/98, 32]

Soon after he turned nineteen, he got a job as a male stripper at a Chippendale club for women. He had tried to get into the club for a drink, but he was turned away at the door and told, "Well, you can come in the bar and drink, but you have to strip."

They handed him a cowboy hat and said, "All right. Use this. If you're good, we'll pay you and we'll have you back, and if you're not, we won't. We won't pay you or have you back."

"So I went out," Stryker explained, "and my whole gimmick was I would swing totally naked dick at 'em. Freak 'em out! They loved it. It's like, 'You can't do that! But please, *do* that!'"

He became part of the club's regular strip show, Fast Freddy and the Playboys.

Despite his exhibitionist bravura, Stryker considered himself somewhat "reclusive," which was reinforced when people in town became aware that Stryker was having an affair with an older man widely known to be gay. The affair lasted three years. As he explained, "If people have any clue that you're gay, the whole town comes down on you.... Everyone was just constantly on me, and I kinda withdrew from society." [R.W. Richards, *Manshots*, 6/89, 51–53]

In 1985, he answered an ad placed in the local paper by a photographer looking for models. The photographer was so impressed he sent the pictures to John Travis, who was similarly impressed.

"I don't have legit modeling," Travis told Stryker over the phone, "but how'd you like to do a movie?"

Though it had long been Stryker's ambition to be in porn movies, he was wary. "I was reluctant because in small cities, they're so homophobic, it's unreal. It would ruin your entire life. I understood that once I got into it, there was no turning back, so it had to be my entire life."

But Stryker decided to accept Travis's offer, and with a "desire to be something else," he left the small town he grew up in.

> "I wanted to be everything, I wanted to be accepted in all. I saw the competition in both— straight and gay porn—I thought, 'I can be number one in both, and it will help people accept other people's sexuality.' Just kind of make it more open, where there aren't these categories branding people and limiting them. A person can do whatever they feel at the time." [Spencer, *Manshots*, 9/98, 32]

The encounter between the veteran porn director/cinematographer and the young man from the Midwest soon blossomed into a more intimate relationship. Within weeks of Stryker's arrival, he and Travis took a trip together to the Grand Canyon to get acquainted. A week or so later, they went to bed together.

"It was never a pushed thing," Stryker remembered.

> "It happened when we felt comfortable with each other. I don't know ... I felt magnetism ... I knew from the second I saw him that he was a great guy and the more I got to know him, the more I cared for him. It was three months before I did my first video." [Richards, *Manshots*, 6/89, 53]

Stryker and Travis lived together for a year. As Travis recalled, "we were very close in the first year that we knew each other, a year and three months."

A STAR IS MADE, NOT BORN

Almost immediately, Travis began to transform Charles Peyton into Jeff Stryker. He sought to build the "star" from the ground up—creating his porn persona, his hair, physique, and sexual image. "I've been groomed," Stryker explained several years later. "My hair was changed—everything.... I owe [Travis] *everything*." [Richards, *Manshots*, 6/89, 53]

Within a few weeks, Travis introduced Stryker to his good friend Matt Sterling, who also quickly grasped Stryker's potential.

> "I could ... see in him a young Marlon Brando and a young Elvis Presley... his passion for motorcycles, for example. So I felt it was a real thing, not a packaged thing. I just wanted to bring out as much as I could of the real, and it worked—he became a hero of sorts in the gay community. I would go places with him and the response was astronomical. Even in blasé Holly-

wood, he would get more interest than some of the major Hollywood stars. So he was definitely a phenomenon. No doubt about it." [Sterling, *Manshots*, 9/88, 50]

Travis and Stryker joined forces and put together a three-year agenda; they planned Stryker's future. They worked out a strategy for his entire career and how it would be done. They believed that Stryker had everything it would take to be a major gay porn star.

Finding a model and making him into a successful performer in porn required an investment of time and money. "I think it requires a certain amount of conditioning and preparation mentally before a new model goes before a camera....," Travis explained. "[You have to] make them feel at ease, make them feel like they're part of the family, answer their questions honestly, and help them through any problems they may have. You've got to put yourself in their shoes." He also carefully vetted their sexual abilities and preferences. "I do test Polaroids. I ask them to go into a room by themselves and get themselves ready.... [A]nd then we sit down and discuss who, where, and when. I try to find out what type of partner they prefer to work with." Travis often took three or four months to prepare a model for film work. "It costs a lot of money to put someone in front of the camera, and if they don't function, you've lost a lot of money. With new talent, it takes time and preparation." [Travis, 3/9, 8-9]

They developed a very specific persona for "Jeff Stryker," one that brought together an almost "classic" gay man's fantasy of a "real man," presumably heterosexual, who also engaged in homosexual sex, with a fantasy that distanced itself from the versatile sexuality that so dramatically marked the seventies: that era of gay promiscuity in which the fluency between top and bottom had apparently contributed to the AIDS epidemic.

Their image of "Jeff Stryker" portrayed him as strong and impassive, guarded and inaccessible: he did not kiss, he did not

suck cock—he only fucked. In a deep growl, he produced a tor-
rent of dirty talk as he got sucked or as he fucked. He was carefully cast only in roles that emphasized his impassivity, his
masculinity, and that excluded the sexual reciprocity and
abandon that characterized gay sex in the 1970s. This sort of
persona, both more ambiguous and more deliberate than the
"straightness" of Jim Cassidy or Jimmy Hughes had ever been,
was something totally new.

Stryker became not just a star but a superstar because he set
out to embody certain gay male values and to project himself as
"bigger than life." Porn stars project themselves both as "active"
figures as well as "objects" of desire; fans both desire and strive
to identify with them. Though both Casey Donovan and Al
Parker were able to animate those sexual feelings, their
"charisma" was not so consciously motivated or maintained—
and the gay male sexual and cultural values they expressed
seemed less relevant during the AIDS epidemic. But the Stryker
persona also limited him to certain genres or settings within gay
porn—it's no accident that a number of his gay films have jail-
house or military settings, or rough blue-collar roles. His persona
as a sexual performer is most credible in those settings. It is only
in the straight or bisexual films that his persona is softer—when
he performs with women.

Travis first cast Stryker in *In Hot Pursuit*, a film he'd
already mostly completed. Stryker appeared in a scene with
Mike Henson, another newcomer. Directed by Travis and put
out by Catalina, where he was the director of production, the
film was originally supposed to be set at a costume party where
each scene was built around the participants' sexual fantasies
of one another. But budget cuts after four scenes had already
been shot forced Travis to tie the scenes together by having
Stryker play an artist sketching the men in different uniforms
or costumes and entertaining sexual fantasies about them—
adding the scene with Stryker and Henson as well. In the film,
the Stryker mystique appears to be fully developed.

Stryker's next film, *Powertool* (1986), was designed specifically as a vehicle for Stryker. It also happened to be Catalina's first movie shot on video. Directed again by John Travis, it was set in a jail, a place where straight men will often engage opportunistically in sex with other men. As the film opens, Stryker is sitting in a jail cell; he overhears two prisoners in another cell having sex and gets up to watch. Toward the end of this first scene, he takes out his eight-and-a-half-inch penis to masturbate as he looks on. In the second scene, Stryker has sex with another inmate, playing the top role; in the next scene three prisoners have sex in a shower, then Stryker has sex with a corrections officer—again topping. In all four of these scenes, there are very rigid roles of top and bottom. The film presumes to show "straight" men having sex with gay men who suck cock and get fucked. There is no reciprocity. The last scene, however, shows Stryker released and coming home to find his male lover having sex with another man. While the two men fuck unaware of his presence, Stryker collects his things and quietly leaves. The sex portrayed in *Powertool* is exclusively the sort of sex that reputedly takes places in jails. It is very limited. The bottoms are rarely erect while getting fucked, there is no reciprocity, and most of the sexual roles are exclusively top or bottom.

While *Powertool* was in production, Matt Sterling was shooting Stryker in *Better Than Life*. Here was the origin of the relationship that emerged years later when Stryker and Sterling became lovers and Stryker went to live with Sterling.

The Switch Is On, the fourth film Stryker made in his first year, consolidated his heterosexual credentials—at least to his gay audience. While bisexual movies typically include heterosexual acts, they are usually directed at gay viewers and are generally considered in the business as a gay genre. Directed again by Travis, it was Stryker's first bisexual movie. It tells the story of a country boy who sets out to make his fortune in Los Angeles. The film featured at least four performers who considered themselves to be primarily heterosexual or bisexual: Jeff Stryker, Jeff Quinn, John Rocklin, and Mike Miller. On the Amtrak train to L.A., Stryker meets a prominent magazine editor played by Ellie Rio. After Stryker fucks her in a train compartment, she introduces him to a Hollywood couple played by Mike Miller and Danielle. The fourth scene also features Stryker in a bisexual three-way with Megan Daniels and Steve Ross.

The following year Stryker went on to star in *Jamie Loves Jeff*, a straight adult film, which was reported to be one of the best-selling straight porn films ever until that time. In it, he plays Rebel Cochran, dressed in jeans and a tight white tank top: a character obviously modeled on Marlon Brando's role in *A Streetcar Named Desire*.

These five films, released back to back in less than three years, established Stryker as one of the most successful male porn stars of all time—and in both gay and straight porn, something no one else had achieved or has since attempted. He was a bigger star than either Casey Donovan or Al Parker, the reigning stars before Stryker's appearance. After completing the five films that launched him, Stryker attempted to break into mainstream filmmaking by appearing in *The Heiress* and going to Italy where he performed in *After Death* (*Oltre la Morte*), an Italian horror film, and *Dirty Love* (*Amore Sporico*).

As the first five films rolled out, Travis and Stryker distributed hundreds of photos to the new gay beefcake magazines that had begun to flourish in the era of AIDS. Over the next three years, dozens of interviews and photographs of Stryker appeared in *Advocate Men*, *Inches*, *Play Guy*, *Torso*, *All Man*, and *Stallion*, among others.

Stryker later felt that the persona John Travis had shaped for him was too limiting. When asked if the dirty talk in his movies came from him or if he was as sexually aggressive in private as the role he played in his movies, he said, "Yes, it's me. But there are also times I get romantic, real soft and gentle. Loving … touching. … In my movies, until just now, they wouldn't allow me to show a softer side, because of the image they'd built." [R.W. Richards, 6/89, 51]

William Higgins, the head of Catalina Studios, where John Travis was employed when he first discovered Stryker, also disapproved of the Stryker persona.

> "I don't like the image that they created for Jeff Stryker, of the macho-put-the-gays-down. That's not the way he is at all, you know. That's a film persona that was created by Matt Sterling and John Travis.... I think Sterling, Travis, and Falcon all believe that the only person that gays are really interested in viewing is the quintessential top man who is essentially trade and is insulting to the gays. And you know I can play along with that when I feel like it, but I don't think it's a persona that I find attractive. I think that Jeff Stryker, more than any model that I've ever known, generates more positive comments and more extremely negative comments that any other model.... I don't find anything attractive or sexual at all about his screen persona." [Douglas, *Manshots*, 2/91, 80]

STRYKER'S CAREER

Careers in the gay male adult film industry are notoriously short lasting, on average rarely more than three or four years. "Listen, kid, you gotta get what you can get. 'Cause you'll have no more than three years at max," Matt Sterling had warned at the very beginning. [Spencer, *Manshots*, 9/98, 32] But Jeff Stryker started making films in 1986 and continued to appear in gay and straight erotic movies until 2001.

Given the success of the promotional campaign Stryker and Travis engineered, Stryker was able to command extraordinarily large fees for performing in his films. Despite the fact that male performers make more money in gay porn than in straight adult films, it is almost impossible for most gay performers to earn a living wage. Performers can typically earn (in 2006 prices) $500 to $2,500 per scene—depending on their popularity, the sexual acts to be performed, and the prestige and wealth of the studio. Thus, if a performer is paid $2,000 a scene and makes a movie every month, his annual income would be $24,000. Major stars, on the other hand, can earn anywhere from $10,000 to $50,000 per film, as Stryker was reportedly paid in the late nineties. [Adams, 2003]

Porn director Kristen Bjorn observed, "One interesting thing about this business is that the longer you are in it, the less money you are paid. Once you are an old face, and an old body, forget it. You're through as far as your popularity goes." (De Walt, 1/98, p. 55). In the porn industry, "old" is a relative term, having little to do with age. The performer who is considered an "old face" or an "old body" is either overexposed or sexually predictable. He has made too many movies in too short a period of time; he has been around too long; or his performances are too similar from movie to movie. Viewers are bored with him and do not expect him to provide anything new. This progression often leads to lower-budget productions as well.

On a practical level, most performers worry, quite reasonably, about "overexposure." The most common way to prevent overexposure is to appear in a limited number of productions, perhaps a handful a year; however, for economic reasons, most successful performers usually pursue a number of different activities and supplement their income from performing in films to performing live as strippers ("dancing") or working as escorts.

To succeed, stars must be personally invested in making themselves into "celestial beings." Stryker was fortunate to have two veterans of the earliest days of gay commercial porn as his mentors. His success gave him the luxury of adopting a different approach. "I never hustled or tricked on the side," he said, "and that way, I was unobtainable."

"The only way they could get it was on video. So

with that in mind, my objective was to make as few movies as possible, but make sure they were the best. That's what I tried to do and to do that, you've got to start out from a position of power. I negotiated deals in which I was covered—my rent and everything, so that I wasn't having to take jobs to get by or to get food, rent or whatever." [Spencer, *Manshots*, 9/98, 33]

Over the years Stryker has licensed or developed a line of merchandise built on his "brand name": two different "realistic" Jeff Stryker dildos, playing cards, T-shirts, lube, and a country music CD. Many porn stars over the years have exploited their "brand identities" to offer related sexual services such as stripping or escorting, but Stryker was the first gay porn star to market his "brand" in order to sell other products.

Twenty years later, Stryker's sexuality is no more known than when he first appeared on the scene. He admits to having sexual relationships with both his mentors, but he has steadfastly refused to call himself gay. "Someone had labeled me a 'straight actor in gay porn,'" he told reporter Jack Shamama, "but 'universal' I think is the only word I could actually use to describe my sexuality." [Shamama] Later in his career he made a number of heterosexual porn movies as well—and tried to branch off into acting in spaghetti westerns and country music.

In the mid-1980s, with AIDS on so many gay men's minds, Jeff Stryker was a new kind of gay porn star. Identified as straight, performing exclusively as a top, exclusively passive in oral sex, and rarely kissing, he offered a stark contrast to Casey Donovan and Al Parker. Their liberated gay personas had been deeply compromised by AIDS—even before the public became aware that they were infected. The egalitarian ethos of the seventies prescribed an exchange between top and bottom roles. The risk of infection was significantly greater for the person taking the passive role in anal sex; hence, an exclusive top would be much less likely to pass on HIV than someone who had engaged in both roles.

Jeff Stryker's incredible success—he is still the *only* gay porn star whose name is known to those outside the gay community—created the niche within the gay porn business for straight male performers, who have become known as "gay-for-pay."

GAY-FOR-PAY

Performers who are predominately heterosexual have played a significant role in the gay porn industry since it started. Producers and viewers responded to a performer's ability to have sex with another man in front of the camera. No one cared whether or not the performer identified as homosexual or gay—his performance was all that mattered.

Gay-for-pay is a much discussed and often misunderstood topic. Performer and director Chris Steele responded to an online discussion of whether or not gay-for-pay performers were "really" straight:

> "Straight, meaning what turns them on or gets their dick hard, is the sight of a naked woman. Because they're willing to get fucked or suck dick for money on camera doesn't change their sexual preference.... Porn is not sex, it is performing. There's absolutely nothing sensual or erotic about the experience at all. It is cold, calculated and structured." [Rad Forums, Porn Star Sightings/WEHT, 6/28/1999]

Today some 35 to 45 percent of performers in gay porn are said to be "gay-for-pay" although the sexual, economic, and cultural rationale for their inclusion is now quite different. In many cases, there is often no evidence proving that gay-for-pay performers are *really* straight or "*actually* gay but in denial." However, performers in the video porn industry, like anyone being paid for sex, must engage in sexual acts they would not otherwise choose to perform and with partners for whom they feel no desire.

Some directors and videographers have found that it's easier to work with straight performers because they don't have any personal investment in the sexual appeal of their scene partners. According to Kristen Bjorn's assistant:

> "Straight men usually have less of a problem getting erections for still photography as well as video. I believe that they are better prepared to come to work knowing that sexual energy must come from themselves through fantasy, memories, erotic magazines, etc. Gay men often come to work thinking that their work is going to be a realization of a sexual fantasy that they have had for a long time. When they realize that they are not in control of the sexual activity, partners, and duration, they become detached and often bored with it and one another. . . . Once a gay model has decided that he is not sexually interested in the other models, it seems most difficult to bring him into the action and get him aroused. Straight boys don't seem to be as dependent upon the excitation of the other models or as concerned whether or not they are exciting their partners. But when a gay model perceives that he is not arousing his partner, as often happens in scenes that involve gay and straight models together, it can make him feel insecure with himself. [Bear, Manshots, 111/99, 3]

While Jeff Stryker originally "popularized" the gay-for-pay performer as an example of passsive masculinity (in which he does nothing to arouse his partner, no cock sucking, rimming, or kissing), many gay-for-pay performers were sexually versatile or bottoms. The most famous such gay-for-pay performer who did not play the trade top in the late eighties was Matt Ramsay, later one of the most popular performers in straight porn.

Brian Estevez, who appeared as a bottom in *Powertool,* claimed to be straight—though in the early phase of his gay porn career he usually bottomed. In an interview, Estevez, a former marine, said that he had originally been approached for "modeling," but he explained: "He then told me that these guys had big companies and that they made movies. I told him I didn't want to do movies—and then he started talking money and I swear ... I don't know ... I guess money manipulated me ... I didn't want to do it!

> **Brian Estevez:** You know, I grew up very straight–never had *any* homosexual tendencies.
>
> **Interviewer:** You didn't connect it in any way to sexual pleasure?
>
> **Brian Estevez:** I didn't get any sexual stimulation from it. Even to this day, even in a sexual act, even if I have a hard-on and everything—I still didn't connect it to "Wow, this feels good."
>
> **Interviewer:** And yet you started in films as a bottom? ... I'd think a straight boy would be a bit put off—that being a top would be more logical ... more straight.
>
> **Brian Estevez**: I know—and that's how I felt. I'd much rather be a top, and in my later movies I didn't do bottom anymore. It's just when they manipulated me into the business, they manipulated me into being a bottom. They told me that I wasn't big enough or buff enough to play a top role, so I was labeled a bottom—a small, hot guy

who gets dick up his ass. [Richards, *Manshots*,
57–58, 1991].

Despite his ambivalence, Estevez had a relatively successful career that stretched from 1985 to 1991, during which he
appeared in twenty-six films.

• • •

The gay-for-pay label was adopted by the industry only after
Jeff Stryker had become a gay porn superstar—this took place
after "gay identity" had become a socially recognized way for
those who are predominately homosexual to identify themselves. But over the years, the gay-for-pay label has been
applied to performers with a number of very different orien-
tations to heterosexuality. There are the men who do it only
for the money. Compared to what male performers make in
straight porn, they earn more than twice as much in gay porn.
Then there are those men who decide to do gay porn because
they are bisexual. Among the bisexual performers there is
enormous diversity. Some may be primarily heterosexual and
emotionally involved with women, but occasionally enjoy sex
with a man. Others have entertained the idea of having sex
with men, but have never gone through with it. Getting paid
for it gives them permission. Others are equally interested in
both men and women.

Another group of performers are those for whom working in
the gay industry serves as a portal into a brave new world of
sex, into a wide-ranging exploration of many different kinds of
sexual possibilities—of different sexual partners (women, men,
and transsexuals), of active and passive roles, dominant and
submissive, anal eroticism, bondage, whips, and discipline.
These men are not necessarily straight or gay, but "sexual."

THE FEW, THE PROUD,
AND THE NAKED

The men of the United States Marine Corps are often considered the epitome of masculinity. Yet the Marine Corps is also an arena of intense homoeroticism. "Marine masculinity," writes fan Steven Zeeland, "is a cultural, historical, and personal human invention, and scrutiny of its displays reveals deliciously perverse—and instructive—flaws and contradictions...."

> "Marines devote attention to appearance so fastidious as to be called effeminate or narcissistic. In building up and exhibiting their hard-muscled bodies, Marines may be mistaken for gay gyms queens. In striving to be 'more man than a man can ever be,' they may be called butch drag queens. And what about the strong sexual undercurrent rippling among men who exalt the masculine over the feminine and who live and work in a 'Spartan' environment?" [Zeeland, 2]

Since World War II, San Diego has been headquarters for the United States Navy's Pacific Fleet. Eleven naval stations are based there, making it the largest concentration of military personnel of any U.S. city. Just north of the city, near Oceanside, lies Camp Pendleton, one of the nation's largest marine bases, home to 44,000 Marines.

San Diego is a magnet for gay men attracted to military men. Among them is businessman Rick Ford, who adopted the name Dirk Yates for his gay/military porn films. Over the course of running a number of gay sexually oriented businesses, Yates sought to serve a clientele who, like himself, were sexually interested in soldiers, sailors, and Marines. For a number of years, he published *Dirk Yates' Military Maneuvers,* a newsletter for military fetishists illustrated with photos of servicemen stripping out of their uniforms.

In 1982, Yates had an affair with a sailor named Steve that

continued even after the sailor was married. Before the attractive sailor was to be shipped to an island outpost in the Pacific, Yates arranged his first photo session. Soon he was using the photos of Steve in his newsletter. Shortly thereafter, he found a marine model who was willing to help him recruit, for a fee, other military men to pose for nude pictures. When the newsletter's readers started writing in requesting photos, Yates started selling them. [AGV, Dirk Yates, 5–7]

Starting in 1989, Yates began to issue the *Dirk Yates Private Amateur Collection*, for which he taped marines and sailors masturbating by themselves as well as having sex with women and men. [AGV, 9–10] Things changed dramatically on August 9, 1993. A headline in the *Los Angeles Times* read "Inquiry Links Marines to Gay Pornography"—about Camp Pendleton Marines posing nude and masturbating for videos being marketed to gay men. [Granberry, *L.A. Times*, 8/9/93, A-3] CBS picked it up later in the day for *The CBS Evening News*. The next morning *The Today Show* (NBC) displayed the box cover of the *Honorable Discharge* (dir. Jerry Douglas, 1993)— All Worlds' latest porn video about the Marines. In Washington, D.C., the debate raged on Capitol Hill about letting openly gay men and lesbians serve in the military. [Zeeland, 200] This was merely the most recent scandal involving Marines and sailors engaged in making pornographic movies and videos. Previous scandals had emerged in 1976 and 1988.

The story about the Camp Pendleton Marine jack-off tapes hit the news on a Monday. By Friday the All Worlds' staff wasn't able to leave their offices because of the presence of cameras and newspaper reporters outside. Later that week on NBC, Tom Brokaw opened with an image of the box cover of All Worlds' video *Honorable Discharge*. Soon All World's landlord would realize that they did not film weddings as Yates had claimed.

Yates received a phone call from a man in Fresno.

"Are you the guy in San Diego who has all those problems going on down there?" businessman Richard Lawrence asked.

"Yes, I am." Yates said

He said, "Can you get me some of those tapes?"

"Well, yeah ..."

And he said, "Well, give me five hundred each, to start."

"Five hundred each!" Yates thought to himself and laughed with disbelief. [AGV, 43]

Lawrence promoted the tapes from his office in Fresno. As he told Yates, he called stores saying, "This is Sergeant So-and-so, and I have these tapes that everyone's talking about in San Diego." Lawrence sold several thousand tapes and gave All Worlds the economic push it needed to compete with Catalina and Falcon.

The national publicity generated a huge demand for Yates's videos. In addition, Yates decided to exploit the scandal by issuing a series of tapes called *The Few, the Proud and the Naked,* which consisted of a handful of the best video scenes of men in marine uniforms from the Dirk Yates Private Amateur Collection. [AGV, 43–47] With the sudden influx of cash in the wake of the 1993 scandals, All Worlds Video was able to greatly expand its production and distribution, thus embarking upon the making of mainstream feature-length gay porn videos.

All Worlds, operating as a legitimate business, was harassed by the media but never prosecuted. It had been a rough year for the military; there had been the Tailhook scandal in Las Vegas over sexual harassment of women in the armed forces and a brigadier general who had said the Marines shouldn't be married. The last thing it wanted was a scandal about Marines being in a "porno ring"—whatever a porno ring was. The naval investigators concluded that only nine Marines had been guilty of improper conduct and that "none engaged in homosexual acts." After the investigation was complete, the official spokesman for the Marine Corps told reporters, "We are still the few and the proud, and I hope something that was alleged but not proven does not tarnish the great reputation we have." [Zeeland, 103]

"This all started," Yates recalled, "when a friend of mine, a drag queen, turned me in out of spite. She wanted a fuckin' ball gown for a drag thing and I wouldn't buy her one. But it turned into the greatest gift. She made me rich!" [AGV, 47–49]

Dirk Yates's pornographic enterprise is built around the Private Amateur Collection. As the name suggests, Yates likes to set up action with performers who are not professional adult performers, see what happens, and tape it. Yates explains that "the naiveness of it is what interests me.... two straight Marines were interested in doing a bisexual video, so I said, 'Come over and let's see if you know what that means.' I laid them side by side and nothing happened." [AGV, 29]

The "amateur" perspective allows Yates's models to act out their own fantasies rather than his.

> "They're exciting to me because I never know what's going to happen. The other night I had this big, hot Marine over and he said, 'I want to get fucked by a tranny.' It certainly made my dick go soft, but that's his fantasy and he trusted me enough to tell me. Here's this big hunky Marine in my bed jacking off, playing with his ass—and his real fantasy is go with a tranny. I never know what they're going to do." [AGV, 55]

Another remarkable aspect of Yates's amateur tapes is the willingness of his models to engage in anal sex. For many straight men, anal sex between men violates deep taboos—about the anus, gender roles, and masculinity. Despite the taboos associated with anal penetration, many men seem to enjoy being fucked—as evidenced by the growing straight fetish genre of female-to-male strap-on videos—while others have found it difficult to shed the belief that bottoming is demeaning.

If the Marines represent the apex of masculinity in popular culture, it is especially ironic that one of the most widely held "stereotypes" among gay men is that Marines prefer to "get fucked" in gay male sex. Taking the bottom role—"taking it like a man"—may give special access to an intense pleasure. The phrase underscores the literal and symbolic centrality of anal sex among gay men, and thus also in gay pornography. "It takes a lot more masculinity," a marine captain has said, "to be a bottom than to be a top." [Zeeland, 3–10]

Most of these Marines are heterosexual. Yates believes that the majority of his models participate in order to experiment.

> "[M]oney makes it all right. The *amazing* thing is how they all talk about it. Gay, straight—it doesn't matter—they all brag about it. The other day this one Marine brought four in.... [H]e was telling his buddies, 'Dirk's in this neighborhood' —and here he brings these four over. Four are ready to do it! I mean why would you boast so much about it?... I beg them '*Please* don't tell your girlfriend.' 'Oh she's different.' She's not different. That's usually where their trouble begins." [AGV, 89]

In addition to paying them for their video session, Yates also arranges heterosexual video sessions for his models. "That always legitimizes it in their eye, if I can get these guys laid." When the scene is heterosexual, "I shoot with a gay eye, I'll be down there, you're looking at a pretty asshole and the camera pulls back and it's on the Marine, not the girl." [AGV, 65]

The gay pornography industry in San Diego continues to attract a steady stream of men, many of them heterosexual, to perform in gay sex videos. One element that accounts for its attraction, observed one highly successful ex-Marine, "is that after guys get out of the military, they're broke and the only thing they can do to make money is porn."

> "That's what happened to me. They're poor for four fucking years in the military, and then suddenly all this money gets thrown at 'em. And there's a market in video work for military men

because people like it. They're a commodity when they get right out, before they lie around and turn to shit." [Hollar, *Unzipped*, 16]

REFERENCES

Adam Gay Video Erotica (AGV), *Dirk Yates: From Sgt. Swann to God Was I Drunk* (Los Angeles: Knight Publishing, December 1999).

J.C. Adams, "Pay4Porn," *Badpuppy*, May 2003.

Bear, "Interview with Buddy Jones," *Manshots*, November, 1999.

Mark De Walt, "The Eye of Kristen Bjorn," *Blueboy*, January 1998.

Gary W. Dowsett, *Practicing Desire: Homosexual Sex in the Era of AIDS* (Stanford, Stanford University Press, 1996).

Brian Estevez, Interview by Robert W. Richards, *Manshots*, April 1991.

Richard Goldstein, "Go the Way Your Blood Beats: An Interview with James Baldwin," *Village Voice*, 1984, reprinted in Quincy Troup, ed. *James Baldwin: The Legacy* (New York: Simon and Schuster, 1989).

Michael Granberry, "Inquiry Links Marines to Gay Pornography," *Los Angeles Times*, August 9, 1993, A-3.

William Higgins, Behind the Camera: Interview by Jerry Douglas, *Manshots*, Part I, December 1990; Part II, February 1991.

Keith Hollar, "Men Out of Uniform," *Unzipped*, March 16, 1999.

Brian Pronger, *The Arena of Masculinity: Sports, Homosexuality and the Meaning of Sex* (New York: St. Martin's, 1990).

Robert W. Richards, "Jeff Stryker: The Man and the Mystique," *Manshots*, June 1989.

Jack Shamama, "Mr. Big Stuff," www.metroactive.com/papers/sfmetro/03.01.99/jeffstryker-9907.html   Retrieved 6/24/2004

William Spencer, "Jeff Stryker," *Manshots*, September 1998.

Matt Sterling, Behind the Camera: Interview by Jerry Douglas, *Manshots*, September 1988.

"John Travis, Behind the Camera:" Interview by Jerry Douglas, *Manshots*, March 1990.

Steven G. Underwood, *Gay Men and Anal Eroticism: Tops, Bottoms, and Versatiles* (New York; Harrington Park, 2003).

Steven Zeeland, *The Masculine Marine: Homoeroticism in the U.S. Marine Corps* (New York: Harrington Park, 1996).

CHAPTER EIGHT

Porn Noir

Noir posits an unstable world in which terror lurks in wait just beneath a deceptively placid reality.

—FOSTER HIRSCH, FILM NOIR:
THE DARK SIDE OF THE SCREEN

... eroticism is linked to the preoccupation with the haunting fear of death ...

—GEORGES BATAILLE, *TEARS OF EROS*

On March 10, 1987, Larry Kramer stood before a large audience of gay men at New York's Lesbian and Gay Community Center in Greenwich Village. Kramer was the country's most vocal critic of both the federal government's and the gay community's failure to address the AIDS crisis. In 1983, he had founded Gay Men's Health Crisis to provide support and social services for the gay men stricken with the disease; two years later he wrote *The Normal Heart*—one of the longest running plays ever at the Public Theater—to dramatize the situation behind its establishment.

On that March evening, Kramer read from his 1983 AIDS manifesto, "1,112 and Counting": "Our continued existence depends on just how angry you can get." Four years later, the number of AIDS cases had reached 32,000. While any number of issues spurred his wrath that evening, the tipping point was the overly restrictive drug testing policy of the federal government's Food and Drug Administration, which thus far had prevented the development of any medicine to treat HIV/AIDS. He was also exasperated by the failure of Gay Men's Health Crisis to lobby or take an advocacy role.

He appealed to his audience.

"Do we want to start a new organization devoted solely to political action?"

A huge "yes" rose up from the audience.

Two days later more than three hundred people met to found the AIDS Coalition to Unleash Power—ACT UP. Their first political act was a large demonstration on Wall Street to protest the lack of corporate initiative on development of drugs to treat HIV/AIDS. In the years that followed, ACT UP gained thousands of members in seventy chapters in the United States and abroad. [Andriote, 185–87].

REQUIEM

Far away from the epicenters of AIDS, Andrew Holleran, who was living in Florida caring for his ailing parents, walked out into the night after hearing of a friend's death. Looking up into the sky at the stars, he thought that his friend, like others, had joined "a constellation not marked in the maps of heavens..."

> "Some of them were stars—to me, or to the homosexual world of New York City, or the world in general. Some of them were famous for designing clothes, or buildings, or interpreting history, or composing music.... Some were stars

in pornographic films—like the man I saw in the slides flashed on the screen of a bar in Washington several years ago, one of the sexual icons of New York, who was in fact withering away even as the men around me paused in the conversation, their drinking, to admire his penis and his pectorals." [Holleran, 213]

For the first time, obituaries were a common sight in gay newspapers across the country. By the middle of the eighties, prominent artists, writers, dancers, and performers were among the most highly publicized victims of the disease. Among them the growing list of porn stars, directors and erotic artists:

Joey Yale, who appeared in *LA Plays Itself*, and who was the lover and business partner of Fred Halsted, died of AIDS on April 18, 1986. He was thirty-six.

J.W. King starred in *Brothers Should Do It* and *These Bases are Loaded* with his fictive brother, Jon King. One of the most popular gay porn stars of the late seventies and early eighties, he died of AIDS in Los Angeles on December 5, 1986. He was thirty-one.

Gay porn film director **Arthur Bressan** died of AIDS on July 28, 1987, at forty-four. His film *Pleasure Beach*, starring Johnny Dawes, won the first annual Gay Erotic Film Award in 1985.

Casey Donovan died of AIDS in Florida on August 10, 1987. None of his friends or family had known he had AIDS. He was forty-three.

John Holmes, who boasted that he had had more than 1,400 sex partners, died of AIDS on March 13, 1988. He was forty-three.

Photographer **Robert Mapplethorpe** died of AIDS in a hospital in Boston on March 9, 1989. He was forty-two. After his death, "The Perfect Moment," a controversial retrospective exhibition of his photographs, opened in 1989.

Bob Damron, the creator of *Damron's Address Book*, one of the most popular gay travel guides, and business partner/publisher of pioneering gay porn photographer and director J. Brian, died of AIDS on June 20, 1989. He was sixty-one.

Johnny Dawes, the star of Arthur Bresson's prize-winning *Pleasure Beach*, died of AIDS on July 25, 1989. He was thirty-four.

Over the next few years, artist **Keith Haring**, age thirty-one, and porn stars **Lance and Tony Bravo** died in 1990; porn director **Christopher Rage**, performers **Lee Ryder** and **Chris Williams** in 1991; porn stars **Tim Kramer** and **Al Parker** in 1992; director **Jeff Lawrence**, porn star **Joe Simmons,** one of gay porn's first black stars, **Jon King**, the superstar butch bottom, and **Lon Flexx** in 1995.

Not all deaths were AIDS-related. Fred Halsted, pioneering director of *LA Plays Itself, Sex Tool,* and *Sex Garage,* committed suicide with an overdose of sleeping pills. He was forty-nine.

In the years since he had made his trilogy of sex films, Halsted had gone on to make a handful of more conventional pornographic movies as well as giving several notable sexual performances in porn movies directed by others—among them Joe Gage's *El Paso Wrecking Co.* (1977)—but he never again made films with the originality and raw energy of his L.A. sex trilogy. Almost immediately recognizing it as a masterpiece of independent art films in the tradition of Kenneth Anger's *Scorpio Rising*, New York's Museum of Modern Art included *LA Plays Itself* in its film collection.

The most significant of his later movies, *A Night at Halsted's* (1980), was shot at Halsted's, the bar he owned, and featured an astounding and sophisticated new wave/punk sound track unlike that of any other gay porn film. Halsted's relationship with Joey Yale, who starred in *LA Plays Itself* and was the young man being whipped and fisted in the last scene of the film, endured for the next fifteen years. But it was a tempestuous relationship, and over its course they split up and got back together several times. When they were together, as with so many relationships of that time, their relationship was sexually open, but it was the emotional foundation of Halsted's life.

After Yale's death, Halsted was without an anchor. One friend noted, "Fred didn't have anybody to tell him what to do." [Moore, 67] Another friend, Durk Dehner, recalled:

> "Joey got Fred off the bottle and various drugs. Fred slipped back and Joey pulled away to help him. Fred had a healthy ego. But that was destroyed when Joey separated from him. He lost his ego, his pride, and his persona. He got so bad that people didn't want to be around him. He ... was a sloppy, sloppy drunk." [Moore, 66]

When Yale died from AIDS in 1986, Halsted had a difficult time earning a living—since he basically made it from sex. He was also losing his struggle with alcohol and drugs. He attempted to sell his memoirs to porn publisher George Mavety, who thought that the book was not publishable. That was the end; Halsted gave up after that.

SIDELINED

As the AIDS epidemic devastated the lives of gay men, more gay men were choosing to stay at home and watch pornography than go out to cruise for sex. At the height of the epidemic, in the fall of 1988, Jerry Douglas launched the first issue of *Manshots*, a new magazine devoted to covering the gay porn films. [Douglas, *Manshots*, 9/88, 65] One of the articles in that issue was about safe-sex videos and another was an obituary for porn star Eric Stryker, a fictive brother of Jeff Stryker, who had died from complications of AIDS. It was the first time any publication devoted to erotic photography and porn had published an obituary of a porn star. It was to be a regular feature of *Manshots*. Douglas felt that it was time for the adult film industry to acknowledge that many performers were dying of AIDS.

By the time he started *Manshots* at the end of eighties, Douglas had already had two successful careers revolving around the gay adult film industry—as a writer/director in his pioneering films of the early 1970s and a journalist and magazine editor.

The theater was Douglas's first love, and he continued to work on the stage throughout the seventies, supporting himself by working as a journalist. By the mid-seventies, a burst of cultural energy within the gay and lesbian communities had spawned numerous publications. *The Advocate*, originally a local newspaper in Los Angeles, had emerged as a national newspaper and Douglas wrote on books and movies for it. He was one of the first journalists to interview Dave Kopay, the NFL football player who wrote about being homosexual in professional sports.

Douglas only managed to eke out a living as a reviewer. Eventually he went to work as a writer on a publication called *Eros* for a magazine packager named Al Weiss. While most of Weiss's magazines were aimed at a heterosexual audience, he recognized that there was also a potential market for gay male magazines. In 1982, Douglas conceptualized *Stallion* magazine for him. Running six years, *Stallion* carried on, in a more explicit vein, the tradition of gay publishing initiated by *After Dark* magazine—publishing articles on popular culture, books, films and theater, and interviews with actors, writers, and celebrities, each issue adorned with erotic photography of men, stopping short of showing erections, oral sex, or anal penetration. The magazine also published pieces about gay male pornography, interviews with performers and directors, and reviews of new releases.

In 1985 *Stallion* published a special issue (Special No. 4) on the "All-Time Best Male Films and Videos, 1970–1985." This was probably the first history of the commercial gay porn industry ever published; Tom DeSimone's historical documentary film *Erotikus* had only covered the first four years after 1968. *Stallion's* survey focused on the fifty best movies released since the release of *Boys in the Sand, Seven in a Barn, Left-Handed,* and *The Back Row.* A vast majority—thirty-two out of the fifty—of the films selected were made between 1981 and 1985, labeled by the magazine's editors as "The Banner Years."

The fifty films were almost all feature films made for theatrical release and directed by men who, for the most part, considered themselves professionals in the nascent gay porn industry. The most glaring omission was Fred Halsted's *LA Plays Itself,* the 1972 landmark S/M film that had been selected to be in the permanent collection of the Museum of Modern Art. Approximately a quarter of the films selected were made by only two men: Steve Scott (eight) and William Higgins (five). Almost another quarter was made by four men: Mark Reynolds and Matt Sterling (four each), and Jack Deveau and Joe Gage (three each). The remaining—slightly less than 50 percent—were directed by fifteen other men.

Of the leading directors featured in the special issue, William Higgins, Matt Sterling, and Joe Gage remain among those best known for porn made in the late seventies and early eighties—Higgins and Gage are still making films. Steve Scott, the man who made eight of the films identified in the special issue, more than anyone else, died in 1987. Two decades later his name is barely recognized—in 2006 *Unzipped* magazine identified "The 100 Greatest Gay Porn Films Ever," which included only two Steve Scott films: *A Few Good Men* (1983), included in the special issue of *Stallion,* and *Games* (1983), which hadn't been included. Nevertheless, Scott's work may be among the best ever produced in the gay porn industry.

In the editorial introduction, Douglas compared the origins of mainstream filmmaking with the development of gay porn:

"During the Twenties, when silent filmmaking was at its zenith, few of its practitioners thought of their work as an art form or imagined one day their 'flickers' would be treasured in museums and archival vaults. Silent filmmaking, if we are to believe the memoirs of Griffith, Chaplin, and especially Sennett, was a carefree, chaotic business in which people were delighted to be paid for being a little bit crazy. Today historians dig with the intensity of archeologists to reconstruct the days and data of this era. We suspect in time the output of the carefree, chaotic business of 'skin flicks' will also achieve the status of treasures, and future historians will likewise try to reconstruct the days of early porn. To that end, this magazine attempts to give some order to the first quarter century of gay erotic filmmaking." [*Stallion*, 3]

In 1987 the publisher of *Stallion* decided to sell the magazine. George Mavety, the new publisher, chose not to keep Douglas on as the magazine's editor. Douglas immediately called Jackie Lewis, one of the freelance writers he had used at *Stallion*. She had become the publisher of *FirstHand*, a magazine of erotic stories, and she hired Douglas immediately as an editor.

Douglas proposed a new magazine to First Hand Publications.

"I pitched the idea of a magazine devoted entirely to gay adult videos. They did some checking around, did some demographics, and found that it was a viable idea. That's how *Manshots* came about. The first issue came out in September 1988.... I did that until *Manshots* was sold—and the new owners didn't want me—and history repeated itself and I had been fucked again." [Douglas, unpublished interview]

The first issue of *Manshots* arrived at a key historical moment—the growing availability of videos and the emergence of the home viewing audience had broadened the reach of pornographic films, and that was reinforced by the impact of AIDS, which by 1987 had become a full-blown catastrophe. Though AIDS had already devastated the gay male community, it was never mentioned in the 1985 special issue of *Stallion* on porn.

The successful launch of *Manshots* also demonstrated that an "industry" had definitely emerged since Douglas quit making films in 1975; several hundred gay porn videos were released every year. The premier issue included a rare interview with the reclusive director Matt Sterling and an article on safe sex in hardcore videos. Other early issues included interviews with pioneering director Tom DeSimone and popular porn star/director Al Parker, and an obituary of straight porn star John Holmes.

It was the launch of *Manshots* that set in motion the third phase of Jerry Douglas's career in adult films. In the course of putting together the first year of *Manshots*, Douglas arranged to interview Dirk Yates, the owner of All Worlds Video. When they met for the interview, Douglas found that Yates was familiar with *The Back Row*—and Yates offered Douglas the chance to return to directing. Douglas agreed immediately—and he began to plan his first film in fourteen years.

SEX AND THE STORY

By the time Douglas returned to porn, he had a new vision—one that told a story through explicit sexual action. Immersed in Hollywood movies and the theater all his life, Douglas applied the principles of scriptwriting to hardcore movies. In Douglas's view, *sex* tells the story. What kind of sex it is and how it is performed reveal aspects of character and the film's underlying themes. Sex also moves the plot along.

> "[I]t came to me in a blinding flash," Douglas recalled. "I just can't imagine why more people

didn't see it. It seems to me absolutely transparently obvious. Just in one example: after Rodgers and Hammerstein's *Oklahoma*, the whole idea was to integrate the musical numbers into the fabric of the story. And in an adult film, I usually know where my sex scenes are going to fall, and then I have to build the libretto or the webbing or whatever you want to call it, around them. If I do it right, the sex scenes will do what a good number in a musical comedy does: it will reveal character, it will push the plot forward, and it will enrich the theme." [Douglas, unpublished interview, 10/1/01]

Nearly all of Douglas's later movies involve a thoroughly worked out script, often as long as sixty pages—even the sex is scripted and is integrated into the plot and character development. Douglas frequently quotes his good friend Stan Ward, a former *Adult Video News* (AVN) editor and fellow porn scriptwriter: "Sex always takes place in context."

In the pornographic film business, narrative or plot has often been seen as incompatible with sexual action—telling a story is seen as unnecessary since the sexual action alone is self-sufficient. Most makers of porn films have gravitated to one pole or the other. Directors like Tom DeSimone, Jack Deveau, and Steve Scott have made hardcore movies that tell a story. Others like Wakefield Poole, Fred Halsted, John Travis, or Matt Sterling more often make films that stress sexual action with only minimal elements framing the sex scene. Someone's interest in a plot may also differ according to his situation—whether he is performer, author, or viewer. Porn actor Gus Mattox recently told an interviewer that "personally I like porn with no plot—that's what I like to watch, but because I'm an actor/writer, it's more fun for me to make porn with a plot." [Shamama, 8] While the use of narrative and character development can contribute to arousal and stimulating one's fantasies, they can also limit the fantasy.

Probably the director with whom Douglas had the greatest affinity was Steve Scott. Scott had died by the time Douglas returned to filmmaking. In his short career, Scott had made both loops and what he called "story films" which had plots and character development. They were more emotionally complicated tales that included explicit sexual action as an integral part of the story. "The most remarkable talent of director Steve Scott," according to *Stallion* staff writer Ted Underwood, "is his ability to create films that embrace both narrative and erotic lines without shortchanging either. Virtually always, his stories and his sex scenes mesh seamlessly; his films are always more than loops, but just as hot." [*Stallion,* 12]

Although Scott wrote and directed most of his films, he believed that the real art of filmmaking took place in the editing room. As he explained,

> "I'm getting to the point where I don't really like to be on the set getting pieces of film I need. Providing I have the pieces, I can create the magic and the magic for me is in the cutting room. A case in point—there have been two films I've done where two scenes were so deadly that I just hated being on the set, so I was very panicky when I went to the cutting room. But with a little editing, some heavy breathing, some music, everybody says 'Oh, that's gotta be the hottest scene in the picture.'" [Douglas, *Stallion*, 3/83, 57]

When Douglas returned to adult filmmaking, he carried on in the tradition that Scott had represented—not only by writing detailed screenplays but also by focusing on the editing process.

RETURN OF THE AUTEUR

In the late sixties and early seventies, many of the hardcore loops or films sold through mail order or released in the storefront theaters did not credit a director—for the most part, to protect the makers from arrest and persecution.

The irony is that the director of a porn movie exercises much more control over the total product than any Hollywood director does. In an adult film, it is the director who creates the film's visual style and sets the stage for the film's fantasy world—locale, lighting, props or costumes, the sequence of sex acts, the choreography of the sexual performances, and the cast that will perform. As a director, Jerry Douglas is the complete master of the worlds he creates in his movies. He is what film critics call an "auteur."

For his first project, Douglas wrote a short script about two brothers and their sexual obsession with each other. Since it was his first film in fourteen years, he sought to make it as "contained" as possible, both thematically and practically; all of the film's action takes place in one house, and only two performers appear in it. Tim Lowe, the lead, was one of the period's most popular stars. Though primarily straight or bisexual, and most frequently a top, Lowe was sexually versatile. Douglas considered him an exceptional performer.

True to Douglas's new style, the sex was carefully choreographed. The film shows the characters' sexual development, first a solo masturbation scene progressing to mutual masturbation, then two-way oral sex, and ultimately penetrative and receptive anal sex.

"I was scared shitless," Douglas recalled. "I remember sitting on the plane, saying to myself, 'Now Jerry, you've got to give as much attention to the sex as you do to the drama.'"

In *The Back Row* and in *Both Ways*, he had left the sex to the performers, but in *Fratrimony* he decided to directly choreograph the sex. He believed that the art of adult films had evolved enormously since he had last shot a film. Not only was sex more actively choreographed. Specific camera angles were now considered necessary, of the oral and anal penetration, which the early films had often been more relaxed about. [Douglas, unpublished interview, 12/4/01] In order to capture as much on film as possible, Douglas asked Dirk Yates for two cameras.

It was unusual for a pornographic film to have only two performers, but the movie was an immediate hit. A master had returned. The film was nominated for AVN awards in Best Gay Picture, Best Gay Actor, and Best Gay Director, with Lowe winning in the actor category. Yates was especially thrilled because no All Worlds film had ever previously been nominated for, much less won, an AVN award.

MORE OF A MAN

The success of *Fratrimony* inspired Douglas to make another film. Almost immediately, the germ of a new idea began to grow. While at the annual AVN award show in Las Vegas, Douglas had seen Chi Chi LaRue—the drag persona of up-and-coming porn director Larry Paciotti—perform and was stunned by her flamboyant presence and style. Larue was a lavish personality who frequently emceed and sang at industry events. Though they had long had a telephone relationship while Douglas was a magazine editor and LaRue the marketing and promotions manager at Catalina, Douglas had never seen LaRue perform. She had recently left Catalina to direct videos for In Hand Productions. After seeing her performance in Las Vegas, Douglas wanted to build a movie around LaRue, but he asked himself "How do I build a gay porn movie around a large drag queen?"

It came to him over a lunch with LaRue, who brought along a handsome brunette performer named Joey Stefano. It was clear that Paciotti was very much in love with Stefano, while Stefano clearly looked up to LaRue/Paciotti as a mentor.

Douglas was touched by their intimacy.

> "The relationship between them was just incredible; they had bonds made of violin wire. I said, 'I'd like to write a movie for the two of you.' And

> Larry said, 'You may have him.' That was the
> most generous thing Larry [Paciotti] could have
> done, and I am indebted to him for the rest of my
> life. So I went right home and wrote *More of a
> Man*—as much for Larry as for Joey." [AGV,
> Jerry Douglas, 45–47]

At lunch that day, Stefano talked about the difficulties he
had had coming to terms with his sexuality because of his
Catholic background. Stefano's struggles gave Douglas an
idea. Just a month earlier, ACT UP had staged a mass demonstration at St. Patrick's Cathedral to protest Archbishop Cardinal O'Connor's outspoken opposition to gay rights and
condom use. "During high mass inside the church, angry pro-
testors," as ACT UP members Doug Crimp and Adam Rolston
recounted, "forced O'Connor to abandon his sermon."

> "Affinity groups lay down in the aisles, threw con-
> doms in the air, chained themselves to pews, or
> shouted invectives at the cardinal. One former
> altar boy deliberately dropped a consecrated Com-
> munion wafer on the floor. (The media had a field
> day with that one: by the day after the event, it
> had become legions of 'homosexual activists' des-
> ecrating the host.)" [Crimp/Rolston, 139]

Within weeks after returning from L.A., Douglas had written a script about a young man's coming to terms with his
homosexuality against the backdrop of the Catholic church
and AIDS activism. Douglas incorporated some aspects of the
relationship between LaRue and Stefano as well.

Douglas felt that *More of a Man* was "[t]he first real film I made.
I think that's the first time I really hit my stride and got it right."
All the elements came together: not only Douglas's extensive experience as a playwright and theater director, his pioneering role as
a director of erotic films, and his wealth of knowledge of the gay
world as a journalist and observer, but also the strong erotic appeal
of the actors, and above all the exact and delicate appreciation of

the historical forces sweeping across the gay world.

The film tells the story of a young man struggling against the Catholic church's prohibitions of his homosexual desires and portrays the furtive and sometimes degrading ways he gives in to them. Eventually with the counsel of a drag queen (played by LaRue) whom he meets at a local bar, he achieves sexual self-acceptance and has a liberating sexual experience with an AIDS activist during the annual gay pride parade.

More of a Man sets the sexual action in the actual context of gay male life in the late 1980s—a time overwhelmed by the AIDS epidemic, filled with the fear of sex, and riddled by doubts that AIDS could be stopped. The main characters represent the two poles of gay male sexual life: one, a construction worker, a young man torn by guilt and self-hatred, overwhelmed with a sense of sin and unwilling to identify himself as gay; and the other a jock and a bartender, a self-accepting gay man in a long-term relationship, an AIDS activist. The young construction worker engages in risky sexual encounters with strangers, anonymous sex in public toilets; the activist uses a condom even during sex with his long-term partner.

The film was made within an industry that had hesitated for years to portray explicit sexual action using a condom. Douglas showed that, within the grim historical setting, powerful and arousing sex could take place. *More of a Man* won four awards at the 1990 AVN awards show, including the Best Gay Video, Best Screenplay, Best Performer (Joey Stefano), and Best Non-Sexual Role (Chi Chi LaRue). It was also the first time a major gay film in which condoms were explicitly used had won a major award since the beginning of the epidemic in 1981.

LEARNING TO SUCK COCK

The success of *More of a Man* may have proven to the industry that All Worlds was not just that "little company in San

Diego," but it didn't necessarily bring in enough revenue to bankroll the next movie. Yates told Douglas that he couldn't afford to produce a movie that year.

But as Yates told Douglas, "I've made a deal with Ryan Idol. He'll do three jerk-off loops for me. That's all I can afford."

The six-foot-three-inch, strikingly handsome Ryan Idol had recently been launched by agent David Forest and billed as Jeff Stryker's successor: as a straight gay-for-pay macho star.

Douglas proposed making a movie around the three masturbation scenes.

"How can you make a movie out of three jerk-off loops?" Yates asked.

"I will do it, I want to work with Ryan Idol."

"You'll never get a movie out of this, Jerry," Yates warned. [Douglas, unpublished interview, 12/4/01]

Douglas chose Axel Garret as the second lead. Beautiful and unattainable—and probably not at all gay—Axel Garret occupied a very special place in the imaginations of Dirk Yates and Jerry Douglas. Yates was overwhelmed by his movie-star beauty; Douglas was mesmerized by him. A former Marine, Axel had shot solo scenes for both of Dirk's series, *The Few, the Proud and the Naked* and *Dirk Yates' Private Amateur Collection*. Like Ryan Idol, Garret was considered straight, and in fact as far as anyone knew he hadn't even had sex with a man at that point.

Douglas was also "schnockered" by Garret. "I have never, ever been to bed with anybody that I have worked with," recalled Douglas, who for more than twenty years has been in a monogamous relationship, "not just in the adult film industry, but in any of the things I've done in my life. You just don't do it. It clouds too many issues.... I came *this* close. Of all the people I've worked with, Axel is the one who pushed my buttons more than anyone else." [AGV, 61]

Douglas struggled with his desires up until the night before filming the first scene.

"I was lying in bed and I thought, 'You have a film to make. You do not have time to indulge yourself or let it get in the way of your work.' And then like a light-bulb going on over my head, I thought, 'Von Sternberg was in love with Marlene Dietrich and … he never got her. So he fucked her with his camera.' And that's what I did." [AGV, 61]

Trade-Off interspersed Idol's three solo masturbation scenes with several other sex scenes, including a bisexual one. The movie translates Douglas's sexual obsession with Axel into its main plotline—Ryan Idol plays a closeted voyeur obsessed with his straight next-door neighbor, played by Axel Garret, who, unbeknownst to Idol's character, obsessively watches Idol back.

Douglas had hoped to make a sequel to *Trade-Off*, again starring both Ryan Idol and Axel, but Idol was no longer available, having priced himself out of the market. Instead, Douglas wrote the sequel for Axel Garret. *Kiss-Off* took up the story again of the closeted voyeur. In the sequel, Garret becomes obsessed with the attractive man who moved into the apartment where Ryan Idol's character had previously lived. Garret's character is a police officer assigned to the vice squad, where he is tempted to indulge in his homosexual desires by both his police work and his corrupt partner.

Both *Trade-Off* and *Kiss-Off* continued to explore the territory opened up by *More of a Man*—the coming to terms with one's homosexual desires and identity. Douglas was "absolutely convinced" that Axel was gay, but "equally convinced that he will never act on it, ever, in his entire life outside a film set." [AGV, 61] But in both of these movies, Douglas exploited the strange doubleness of porn—it is *both* a fantasy created by actors *and* an enactment of the fantasy through real sex (that is to say, real erections, real penetration, and real orgasms)—to challenge the sexual presumptions of his stars.

The leading actors in both films were ostensibly straight. In

Trade-Off neither one had engaged in sex with a man, but in *Kiss-Off* Douglas put Axel Garret into sexual encounters with several other men—a tearoom scene in which he gets a blow job, an outdoor scene in which he tops Danny Sommers, and a scene with his corrupt undercover partner in the backseat of a limousine. Although Garret required magazines and videos to get himself primed, Douglas felt that Garret's performance "was so naked and so true and revealing.... I wrote the script because I knew that's where he was in life. And I made him tap into those things."

Douglas has been called the "Stanislavski of smut" after the Russian director and teacher who pioneered "method acting" because he applied the technique to adult movies. Method acting is a technique by which actors attempt to replicate real experiences and feelings in order to give an accurate, life-like performance of the characters they portray. Since the sexual action in pornographic films was always "real"—real sex with real erections and real orgasms—performers in porn often experience the kind of awareness that the method provides.

In *Kiss-Off* there is a scene that takes place in the limousine where one of the cocaine dealers initiates sex with two undercover cops. He says, "Flip a coin, and one of you is going to have to fuck the other one."

When Douglas and Garret discussed that scene before shooting, Garret told Douglas, "I was scared when I got to that part in the script, I thought I was going to have to suck cock." The straight actor would have to learn to suck cock by sucking cock.

Douglas was sure Garret would have it on his mind when he played the scene.

"That moment when Mitch Taylor says to flip a coin," Douglas recalled, "the look on Axel's face is real! The first time anybody rimmed Axel was a *moment*. I wish I'd gotten a facial reaction to it. I think it never occurred to him that people did things like that. The look on Axel's face was just priceless." AGV, 78]

Over the next four years, Douglas continued to produce one movie a year—he made *Jock-A-Holics* (1993), a takeoff of Arthur Schnitzler's classic erotic play, *La Ronde*; and *Diamond Stud* (1995), a reworked version of *Pay-Off*, which was to have been the third play of his Ryan Idol/Axel Garret trilogy; and *Honorable Discharge* (1993), his takeoff on then currently debated issue of gays in the military and above all, a tribute to Dirk Yates's erotic obsession with Marines.

Douglas considered the making of *Honorable Discharge* "a labor of love."

"I was fascinated by all the anthropological and sociological implications, of these straight guys who are willing to have sex with another man." He wanted to explore the widespread belief that "sailors suck cock and marines fuck—or get fucked."

> "I never understood why. This is my thought on it: The Marines are the most macho American image in existence, and if you have any doubts about your sexuality, that's where you go to prove you're a man." [AGV, 90]

MOURNING AND MELANCHOLY

From 1995 on, Jerry Douglas made a movie almost every year. *Honorable Discharge* was released in 1995. *Flesh and Blood* came out in 1996. *Family Values* (Odyssey) came out a year later. In 1998 *Dream Team* (Studio 2000) was released. That year Douglas was elected to the AVN Hall of Fame, and in 1999 he received the Lifetime Achievement Award from the Free Speech Coalition, the adult industry's political lobby group.

Flesh and Blood (1996) is Douglas's tribute to Alfred Hitchcock and film noir. The film tells the story of Derrick, played by Kurt Young, investigating the murder of his identical-twin brother, Erik (also played by Young). Derrick, who mentions soon after his arrival that he is engaged to be married, discovers that his brother left behind a series of betrayed sexual partners, both male and female. Initially, all characters are suspects, but they all declare their love of Erik and tell Derrick the story of their sexual relationship with Erik in a self-serving way that suggests their innocence. Flashbacks reveal the false notes, delusions, and lies in their stories as well as Erik's unscrupulous manipulation of his partners through seduction, misrepresentation, and lies.

Flesh and Blood exploits many of the motifs and conventions of film noir. As a genre of film production, film noir flourished in the forties and fifties, but it became particularly influential in the last quarter of the twentieth century. It almost seemed to be a kind of popular mythology. Sexual desire, paranoia, and murder are central. Sex rarely occurs in a romantic context, but one in which sexual desire is driven by obsession and provokes criminal acts. According to Foster Hirsch, it is "an unstable world, in which terror lurks in wait just beneath a deceptively placid reality.... In noir no one is safe from himself or from others—and those others include spouses, siblings, neighbors, best friends." [Hirsch, 182] Between 1985 and 1999, a mood of extended grieving and melancholic nostalgia had settled over the gay male community populated by traumatized men whose sexuality was hemmed in by death, religious bigotry, and homophobia. It defined an era of gay noir. "Silence = Death" is the motto of the gay noir sensibility.

The sexual action of each scene reveals the psychological character of the person who relates the scene and shows us how, in each case, the narrator's own delusions about Erik's sexuality or about themselves allowed Erik to manipulate them sexually. His sex with Kenny, the young man who claims to be Erik's boyfriend, is not reciprocal, which suggests that Kenny's love was not reciprocated. The flashback also demonstrates that Kenny's vulnerability lies in his romantic naiveté. The bisexual three-way that Marilyn, who claims to be Erik's fiancée, gives as proof of she and Erik's sexual openness and of their trust in one another, instead reveals her self-delusion; Erik only has sex with the man. Erik's sexual manipulation of a young man who insists that he is straight shows that the young man is also self-deluded about his sexual desires. Each of Erik's suitors fantasizes about Derrick as a possible replacement for the murdered brother—another aspect of their self-delusion. When the supposedly murdered Erik suddenly comes out of hiding, Derrick must engage in sex with his brother in order to solve the psychological mystery. But like the others, Derrick succumbs to Erik's ruthless domination because he too is self-deluded—about his own sexual desires and his brother's thirst to destroy. Derrick has risked everything, but he fails.

Few porn films are predicated on the relentless exploration of the characters' delusions about sexual relationships, their sexual desires or identities, or a narrative that begins with and ends in murder. The title, *Flesh and Blood*, alludes both to family ties and to the mythology of film noir—invoking the claustrophobia of forbidden sexualities, incest, and secrecy. Through the positioning of the camera as a spectator within the internal space of the scene, the dark angular lighting, and the claustrophobic set, Douglas's *mise-en-scene* replicates the visual style and mood of the traditional noir film. Within the film's narrative, the explicit sexual action contributes to the development of each of the film's characters, revealing their illusions and in some sense illustrating the danger of deluding oneself about sexuality—so commonly the topic of traditional film noir.

● ● ●

In the summer of 1991, Douglas attended a lecture at Carnegie Hall on "Gay Pornography, 1900–1970." It was an odd venue for such a presentation, and the speaker knew little about the material he showed or about gay life. The lecture consisted mostly of clips from old stag films and underground movies. Douglas found it quite boring and was about to fall asleep when the lecturer introduced one clip by observing that he was "almost positive" it was shot in the Midwest around 1932 or 1933. Douglas was born around that time and grew up in the Midwest, so he perked up.

> "I started to watch it and the man who was doing the fucking looked exactly like the pictures of my father at that time in his life. Of course, my father was about as straight as you can get— although he was adventuresome sexually, so it's conceivable that it could have been, but I think it's very unlikely. But the light-bulb went on and I thought, 'What if a kid found his father was a porn star?'... [T]hat's how *Family Values* came about.... It wrote itself effortlessly." [AGV, 94]

The title *Family Values* suggested that it was a movie about the Christian right's war on porn, but instead the film is a series of scenes between men of widely disparate ages. To realize that theme, Douglas wanted to bring together some of the "classic" porn stars of the seventies with a younger generation of porn stars from the mid-nineties.

The AIDS epidemic played havoc with some of the cast Douglas had originally had in mind. He had originally hoped to cast Al Parker as the father and Johnny Rahm as the son. Al Parker agreed, only to withdraw shortly afterward because he had become too ill. He died soon after. Then Douglas approached Richard Locke, the star of Joe Gage's 1977 *Kansas City Trucking Co.* He agreed, but he also had to withdraw because he was sick. When he approached Derrick Stanton, who had starred with Kip Noll in several of William Higgins's early movies, Stanton told him that he did not want to return to making adult films. At that point, Douglas decided to drop the project. However, four years later, Stanton had changed his mind. And at that time, Douglas began to shop the film that became *Family Values* around. He signed on with Men of Odyssey.

Douglas cast Kurt Young as the son who discovers that his

father had been a gay porn star in the seventies. Douglas managed to recruit a number of popular early porn stars—in addition to Derrick Stanton, there were Steve York and Erich Lange—to play the older men in scenes with younger porn stars. While there is nothing controversial about young gay men having sex with older men, many viewers and critics were shocked and disgusted by a scene that showed a son (Kurt Young) and his father (Derrick Stanton) having sex.

Douglas also cast another performer from *Flesh and Blood* in *Family Values*—Bryan Kidd, the young man who had played Kurt Young's boyfriend. Though Kidd was easygoing and cooperative, his presence on the set of *Family Values* was potentially disruptive. The filming took place with the dramatic cross-country killing spree of Andrew Cunanan as a backdrop. Cunanan had killed two of his friends in Minneapolis, along with another two men on his way to Miami, where he then murdered fashion designer Gianni Versace. Bryan Kidd and his boyfriend Ryan Wagner, who was also a porn star, knew Cunanan from San Diego, where they all lived. Photographs of both of them with Cunanan appeared in the *National Enquirer* and other tabloids. During the making of *Family Values*, Kidd was constantly on the phone with reporters. The FBI had Kidd and Wagner, like some of Cunanan's other friends, under protective watch the entire time.

Douglas's next movie was *Dream Team* (1998), an autobiographical film set in Iowa during the fifties. As the filmmaker explained it, "I've always thought of *Dream Team* as a very simple little film. It's basically the story of my coming out. Every scene in that film, with some dramatic license happened to me, back in Iowa, in the fifties." [interview, 10/1/01]

The producer of *Dream Team* was Scott Masters. "The joke on the street," Douglas recalled, "was that it would never be finished because Scott Masters and I would kill each other because we're both such control freaks." [AGV, 96] Nevertheless, the film went smoothly. "We had one very bad fight that was resolved relatively soon.... It was an absolutely joyous experience, but it was rough work."[AGV, 96]

Dream Team was both an autobiographical film and a historical allegory illustrating the significance of gay liberation. Set at the five-year reunion of Herbert Hoover High School, the film brings together the seven members of Hoover's hapless basketball team—who have gone through entire seasons without a victory. The team was made up of three or four closeted young men and some "straight" boys who enjoyed sex with guys. The high school sex scenes captured the loneliness, guilt, and transgressive nature of sex in the closet in small-town America during the 1950s. They are contrasted with the joyous sex that took place at the reunion, which was after Stonewall. The film, with its romantic stories and happy endings, offered a historical antidote to the grim atmosphere of the AIDS epidemic—despite AIDS, gay liberation was a major step toward sexual happiness.

While Douglas continued to make one movie a year, he continued editing *Manshots*. It was a unique publication in that it was virtually a magazine "of record" for the gay porn film industry. While it was not a trade publication per se, it methodically covered the industry as it developed—reviewed new releases and old classics, published photo layouts of high-profile movies in every issue ("the Picks") and included in-depth interviews with established stars, up-and-coming performers, directors, and all kinds of people who worked behind the camera.

Toward the end of 2000, *Manshots* magazine was sold. The last issue Jerry Douglas edited came out in November 2000. No new issue of *Manshots* showed up on the newsstands until March 2001, then months went by before another issue came out—a June–August 2001 issue. After that, no other issue was ever published. When Douglas was fired by the *Manshots'* new owner, he decided to retire.

REFERENCES

Adam Gay Video (AGV) Erotica, *The Films of Jerry Douglas from Fratrimony to Top Secret* (Los Angeles: Knight Publishing, December 2002).

John-Manuel Andriote, *Victory Deferred: How AIDS Changed Gay Life in America.*

Douglas Crimp with Adam Rolston, *AIDS Demo/Graphics* (Seattle: Bay Press, 1990).

Jerry Douglas, unpublished interview by Jeffrey Escoffier, October 1 and December 4, 2001.

Jerry Douglas, "Steve Scott: Class Act of Porn," *Stallion*, March 1983.

Jerry Douglas, "Parting Shots," *Manshots*, September 1988, premiere issue.

Foster Hirsch, *Film Noir: The Dark Side of the Screen* (New York: Da Capo Press, 1983).

Andrew Holleran, *Ground Zero.*

Patrick Moore, *Beyond Shame: Reclaiming the Abandoned History of Radical Gay Sexuality* (Boston: Beacon Press, 2004).

Jack Shamama, "Gus Mattox: An Interview," *Adam Gay Video XXX Showcase*, October 2004.

Stallion Editors, "Stallion 50 Best," *Stallion.*

PART III

SEXUAL
SPECTACLE

CHAPTER NINE

The Perfect Orgy

Chemistry between performers makes a scene work. You can't fake true chemistry between performers.

—CHI CHI LARUE

To me sex is one of the highest artistic acts.

—ROBERT MAPPLETHORPE

On June 13, 1989, Christina Orr-Cahill, director of the Corcoran Gallery of Art in Washington, D.C., canceled "The Perfect Moment," a large-scale retrospective show of Robert Mapplethorpe's photographic career due to open at the Corcoran on July 1. It covered the full spectrum of his work including celebrity portraits, spectacular photos of flowers, self-portraits, and homoerotic and sadomasochistic photographs.

While the show had appeared without controversy in Philadelphia and Chicago, Orr-Cahill decided to cancel in order to avoid playing into a growing controversy over funding from the National Endowment for the Arts (NEA). Her decision to cancel triggered a dramatic explosion between conservatives and the art community. Two days after 108 members of Congress filed a complaint against NEA for using federal funds to support indecent and immoral art, artists and members of the arts community also protested Orr-Cahill's decision. The Corcoran lost members, several curators and other staff members resigned, and artists who had scheduled shows at the Corcoran canceled them.

Republican Senator Jesse Helms of North Carolina led the opposition to the show. He regarded some of Mapplethorpe's photographs as pornographic and produced a packet of four Mapplethorpe photographs, one of which was the famous "Man in Polyester Suit" which showed the torso of a black man clad in a polyester suit, his large uncircumcised penis dangling from his fly.

Helms sponsored an amendment to an appropriations bill to bar the National Endowment from funding "obscene artwork" and to exclude the organizations that had organized the Mapplethorpe and other shows from federal funding for five years. The Helms Amendment forbade the NEA to fund:

> "...[O]bscene or indecent materials, including but not limited to depictions of sadomasochism, homoeroticism, the exploitation of children or individuals engaged in sex acts; or material which denigrates the objects or beliefs of the adherents of a particular religion, debases, or reviles a person, group, or class of citizens on the basis of race, creed, sex, handicap, age or national origin."

Mapplethorpe himself never saw the show. Three months earlier, on March 9, he had died of AIDS. [Steiner, 19–22]

THE PERFECT MOMENT

The controversy around "The Perfect Moment" illuminated the significance of the erotic in art and how it intersected with obscenity and pornography. The show was originally conceived and mounted by the Institute for Contemporary Art in Philadelphia. Mapplethorpe's work had been controversial since the late seventies, when he had become known for his erotic photographs and his collages of pornographic images. Among the most controversial of those early photographs was *Self-Portrait* of 1978, in which Mapplethorpe posed bent over with his back to the camera and his head turned around to face it, wearing leather chaps, vest, and boots, and with the handle of a bullwhip penetrating his anus.

Galleries that mounted the exhibit were legally obligated by the artist's estate to mount all 175 photographs in the show, including the controversial X, Y, and Z Portfolios: the nude and sadomasochistic images in X, the flowers in Y, and the provocative studies of human figures in Z. The 1978 *Self-Portrait* was also included. Curators in Philadelphia and Chicago cautiously segregated the most controversial images in special galleries with warnings posted for spectators.

When the Corcoran canceled "The Perfect Moment," a small local arts organization called the Washington Project for the Arts mounted the exhibit. Whereas the Project for the Arts averaged forty visitors a day, more than four thousand people attended on the first weekend. The show traveled to the University Art Museum in Berkeley, then on to the Contemporary Art Center in Cincinnati. There, on the exhibit's opening day, police closed the show temporarily in order to videotape it as evidence for an obscenity indictment brought by the county prosecutor. Both the center and its director, Dennis Barrie, were indicted on charges of pandering obscenity and child pornography (the show included several photographs of unclothed children).

The indictment cited the 1973 Supreme Court ruling in *Miller v. California*, the same Supreme Court opinion that had been so influential on the porn film industry's adoption of plots and narrative to qualify for "serious literary, artistic ... value." *Miller v. California* ruled any work obscene that "taken as a whole, appeals to the prurient interest in sex; portrays in a patently offensive way, sexual conduct specifically defined by the applicable state law; and taken as a whole, does not have serious literary, artistic, political, or scientific value." [Slade, 216–217]

The controversy over "The Perfect Moment" was where the world of high art merged with the world of commercial pornography. Mapplethorpe drew his inspiration from early beefcake porn and went on to explore the world of sadomasochism and present it to the world. Commercial gay pornography portrayed explicit sexual activity between men and gave it affirmation. From Robert Mapplethorpe to Tom of Finland to Joe Gage and Chi Chi LaRue, the portrayal of sex and the representation of erotic images seem to inhabit the same world.

THE FANTASY BUSINESS

In 1988, "The Perfect Moment" was in Chicago while the AVN award show was in full swing at the Tropicana Hotel in Las Vegas. It was only the fourth year that the AVN had recognized gay videos. Falcon Studio's *Touch Me* won the AVN award for the Best Gay Video of 1988. It was the first time Falcon had won an award for one of its films.

That *Touch Me* won the award was ironic. Falcon movies were known for their unsentimental, unplotted sex scenes, but *Touch Me* was atypical in two important ways—first, it was a love story, and second, it had kissing in it. It was also the first film conceived and directed by Steven Scarborough. Early winners in the gay categories at the AVN award show had been veterans from the first days of gay hardcore movies: Tom DeSimone (as Lancer Brooks) for *Bi-Coastal* (Catalina, 1985), Matt Sterling for *Inch by Inch* (Huge Video, 1985), and John Summers for *Rock Hard* (L.A. Video, 1987).

When Scarborough first approached him with the idea of producing a love story, Chuck Holmes had declared, "I don't want any fucking kissing in my films."

Scarborough protested, "I want to have this great love scene," he told Holmes. "Let's do something that people can relate to, a lover gets caught cheating, the one lover tries to walk away, yet he can't. He comes back." He persuaded Holmes to let him make such a film under Falcon's aegis. [Scarborough, *Manshots*, 8/96, 68]

• • •

Scarborough's arrival at Falcon was a significant event both for the studio's creative approach as well as its business strategy. His reorganization of Falcon's production process helped to establish the economic foundation for Falcon's preeminence over the next two decades.

Scarborough thought that Holmes was "the smartest, most successful man in gay porn during his lifetime. Yet he was not the innovator. He had to be dragged kicking and screaming into every change we ever made." [Moore, 98] Known for his strong likes and dislikes (about talent and sex), he was more of a businessman than a director. After John Travis left Falcon and went to work for Catalina in 1984, Falcon struggled to stay afloat. It had long survived by producing loops and packaging them together in "Falcon Video Packs." Steven Scarborough arrived in San Francisco in 1974 when he was twenty-one. Though married, he was actively bisexual and had even had an affair with one of his wife's former boyfriends.

After a couple of years, he opened a health food store on Castro Street across from Harvey Milk's camera shop. He met a local sales clerk, Dick Fisk, who worked at a clothing store named Rugby, which was owned by John Summers and Matt Sterling. Fisk was one of the stars of Falcon's hugely successful *The Other Side of Aspen* (1977). It wasn't long before Scarborough met Chuck Holmes, and the two men became friends.

"Chuck was enamored of me," Scarborough admits. Holmes, who was seven years Scarborough's senior, had just broken up with a boyfriend of ten years. Soon Scarborough and Holmes were caught up in a "crazy, torrid six-month" affair. Throughout their relationship and even after Scarborough broke up with Holmes, he would ask, "Why did you do that?" or go so far as to say "I'd have done that." Finally Holmes had heard enough, and Scarborough remembers him saying: "Listen big mouth, why don't you come down ..."

Scarborough agreed, "but on the first day I was supposed to shoot, I didn't show up." Scarborough recalled. "I couldn't... So [Holmes] sent somebody to come get me, and they brought me to the set, and I was very, very shy. I knew what I wanted to see, and I had considerable experience in sex. But I never had technical movie training. I was very timid. I would whisper '... is it possible to do this?'" [Scarborough, *Manshots*, 8/96, 66; Jansen, 16]

"I was a sexual person, but I was a very private person," Scarborough explained.

> "I think I had a reputation because Chuck and I had been involved, and for some reason, I had several porn stars who had become long-term sex partners. I wasn't a bathhouse kind of person. If I went to the bathhouse, I went to look or maybe gather. But I was very private about what I did. And I think that coming forward like that I felt exposed.... So when I first came on the set—I would say to whoever was sitting next to me: [*whispering*] 'Tell them to do this. Tell them to do that.' I was afraid to speak up, I felt so exposed." [Scarborough, *Manshots*, 8/96, 66-67]

From the start, it was clear to Scarborough that Falcon's operations were not very efficiently organized. Its production team had worked together for a long time, but they had spent the last six months of 1987 making only one movie, *Perfect Summer* (Falcon Video Pac 57); Scarborough came in and finished it in no time.

"When I came to Falcon they didn't have one designated director. It was done by committee. I don't have any film background. I had no video background, I had no production background. What I had was a sense of business and sense of compulsion and a sense of organization.... And I've been very successful at getting people to work together. And that's basically what I found a director did: bring all these talented people to get them to work together." [Scarborough, 66–67]

At the time, Falcon had a camera crew that had worked for the company for years. It was based in Los Angeles, and most Falcon films were shot in northern California or on location. While the film's director may have often worked from a script, the production crew worked with "a general idea of what they were going to do. And they just kind of all wandered onto the set and they spent a lot of time arguing. I watched them argue a lot in the beginning ..." [Scarborough, *Manshots*, 8/96, 67] Once a movie was shot, the camera crew returned to Los Angeles to edit it.

Scarborough thought that Falcon needed to make more movies in order to generate a more continuous revenue stream—and in line with that he thought that the editing should also become a continuous process. He concluded that the Los Angeles-based team should focus exclusively on editing, while a San Francisco-based camera crew shot the film. Holmes resisted; he wanted "people who've shot sex." Instead, Scarborough argued for "really good technicians ... kids, fresh out of school who have something to prove—who are really good, know their equipment, know lighting, have a lot of energy, really want to work hard." Scarborough prevailed.

They hired two young men, fresh out of the film program at San Francisco State—John Rutherford and Todd Montgomery, who at the time were boyfriends. The L.A. camera crew came up to San Francisco to train them. When Montgomery wanted to relight everything as if they were shooting a commercial, a member of the old crew just countered with "Goddamn it, just pull in the lights and keep shooting, 'Cause when you've got a hard-on, you gotta shoot." {Scarborough, *Manshots*, 8/96, 67] But their youth and technical savvy gave Scarborough the freedom to focus on directing the sex and managing the models.

With a full-time production unit in place, Scarborough had greater control over quality and consistency. In order to keep the production unit busy and further increase revenues, he upped in-house production for two other Falcon lines: Jocks and Mustang. He used the subsidiary lines to audition and build new talent "like the farm teams" do for major league baseball. Chi Chi LaRue and Bruce Cam were hired to direct for those lines.

Chuck Holmes was known for the strict guidelines he imposed on Falcon performers: white, "All-American" young men, no body hair, especially no chest hair, no body builders, and no tattoos. The approach was often called "the Falcon car wash," ensuring everything was "clean" and hairless.

When Scarborough first started at Falcon, casting usually began with a script that often took months to develop. He modified the process and began to work with a simple "treatment" that was nothing more than an outline. More important than having a finished script was knowing which performers were available. [Scarborough, *Manshots*, 8/96, 67–68]

Scarborough may have been timid at the beginning, but he soon developed a reputation for being demanding on the set, especially when dealing with performers.

> "I don't talk very much.... Once it gets going. I like to—I challenge the models a lot. I have a whole grab-bag of directorial tricks. I think you have to be a psychologist and you have to know who to push, who to coddle, who to encourage, who to stop, who to time and talk to, and who needs personal attention. I say, 'You call that

fucking? I don't call that fucking!'... Sometimes,
it'll challenge them." [Scarborough, *Manshots*,
8/96, 11]

Scarborough's approach was very effective with performers
who considered themselves straight.

"With these straight boys, I don't care what they
do. I don't care if they call themselves Martians
or what their sex lives are about. In my book, if
you wanna come down and work in gay movies,
then by God, you're gay for the day. 'Cause it's
insulting and demeaning and degrading for these
straight guys to come on these sets and act like
they're better than these gay models. We're gay
men making gay movies for a gay audience."
[Scarborough, *Manshots*, 8/96, 70]

Another important development during the Scarborough
years was the policy of signing performers to "exclusive" contracts—contracts that did not allow a performer to appear in
the videos of another company for a limited period, usually for
a year. The "exclusive" performer was a form of investment
that was meant to guarantee movie sales. In exchange, an
exclusive contract promised the performer a guaranteed number of film appearances (five over the course of a year) and a
higher fee per scene than performers without an exclusive contract. The studio strictly regulated the careers of its exclusives
by controlling their access to the gay press, their sexual repertoires, and the characters they played. The policy helped to
limit a performer's "overexposure" and to carefully stage the
expansion of his sexual repertoire.

It was not, at first, a systematic policy. The earliest mention
of anyone "exclusive" was in the Falcon marketing brochure
for *Out of Bounds* (FVP 53, 1987), which stated that the film
was "Starring Falcon's exclusive discovery, Chris Williams."
The next exclusive wasn't announced until 1990 when Jack
Dillon was listed as "our newest Falcon Exclusive superstar,

'Big' Jack Dillon." Thereafter, the "exclusive" became an essential component of the studio's promotional and marketing efforts.

Scarborough's major achievement as a director at Falcon was the Abduction series—*The Abduction* (1991), *The Conflict* (1993), and *Redemption* (1993)—in which he pushed beyond the long-standing Falcon formulas to explore a "world of uniforms, humiliation, and discipline." Originally inspired by a location Scarborough came across while shooting a Jocks video in Los Angeles, *The Abduction* was shot in a vast underground cavern on an old evacuated military base in the mountains outside Los Angeles. From the minute he saw it, he had envisioned fascist "goons marching" across the large empty space—men abducted from their homes and brought to a torture dungeon to be searched for a mysterious roll of film. They search every orifice with cocks, dildos, and fists. Candle wax, anal beads, gags, enemas, and auto-fellatio supplement the whips and riding crops. *The Conflict*, its sequel, was even more brutal and scary, continuing the extreme leather play and extensive butt-play with toys, dildos, and fists—with spitting, pissing, and boot licking. *Redemption*, the last installment of the trilogy, continued the same round of intense kinky sex.

In the Abduction trilogy Scarborough articulated his most fundamental vision of extreme sex. John Rutherford, his assistant at Falcon, has said that "Steven has always been extremely charismatic. Something that stands out for me when looking at Steven's movies is the character and sexual chemistry between top and bottom. Steven's always had a creative mind in coming up with scenarios of fantasy and playing roles of dominance and submission. He does this like no other, and continues to set the bar." [Jansen, 18]

While working on *The Conflict* and *Redemption*, Scarborough and Holmes were caught up in a fierce conflict over various aspects of the production. But it was both a clash of wills and a matter of creative differences. Their conflict provoked Scarborough's departure. "The straw that broke the camel's back was about a camel in *Conflict/Redemption*, having a camel walk across a scene. And that's basically what the whole issue was around. But it was a control issue." [Scarborough, *Manshots*, 8/96, 14]

Years later, Scarborough reflected on their conflict.

> "Now I look back and see it was just stupid. But there was a struggle going on, where I was becoming my own person. I'd found my voice and identity, and yet I had been tied to Chuck. He was my protector, my boss, my lover ... It was a very complicated relationship." [Moore, 98]

Scarborough left Falcon after six and a half years—during which time he had virtually remade the studio. He took the savings he had planned to buy a house with and formed his own company, Hot House—where the vision he had articulated in the Abduction series would serve as the foundation of his future work.

BORN TO PORN

A poster of Jeff Stryker wearing white gym pants, his large, partially erect penis straining against the pant leg, was what lured Larry Paciotti to Los Angeles from St. Paul, Minnesota. He'd seen the poster for *Powertool* and knew his future lay on the West Coast.

Within days of arrival, Paciotti landed a job at the legendary Catalina Video as a sales agent. Catalina had just released *Powertool*, Stryker's breakout movie. He got the job because he knew a great deal about gay porn. "It ... was a case," he explained, "of my life's devotion to pornography actually paying off." [LaRue/Erich, 50]

Paciotti was born in 1959 in Hibbing, Minnesota (also the hometown of Bob Dylan). The persona of Chi Chi LaRue first emerged as a personality and a performer in a group of drag queens known as the Weather Girls. Paciotti is a big man—well over six feet and somewhat heavy, even by his own admission. In drag, his dimensions are amplified, adding to his mesmerizing presence.

Initially, he had to overcome the resistance of adult video producers allowing him to direct gay films under the name Chi Chi LaRue. For several years after he started, he worked under a variety of other pseudonyms, such as Taylor Hudson and Lawrence David, but eventually, even Falcon, a bastion of gay male machismo, permitted him to use his drag name.

Paciotti's ambition was to direct gay porn films, and he energetically pursued that goal. At Catalina, he moved from sales agent to a job in Catalina's promotion department where he supervised the design of box covers and ads.

Eventually, William Higgins, the owner of Catalina at the time, relented. He told LaRue, "Come up with a concept and lighting scheme for a segment in our Hard Men series, and you can go to San Francisco and direct the segment."

"That was the first thing I ever directed," Paciotti recalled, "and it was the best in the series."

Higgins sold the company before Paciotti ever got the chance to make another film. Scott Masters, who was Catalina's director of production, refused to let LaRue direct.

"He thought I was too big and too loud and too fun and too into everything. He said I'd never direct unless I lost one hundred pounds—and he was a heavy guy!" [Isherwood, 23]

One friend summed up his opinion on the industry: "Why should a big fat femme drag queen be telling gorgeous guys how to have sex?" [Isherwood, 25]

In 1989, LaRue left Catalina to take charge of marketing at InHand Video, where he was also given a chance to direct. The budgets were much smaller at InHand, and many videos were shot in a day or even in hours—but LaRue was given free rein. He made gay, straight, bisexual, transsexual, and lesbian porn, and he began to develop his style—a wild mix of imaginative sex, humor, and energy. While his "drag name" appeared in the credits, he did not direct his gay or straight movies in drag.

As LaRue explained, "I had no training; I didn't know what to do. They just kind of threw me into the job." [GayVN.com, 9/07, retrieved 10/21/07]

He made a handful of gay videos at InHand before moving on to Vivid Man, the gay line for Vivid Video, one of straight porn's largest and most profitable firms.

By the end of 1989, after only two full years of directing, LaRue had directed almost twenty gay videos. And he began to work for Catalina again. His first film after he came back was *Billboard*, which starred his "discovery" Joey Stefano, who would go on to become one of the major stars of the early nineties.

In 1990, LaRue won the AVN award for Best Director for his Catalina video, *The Rise*, which starred another "discovery," Ryan Yeager. By the end of 1991, he had made a handful of videos for Catalina and had been signed by Steven Scarborough to direct for Falcon's Mustang line. That same year, *Jumper*, one of the videos he made for yet another company, HIS Video, won the AVN award for Best Gay Video.

By the end of 1992, not even five full years after LaRue entered the industry, he had directed at least sixty videos. He made more than twenty videos in 1992 alone—mostly for Catalina and Falcon's Mustang line. And he again won the AVN award for Best Director of a gay video—for *Songs in the Key of Sex* (HIS Video), probably his most ambitious film to date.

LaRue's most ambitious as well as his most award-winning work in these early years was made for HIS Video, a subsidiary of VCA, one of the major straight porn companies. Both *Jumper* and *Songs in the Key of Sex* had well-developed scripts by Stan Ward (stage name Stan Mitchell) that required some degree of acting in addition to skills as an adult performer. *Jumper*, modeled somewhat on the 1978 Hollywood movie *Heaven Can Wait*, tells the story of a restless young man in Heaven, a former soldier who died in the Revolutionary War of 1783. He persuades the authorities in Heaven to let him come back to live out some of his unfulfilled dreams. *Songs in the Key of Sex* is about a young gay man, played by Randy Mixer, who is trying to make his way as a singer. He breaks up with his long-term boyfriend and gets involved with an alcoholic man, played by Jason Ross. *Songs* has original music and songs (lip-synced by Randy Mixer) in addition to nonsexual dramatic roles.

LaRue was astonishingly prolific. Over the next eight years (1993 to 2000), LaRue would make on average one video every other week—most directors might make one a month. He continued to work in a number of different genres. *Lost in Vegas* (1993) was an ambitious narrative movie based on the mainstream movie hit, *Leaving Las Vegas*—and dealt, like *Songs in the Key of Sex,* with the impact alcoholism on gay men. *Idol Thoughts* (Catalina, 1993) and *Idol Country* (HIS Video, 1994) were vehicles for superstar Ryan Idol. LaRue counted *Idol Country* as one of his best movies—in a comment made in 1999, LaRue put it his "top four." LaRue won the 1995 Gay Erotic Video Award for Best Director for his work on *Idol Country.* [Adam, 1999, 37]

Increasingly, he became known for his "wall-to-wall" sex films—often involving large groups of men, broken into smaller overlapping combinations of three or four men and climaxing in a large orgy scene. Wall-to-wall sex is one of the standard categories of modern pornographic videos. Nevertheless, wall-to wall sex movies require considerable planning and advanced preparation.

One of LaRue's biggest commercial successes was the Link series of all-sex movies (1997 to 2007). They were shot in a San Francisco leather bar, and the performers are dressed in leather, harnesses, chaps, and black denim. The sexual action takes place in dark, dimly-lit rooms, in slings, through glory holes, and in an enclosed area of chain-link fencing; there are fisting, a beer enema, and mild water sports. Many of the group sex scenes are performed by muscular, hairy men. The set, costumes, casting, and lighting create an atmosphere of underground and hidden places and rough, uninhibited sex. Despite their darkness and sexual intensity, LaRue himself characterized the *Link* movies as "leatherette movies because they're not heavy leather, even though they are total sex pig movies."

LaRue initially thought of *Bolt* (2004), one of his most successful recent movies, as another *Link*, but he took it in a completely different direction by making it bright and "clean" ("not the sex, the sex is dirty") rather than dark and dingy by using silvers, chromes, and Lucite [LaRue, unpublished interview]. In conjunction with *Bolt*, LaRue's company introduced a large industrial-style metallic bolt as a dildo, which is used throughout the movie. *Bolt*, like *Link*, is also a "total sex pig movie" though with a different sort of casting—younger men, more blondes, and the wearing of torn white jockey shorts and tank tops rather than leather. Consequently, it conveys a very different erotic atmosphere and mood from the Link movies.

LaRue is especially well-known for his orgy scenes. Group sex, particularly if it is a large group, is very difficult to choreograph. All-sex movies and orgies often have no discernable narrative structure, other than that they will start with oral sex and kissing, move on to rimming and fucking, and culminate in the money shots. However, the sexual activities are usually cumulative—the sucking, kissing, and rimming are added step by step. Only orgasms bring the sexual narrative to a conclusion.

Among the notable "wall-to-wall" sex movies are *Boot Black 1* (1994) and *Boot Black 2: Spit Shine* (1995) for HIS Video, *Dirty White Guys* (1996), *In the Mix* (1997) with an interracial cast, and the leather-themed *Link* series (*Link*, 1998, *Link 2 Link*, 1998, and *The Final Link*, 1999) for All Worlds, and a series of feature-length orgy videos for Jocks (*The New Pledgemaster*, Jocks, 1995; *Stock: Released*, Jocks, 1998; *Stock: Sentenced*, Jocks, 1998).

Casting was the key to the success of LaRue's erotic filmmaking—together with his skill for directing sex, his unparalleled talent for casting, and his ability to work fast and on small budgets. He could rapidly put a concept together and just as quickly make a video on a relatively low budget. By one estimate, he made more than a dozen movies for at least three different companies—InHand, Vivid, and Catalina—in his first year in the business.

From the very beginning of his career, LaRue found young men willing to appear in his videos—and from his first videos he was able to draw out strong sexual performances from them. He and William Higgins would often egg each other on when Higgins stopped by the Four Star every Friday night to catch LaRue's drag show.

"[H]e and I would dish about the cute boys in the bar," LaRue recalled. "He'd say, 'Go up and ask that one if he wants to do movies.' And I'd do it."

"I used the same formula for every person I've ever approached," Larue told Jerry Douglas.

> "I don't lie. I don't put across any fakeness. I'd walk up and I'd say, 'Hi, have you ever thought about doing porno movies?' Most of them answer, 'No, I've never thought about it.' or 'No, I could never do it.' But every once in a while, a cute one will say: 'Yes, I've thought about it.' And then I pursue it from there, the next step is I tell him how good-looking I think he is, would he like to come in for an interview?" [LaRue, *Manshots*, 10/91, 15]

Among the earliest of LaRue's major discoveries were handsome brunette top Ryan Yeager and pouty straight boy Andrew Michaels. LaRue had cast Michaels in *A Friendly Obsession*, one of the first videos he shot for Vivid Man. "I brought something out in him," LaRue recalled.

> "I got this little straight boy, who wouldn't do anything, [but] he progressively did more and more things for me as time went on. He was and always will be one of my favorite models.... He was such a good worker. He could get it up for

any woman, any man. He never had any trouble keeping a rubber on. He always did what I told him to do, and there was never a problem." [LaRue, *Manshots*, 10/91, 17]

Yeager had sent photographs of himself, wanting only to model for magazine layouts until LaRue explained there was little money in it. But over the course of four or five months they spoke regularly on the phone. Eventually, Yeager agreed to appear in *The Buddy System* (Vivid), a military-themed video LaRue had written specifically for him. In no time, LaRue knew he had a "natural."

"He arrived at the airport at two in the afternoon, I drove him to the location, and at four o'clock, shoved him in front of the camera for his first scene.... He was flawless. He gave me two cum shots in his very first scene, got fucked, and bit a chunk out of the ladder. He was a director's dream come true. He is a natural actor, he is a naturally nice guy, and he's naturally sexual. His dick stays up forever."

This was 1989, before Viagra.

One reason for LaRue's success is his ability to anticipate sexual chemistry between performers. Nevertheless, it's always a process.

"I talk to them and find out what they like before I put them together.... I make the set so comfortable for them they become compatible even if they're not. I let people do what feels good to them. If I want to see something specific, I'll tell them. If somebody wants to do something, I'll let him try it.... if there's a secret to my getting good sex, it's that it's a comfortable situation from the initial interview till we walk out the door and say it's a wrap." [LaRue, *Manshots*, 10/91, 16–17]

The biggest discovery of LaRue's early career was Joey Stefano, whom he described as having "that special something."

> "It's all about star quality, that great indefinable aura of glamour and fabulousness. If you have that trait, you can't hide it. Heads will turn when you walk into a room, and prospective sexual partners will throw themselves at your feet.... If you don't have it, you can't fake it. You'll just never have it.... [W]ith ... Joey Stefano, I knew it from the second I laid eyes on him." [LaRue/Erich, 111]

For LaRue, it was also love at first sight. And he didn't hesitate. He immediately cast Stefano in *Sharon and Karen*, which starred veteran porn actress Sharon Kane and drag performer Karen Dior, in a scene with Kane and Andrew Michaels, LaRue's "gay-for-pay" discovery.

In their scene, Kane was asked to fuck Stefano using a strap-on. "He brought his own," she recalled, though she was "amazed at how big it was. I thought he was an amazing performer—he was quite relaxed about it. That's when I fell in love with him."

Though both LaRue and Kane were in love with Stefano, they remained close friends and frequently worked together. Charles Isherwood, Stefano's biographer, was impressed that "the complexities of their romantic or emotional or sexual attachments didn't destroy their friendship.... Perhaps because they had sex—or orchestrated it—for a living, they didn't overvalue its importance as a validation of an emotional or spiritual bond." [Isherwood, 35]

• • •

Born Nicholas Iacona, Stefano grew up outside of Philadelphia in Chester, Pennsylvania. He dropped out of high school in 1983 not long after his father died—and quickly moved away from his family. He told LaRue and others that he supported himself by hustling.

From an early age, he was a serious user of drugs, including cocaine, heroin, and angel dust (PCP). He also had an avid interest in porn and an encyclopedic knowledge of performers in both gay and straight video. He was so knowledgeable, in fact, that he could identify a performer solely on the basis of an anatomical close-up.

Stefano's fascination with porn led him to attempt to pose for magazines, but not knowing anyone in the business, he went to the Jock Theatre in Manhattan where porn stars sometimes stripped, hoping to make a connection to the industry.

> "So I went to pay to watch one of these porn stars [Tony Davis]. I never heard of him before, because my porn star favorites are older guys from way back. I wound up talking to him, and he took my pictures and said he'd see what he could do because he knew some people. I called him a week later and bugged the shit out of him. He told me to come on out." [Isherwood, 15]

That's when Stefano flew out to Los Angeles and Davis took him to meet LaRue. From that point on, it was a "long, emotional roller coaster ride.... [A]nd it didn't end until Joey's death five years later." [LaRue/Erich, 113]

As LaRue remembers, "Joey did bang-up jobs for me in films like *Songs in the Key of Sex* (HIS Video, 1992) and ... InHand flick called *Fond Focus* (InHand, 1990). As time went on, though, the temptations of the fast-paced porn world began to take their toll on him. His drinking and drug use increased, and he got in this downward spiral that no one could seem to break him out of." [LaRue/Erich, 114]

The depth of LaRue's feelings for Stefano caused him a great deal of pain.

> "Joey could do no wrong in my eyes.... I was blinded by my affection for him, and anything he

did to me, no matter how cruel or thoughtless, I
could always find it in me to forgive. We never did
have sex.... It was a long period of hell for me;
many times I would drop him off at his place or
at a friend's, then drive home crying to myself out
of frustration and my love for him." [LaRue, 200]

The end finally came in 1994, while LaRue was out of town
shooting a film for Falcon. LaRue and the cast were waiting
for Joey, who was supposed to be in a scene. Stefano had promised LaRue that he'd remain sober. But when Stefano didn't
show, LaRue recalls:

"(I) started to get a really bad feeling. I called
home to check my messages, and there was one
... telling me that Joey had overdosed and was
in desperate condition at Cedars Sinai Medical
Center.... John Rutherford and I jumped in his
truck and rushed immediately to the hospital....
He was gone of an overdose—heroin and special
K, an animal tranquilizer—at the tender age of
26. Whether it was a suicide or a tragic accident
is something that's never been fully determined."
[LaRue/Erich, 115]

Throughout his career, LaRue produced a constant stream
of young men who wanted to work in porn. For several years
in the mid-nineties, his house was called "the Porn Motel"
because there would always be three or four performers staying there. The list of his discoveries—probably more than a
hundred—comes right up to the present.

In gay porn there is no greater master of the "all sex" video
than Chi Chi LaRue. Widely considered the best and most original director of sex scenes in gay porn today, he is also far and
away the most prolific director (probably approaching five
hundred or more videos) in the history of gay porn. Since the
late 1990s, he was also one of the leading directors of straight
porn—being the preferred director of such leading female per-

formers as Jenna James and Tara Patrick—though he left the straight industry when using condoms ceased to be required.

"I don't write stage directions on my scripts," LaRue told me, "only the dialogue. All the sex, all the movement comes out of my head. Sitting right there.... I'm a sex director." LaRue's improvisational style extends even to the preparation for future movies—visits to the hardware store can yield material for his next film: "I love water sports, so I do as much dirty water sports as I can get away with.... I'll go to a hardware store and look at anything weird that's used for gardening or hosing off the driveway and I'll think, 'Oh that'll look great up a butt!' and I'll buy and use it in a movie." [LaRue, unpublished interview]

Another notable aspect about LaRue is his directing style. He shouts out instructions ("Go down on him!"), encouragement ("Yeah, that's fucking hot! ... Harder, harder..."), and exclamations ("That's hot!") as he coaches the performers step by step through the sexual scene. He literally supplies the "sexual script" to the performers, the videographer, and the film crew while at the same time establishing his own sexual script as a framework. Although some performers are uncomfortable with LaRue's method, most find it valuable. Usually the biggest problems created by this approach occur in post-production when the sound editor must go through and meticulously strip LaRue's voice from the recorded sound track.

Through his drive, fertile erotic imagination, and prolific production, Chi Chi LaRue has emerged in the last decade as the dominant personality—director, impresario, and producer—of the gay adult entertainment industry. He has made hundreds of gay porn movies and many straight videos; has organized and continues to organize live strip shows and charity events around the country; has recruited and directed hundreds of performers; has published photo books of his stars; has founded one of the first popular internet live sex websites; and has started his own production company—within the last three years Channel One, his production company, has purchased All Worlds and Catalina Video to emerge as the largest company in the business.

So many of those who work in the adult film industry have ambitions to cross over and work in the mainstream film industry or some other area of entertainment. But LaRue says he has no interest in doing that: "For me the sex is it. I will make porn movies for as long as I can."

COMPANY MAN

In August of 1993, Chuck Holmes walked into John Rutherford's office and offered him the job of director of production for all four Falcon lines—Falcon, Jocks, Mustang, and Falcon International. Steven Scarborough had left in the middle of making the last two installments of his Abduction trilogy, and Rutherford and his team were in the midst of finishing it.

> "I shook in my shoes," Rutherford recalled. "I was thinking, 'Me?' I mean, with *Abduction 2* and *3* (*Conflict/Redemption*) I'd really been directing a lot. I mean directing, directing, directing, and thinking it was easy for me to be in that position because I could make all these great, great decisions, let my creativity flow and never have the responsibility of being told by the owner of Falcon, 'That's not a good idea.' And at that point, that came into my mind: 'Now I have to do the best job I can do. And I have to answer for it.'" [Rutherford, *Manshots*, 10/95, 13]

John Rutherford grew up in Redwood City, south of San Francisco. He attended college in the area, but was not sure of what he wanted to do. He thought about business, but wasn't good at math. He decided to go to school in Paris. He knew he was gay, but denied it to himself and continued to date girls. While in Paris, he met a young woman who worked as a movie extra.

Intrigued, he went with her to work. As he watched the director and the production crew at work, he thought: "God, this is fabulous. I want to do this."

He took some classes in Paris and worked frequently as an extra. When he returned to the United States, he attended the film production program at San Francisco State University, where he met a fellow film student, Todd Montgomery. They immediately fell in love.

After Rutherford graduated, a friend of his who put on strip shows using Falcon performers told Rutherford that Falcon was looking for production crew members. He asked if Rutherford was interested. Rutherford replied, "Are you kidding? I graduated with a degree. I'm doing corporate videos at Hewlett-Packard and ... production management on low-budget? There's no way I'm going to do that." [Rutherford *Manshots,* 10/95, 66–67; Barker, 24]

Rutherford reconsidered the suggestion when a couple of months later he wasn't making enough to pay his bills. Finding that the job was still available, he went into the Falcon offices to talk with Chuck Holmes.

"[W]hen I met Chuck Holmes and went to visit the offices, it was like going into the corporation I worked with in Silicon Valley—very well run, efficient. And I was very impressed." [Rutherford, *Manshots,* 10/95, 67]

Rutherford was hired as Steven Scarborough's assistant director. Slowly, he developed his own approach to erotic filmmaking. Initially, he felt creatively stifled.

> "I was doing what others wanted me to do. And I didn't feel that any of my other input was being utilized in the first year.... I take my jobs very seriously. I become a company man. I'm quiet for a long time, because I study things. I study the way people are. I study what they expect of me, how I can become most efficient.... [A]fter I got a grip on it ... then I started pushing my way in."

In his first year at Falcon, he was still in the process of coming to terms with his homosexuality. "It was like a puzzle. It just fit.... I was very closeted. My mother's a lesbian, and I think for a long time, it was hard for me to accept her sexuality because I was trying to deny my own." [Rutherford, *Manshots*, 10/95, 68]

Since Holmes had started the company, there had never been any production credits on Falcon films—neither the cinematographer, the director, nor the producer received any credits. For many years, the name "Bill Clayton" was used to identify anyone who spoke for Falcon—whether it was Chuck Holmes himself or one of his directors/cinematographers such as Matt Sterling or John Travis. This tradition of anonymity continued with Steven Scarborough. Rutherford, the company man, more than anyone, came to exemplify this tradition.

"There's a philosophy that Chuck [Holmes] started 30 years ago," Rutherford told *Blueboy* magazine.

> "It's not important who's making the movies. The most important thing is what you're seeing in our product and that you get off on that. And until recently there were no titles on Falcon movies, no credit for crews.... The reason why Falcon videos are Falcon videos is because there's a team here and there's a philosophy of how we do things. Seeing credits, 'John Rutherford,' is fun for me and it strokes my ego because I'm human, but I'm not the most important person here." [Barker, 24]

Under Rutherford, the development of a Falcon film continued to be, as it had been almost from the beginning, a group effort. It began with a meeting of the development director, production manager, and Rutherford as director of production. The planning started with the review of a list of performers who had been interviewed by the development director or who had contacted Falcon. The planning committee selected the models and then built a movie around them and specific locations. Then elements, ideas, and story lines were developed.

When a strong idea emerged Rutherford asked whoever had come up with it to write a script. When the script came back, Rutherford took it to Chuck Holmes, who would either give it the go-ahead or suggest changes.

• • •

Within a year of taking over from Scarborough, Rutherford began to put together his first major project as head of production. "Everyone was talking *Abduction 4*," Rutherford explained.

> "Now that wasn't me. *Abduction 2/3* was a part of me, but I wanted more story line. I wanted more than just sex. I wanted character development. Chuck [Holmes] believed in that. Chuck wanted that too. We all wanted it.... We wanted something that would bring back the *Touch Me* days, when we got the best picture for *Touch Me*. We wanted something with story line, character development, good sex in it.... I wanted to do something like [*Thelma and Louise*]." [Rutherford, *Manshots*, 12/95, 14]

In 1994, Falcon released *Flashpoint*, its annual big-budget feature and the first major feature produced under John Rutherford as head of production. *Flashpoint* is a road movie about the sexual adventures of Hal Rockland and Scott Baldwin. Like *Touch Me*, *Flashpoint* won the AVN Award for Best Gay Video as well as the Gay Erotic Video (GEV) award for Best Video, while Rutherford won both the AVN and GEV awards for director.

Like Chi Chi LaRue, Rutherford stresses the importance of the filmmaker's attitude toward performers—he believes that filmmakers should do everything to keep alive that sense of possibility and desire. "It's really very important to keep the sexual energy and tension going, which ultimately passes on

to the viewer.... The viewer is alone in his living room enjoying the fantasy and maybe daydreaming about our guys."

In 2000 Rutherford made one of his most ambitious films—
the annual Falcon big two-part "travelogue" called *Out of
Athens*—starring Falcon exclusives Johnny Brosnan, Travis
Wade, and Cameron Fox. Based on Rutherford's own experience as a young man, "*Out of Athens* was my story, I decided
to take three months off and go to Europe after high school.
And I traveled around Greece.... I did a loose story [based] on
my travels and the conflict of being who you are." [Barker, 25]

DECLINE AND FALL

In September 2000, Chuck Holmes died from complications of
HIV/AIDS at age fifty-five. Within a short period of time, Falcon Studios found itself in a dramatically altered situation.
After twenty-eight years, it not only had lost its fiercely opinionated and iron-willed leader, but in his will, Holmes established the Charles M. Holmes Foundation to promote gay civil
rights and gave the foundation complete ownership and control over Falcon Studios and all its subsidiary businesses,
including the website, streaming videos, and sex accessories.

Rutherford, who had served as the executive vice president
and director of production, was named president of Falcon Studios—Conwest Resources was Falcon's corporate name. Terry
Mahaffey, who had come to Falcon in 1996 from the old-line gay
porn producer Le Salon and had served as controller and vice
president of finance, became the chief financial officer.

Holmes's will also established a board of directors that consisted of the company's high-level management to guide the
studio in the immediate aftermath of his death—specifically
mandating that it continue to produce adult films "in the Falcon style," which was spelled out in detail in the will.

Holmes's death brought a new player onto the scene: Terry
Bean, an Oregon-based real estate developer and gay political

activist, was named executor of Holmes's will. Holmes and Bean had become close friends when they served on the board of the Washington, D.C.-based Human Rights Campaign, the nation's largest and most influential gay rights lobbying group. As the executor of Holmes's estate and later as the president of the Holmes Foundation (which was established in 2002), Bean played an active role in the direction and management of Falcon Studios—though he knew nothing about the adult entertainment business.

Over the years, Chuck Holmes often told John Rutherford, "When I die, I don't want those lights to flicker." At the time of Holmes's death, Rutherford was in the middle of shooting *Bounce*, a vehicle for "Lifetime Falcon Exclusive" Matthew Rush—a young bodybuilder of mixed racial heritage who was the biggest gay porn star of the late 1990s. [Barker, 24] Though Rutherford grieved Holmes deeply, he decided not to stop the production. Instead, he asked his close friend and longtime Falcon colleague Chi Chi LaRue to direct two of the scenes. It was the first time LaRue directed any scenes for a Falcon movie since he had been hired by Steven Scarborough in 1991 to direct the videos for the Mustang- and Jocks-branded lines.

Once *Bounce* was completed, Rutherford went on to shoot *The Other Side of Aspen 5*, the latest installment of Falcon breakthrough films from the late seventies. As soon as the first sex scene was shot, Rutherford instinctively went to call Chuck Holmes and tell him about it when he realized "'There's nobody there to call; I'm the last stop.' ... that was difficult. It made me nervous." [Barker, 25]

Rutherford lamented:

> "After [Holmes's] passing Falcon was run by a board of directors that he elected in his will to run the studio. After the first year, I quickly noticed that everything had changed ... the sprit that once was, was no longer—it became a business. The board focused more on trying to meet

projections and goals, rather than on what Chuck and I believed was the recipe for Falcon's success—making damn good movies with the world's best looking men." [Rutherford, interview, 12/06]

Rutherford understood that success involved more than mere formula. "Both desire and passion must be present in front of the camera and behind the camera as well. If you don't like, enjoy and believe in what you do, you won't be successful in this business." [Clarke, 59]

When Rutherford and LaRue tied for Best Director at the 2000 GayVN award show—Rutherford for *Out of Athens* and LaRue for *Echoes*—they discussed making a movie together. Working together on *Bounce* reinforced that idea. In 2002, Rutherford and LaRue moved ahead on the idea of codirecting. The video they made was *Deep South: The Big and the Easy* (FVP 144), one of Falcon's big annual feature productions, another "travelogue" to be shot in New Orleans. It follows a private investigator played by Falcon Exclusive Josh Weston, who must go to New Orleans on the trail of the missing Jeremy Jordan.

The movie was huge commercial success. Reviewer Brent Blue concluded, "It's been a long time since there was a porn extravaganza with the magnitude and force of *Deep South*. Directors Chi Chi LaRue and John Rutherford absolutely outdo themselves in creating a vivid piece full of complex characters, a sturdy well-developed plot, thanks to [writer] Jordan Young and some of the most gnawing sexual force you're likely to find any time soon.... Put simply, this is gay porn at its best." [Blue] (http://mannet.com/cgi-bin/ultimatebb-cgi?ubb=get _topic&f=2&t=000569, retrieved on 9/7/2008)

• • •

While Chuck Holmes was alive, he had been an active participant in Democratic Party politics as well as a major financial contributor, his goal being to promote gay rights in the United States. After his death, Terry Bean sought to continue that work by providing funds from the estate to host meetings with President Bill Clinton and other Democratic leaders in Washington to discuss gay issues. Between 2000 and 2002, the Holmes estate made major donations to a number of Democratic causes in Oregon, including the gubernatorial race of Ted Kulongoski. When it became known that contributions had come from the estate of a producer of gay porn videos, Kulongoski's campaign returned a $15,000 donation.

Bean sought to downplay the significance of Falcon's adult video business—at one point telling *The Oregonian*, the state's leading newspaper, that "Conwest does produce some male erotic videos. It also does a lot of other post-production things and documentaries in other arenas." As Bean explained, "the adult video portion—primarily Falcon Studios—is less than half of Conwest's business, although he could not provide specifics or estimates of the company's overall revenues." [Hogan, 6/26/02]

Under Bean's direction, the estate and the foundation continued to support many of Holmes's causes and made contributions to many organizations serving the gay community, notably the Human Rights Campaign Fund and the San Francisco Lesbian, Gay, Bisexual and Transgender Community Center—which renamed its building in honor of Holmes when the estate pledged $1 million.

However, by 2002, the foundation's board increasingly found the Falcon legacy a liability in its attempts to advance its political and philanthropic mandate. On the other side, many of those managing Falcon Studios felt that Terry Bean knew nothing about the adult industry and had no interest in it—though it was the primary source of the estate's endowment.

Discussions soon began to take place about the possibility of selling Falcon Studios/Conwest Resources. Rutherford, the man most committed to upholding the Chuck Holmes legacy, proposed that Conwest purchase Colt Studios, which had been put up for sale by its founder Jim French. Colt was a classic "beefcake" studio and was considered more "artistic" and less "pornographic" than Falcon. Rutherford thought that such a move presented a "great opportunity" for Falcon. The Foundation rejected the idea. Rutherford also seems to have made an offer to buy Falcon from the foundation, but was again rebuffed. [Rutherford, 2008]

On April 4, 2003, Rutherford resigned from Falcon Studios. In June of that year, he and his partner Tom Settle announced their purchase of Colt Studios. Terry Mahaffey, who had been at Falcon since 1996 as the controller and vice president for finance, was named president, chief financial officer, and chief creative officer. Todd Montgomery, a business consultant who had worked at Levi Strauss for many years, was named vice president and chief operating officer.

With Rutherford gone, Chi Chi LaRue emerged as the lead director for Falcon and continued to direct movies for all Falcon brands. In March 2004, LaRue suffered a mild heart attack just as he was about leave for London to direct *Taking Flight*, Falcon's annual two-part "travelogue." Since it was too late to cancel the production, Falcon hired Chris Steele, the script's author and a former performer, who had directed only one video previously. Nevertheless, *Taking Flight* became one of Falcon's all-time best-selling videos.

Soon Steele was named Falcon's new director of production. It had been almost a year since John Rutherford had vacated that position. Almost immediately, Steele and the Falcon management began planning for the next year's big-budget two-part production. They selected a script (*Cross Country*) by Jack Shamama and Michael Stabile, the authors of *Wet Palms*, a highly publicized gay porn soap opera serial that ran on the Naked Sword porn website.

When LaRue recovered from his heart attack, he decided, after ten years of working for Falcon, to limit his directing to videos for his own company, Rascal Video. His last video for Falcon was *Heaven to Hell*—the story of an angel sexually tempted by the Devil and cast into hell. It was shot in December 2004 and released in 2005. It was the only movie in the history of Falcon Studios in which the cast consisted entirely of Falcon exclusives.

● ● ●

In August 2004, Conwest Resources, Falcon's corporate parent, announced that it had agreed to sell itself to the newly formed 3 Media Corporation for an undisclosed amount. 3 Media was owned by two of Falcon's managers, Terry Mahaffey and Todd Montgomery (not the well known videographer of the same name), in partnership with former Conwest board member Steve Johnson. Mahaffey remained as Falcon's CEO and chief of production, and Montgomery became president and CEO of 3 Media.

Once LaRue left at the end of 2004, except for Terry Mahaffey, the creative direction of Falcon was almost entirely in new hands—with Chris Steele as director of production. He was joined by Rod Barry as the new director of talent development. Production on Jocks and Mustang was suspended pending "rebranding" and repackaging of the subsidiary lines. In early 2006, John Bruno, the owner of Massive Video, was brought on to relaunch the Mustang line around the beefy muscular models he used in his own Massive movies. Later that year, Chad Donovan, a director and former Falcon performer, took Barry's place as the head of talent development. In November 2006 Steele resigned from Falcon. Donovan briefly took over as the director of production. Then he, too, left.

In May 2008, Todd Montgomery, the managing partner since Rutherford had left, was forced out. Steve Johnson, the last of the original three partners who had purchased the studio from the Chuck Holmes Foundation, took over the reins. Today, the Falcon brand is in crisis. Rutherford's departure initiated years of turmoil and change, marked by a seemingly accelerating turnover in personnel that dramatically affected Falcon's role as the industry leader and as a commercially successful business.

At the time of Holmes's death, Falcon Studios, along with All Worlds Video, was one of the largest companies in the gay porn industry. Although they operated with diametrically opposite business models, they were the dominant companies of the 1990s. While Falcon continues to put out releases on its Falcon, Jocks, Mustang and Falcon International lines, the traditional Falcon packaging has been dropped. It is constantly tinkering with different packaging styles and has even gone so far as to retitle earlier films. The company appears to be lurching from director to director, releasing videos in a number of different styles. There is no longer an identifiable Falcon style.

REFERENCES

Adam Gay Video (AGV) Erotica *The Top 40 Films of Chi Chi LaRue* (Los Angeles: Knight Publishing, 1999).

Adam Gay Video (AGV) Erotica *The Falcon Movies of John Rutherford* (Los Angeles: Knight Publishing, 2000).

Keith Barker, "The Emperor of Erotica," *Blueboy*, October 2001.

Georges Bataille, *The Tears of Eros* (San Francisco: City Lights Books, 1989).

Brent Blue, "Deep South," Review, Mannet.com

Ethan Clarke, "John Rutherford: Falcon's Top Man," *All Man*, January 2003.

Dave Hogan, "Democratic Contributor Linked to Gay Porn," *The Oregonian*, June 26, 2002.

Charles Isherwood, *Wonder Bread and Ecstasy: The Life and Death of Joey Stefano* (Los Angeles: Alyson, 1996).

Brady Jansen, "Phoenix Rising," *GayVN*, Supplement to AVN, November 2007.

"Chi Chi LaRue, Behind the Camera:" Interview by Jerry Douglas, *Manshots*, October 1991.

"Everything's Coming Up Chi Chi LaRue," GayVN.com, September 21, 2007.

Chi Chi LaRue commentary, *More of a Man* (Douglas dir: Channel 1 dvd, Platinum Collection Edition).

Chi Chi LaRue with John Erich, *Making It Big: Sex Stars, Porn Films and Me* (Los Angeles: Alyson, 1997).

Parker Moore, "Man of the House," *Men Magazine* (Hot House, special collector's edition), May 2007.

"John Rutherford, Behind the Camera:" Interview by Jerry Douglas, *Manshots*, Part 1, October 1995; Part 2, December 1995.

John Rutherford, interview, GayNYCity.com, February 2006.

John Rutherford, johnrutherfordblog.blogspot.com/2008 Retrieved 9/18/2008.

"Steven Scarborough, Behind the Camera:" Interview by Jerry Douglas, *Manshots*, August 1996.

Joseph Slade, *Pornography in America* (Santa Barbara: ABC-CLIO, 2000).

Wendy Steiner, *The Scandal of Pleasure: Art in an Age of Fundamentalism* (Chicago: University of Chicago Press, 1995).

CHAPTER TEN

Star Power

Stars are essentially worthless and absolutely central.

—WILLIAM GOLDMAN, QUOTED IN
THE STAR MACHINE [523]

Early in the morning of March 20, 1998, Ryan Idol jumped or fell—it's unclear which—three and a half stories onto the street below. He was wearing only his boxer shorts. After falling to the pavement in a fetal position, he was, amazingly enough, only mildly injured—a few cracked ribs and a broken elbow. He also fractured his pelvis. He spent four days unconscious in the hospital, and when he woke, he could remember nothing about the fall. It took place only four days before his debut in the off-Broadway nude comedy, *Born for Porn*.

Since his entry into the world of gay porn in 1990, Ryan Idol had aspired to Jeff Stryker's superstar status. Discovered by Matt Sterling, Idol was six-feet-two, matinee-idol handsome, and muscular. He was following in Stryker's footsteps: purportedly straight, obviously masculine, and sexually dominant. In his first movie, *Idol Eyes*, he was strictly trade: no kissing, no sucking his partner's cock, only getting his own sucked and then fucking Joey Stefano. As the title suggested, he was there to be worshiped, for spectators and his costars to *idolize*. His movies sold extremely well, and he went on to a handful more before drugs, alcohol, and his longstanding ambivalence about his sexuality took their toll.

LAST DAYS OF THE SUPERSTARS

Ryan Idol's career as a superstar started to unravel before the fall. In 1995 he had inexplicably withdrawn from a major two-picture deal for which he was to be paid $50,000—a fee considerably in excess of the $2,000 most top performers were paid per scene—and in the following year he had drunkenly trashed a New York hotel room. Police found evidence of his work as an escort, which led to the arrest and conviction of his agent, David Forest, on pandering and tax evasion charges. [Groff, 43-50]

In January 1995, Idol won the AVN award for Best Gay Performer for his performance in *Idol Country*. The film received rave reviews. *Manshots'* reviewer concluded:

> "*Idol Country* represents a high-water mark for all concerned. Director Chi Chi LaRue has never been better, guiding the video with the sure hand of a master at the top of his form. The script ... tells a story that never gets in the way of the sex, (but rather) moves the action forward with tension and intelligence.... The cast is, without exception, terrific... which brings us full circle back to Mr. Idol who is quite simply magnificent.... He has managed to enter *Idol Country* a super star and emerge a legend." [Richie, *Manshots*, 8/95, 64]

Idol Country sold so well that VCA/HIS Video, its producer, offered Idol $50,000 for his next two pictures. Developed by the same team that made *Idol Country*, the new film, set in jail, was called *Idol Corruption*. However, just days before shooting was due to start, the film was canceled. Just as quickly, it was revived—with a new director, Gino Colbert, a new script about a closeted Hollywood movie star, and a new title: *Matinee Idol*. Colbert, a former gay and bisexual performer, had practically grown up in the business—his parents owned a burlesque palace; he also served as a bridge between the straight and gay sides of the industry. Brought in by VCA to save the movie, Colbert worked out a deal with Idol's manager in which Idol would perform in three of the film's seven scenes: he was to be orally serviced in the first scene, and he would perform fellatio and rim in the other two. Idol had final say for the casting of his onscreen sex partners, and he would insist on their taking HIV tests—despite the fact that condoms would be routinely used in the film. [Kazan, *Manshots*, 4/96, 12]

Colbert planned to start shooting on May 22, 1995, but as the first day approached, filming was again postponed, this time because Colbert had not been able to find a costar who satisfied Idol. Shooting was postponed three more times: once because Idol had caught his penis in his fly and was too injured to perform, another time because he had again exercised his veto on a scene partner and requested a new model, who had to be flown in from Atlanta, and a third time because he had been on a dancing gig out of town, had partied too much, and was hospitalized with an unspecified ailment. By then Forest told Colbert that Idol wanted to opt out of the project altogether and had decided not to make any more gay porn movies.

At that point, an exasperated Colbert called the producers and proposed replacing Idol and making the movie with another star. Otherwise, they would lose their investment. They agreed, and Colbert shot two scenes with the cast who had been hired—neither of which ever made it into the final cut of *Matinee Idol*. Colbert approached David Forest about another performer he represented, Ken Ryker.

Following in the footsteps of Stryker and Idol, the muscular and blond Ken Ryker has been groomed to be the next superstar. And like those before him, Ryker identified as a gay-for-pay top. Six feet four inches tall with a twelve-inch penis, Ken Ryker had been discovered by agent Dan Byers, of Denver, Colorado.

• • •

Several years earlier, Ryker had moved to the San Fernando Valley just north of Los Angeles, where he was employed as a construction worker. Every morning on his way to work, he noticed a group of handsome and well-built young men with expensive cars and attractive girlfriends lounging by the pool of his apartment complex. They were Aaron Austin, Derek Cruise, and Ty Russell—three of gay porn's biggest names at the time. His curiosity piqued, he asked Austin, who was his next-door neighbor, what they all did for a living.

Austin answered, not too convincingly, "We're dancers."

If that was what they did, Ryker said that he wanted to dance too.

Not sure what to say next, Austin conceded, "We do gay porno."

"But you all have girlfriends?" Ryker asked uncertainly.

"Yeah ... it's great money," Russell explained.

Ryker decided that he wanted to make some gay porno too. Austin put Ryker in touch with Dan Byers. After seeing some Polaroids, Byers flew Ryker out to Denver. "He was a beautiful young man with humongous piece of meat, and the instant I saw him, it clicked, he's going to be a star. The only thing was that he never had sex with a guy...."

As he's done with many of the straight and bisexual men he represents, Byers personally taught Ryker how to have sex with a man—how to suck cock, how to work up his saliva, how to control a money shot, how to use a condom.

When it came time to demonstrate anal sex, Byers brought in someone else. "I don't bottom, so I had him fuck another guy for me to see how that went; I taught him everything....

They know and trust me and I'm not using them as a sexual toy. These are guys who have to learn how to get turned out by another guy." [Skee, 33, 82]

Ryker signed on for *Matinee Idol*, which, once it was recast, was shot in a week. It became one of Colbert's most successful movies—according to reviewer Jerry Douglas, his "finest film thus far."

• • •

A recent poll published in *Men's Health* magazine (January–February 2006) found that for most readers, becoming a porn star was their number-one fantasy career. But in the 1980s and 1990s, growing up and becoming a *gay* porn star was probably not a very common fantasy among young men— even young gay men. Discovering one's "talent" for performing sex in public was not so obvious in the age before the Internet and webcams. After all, sex wasn't yet a spectator sport, like basketball or tennis. Porn stars are made, not born.

Jeff Stryker, Ryan Idol, and Ken Ryker were not only performers; they were also a form of human capital—an investment to help guarantee the sales of gay porn movies. Like any other kind of human capital, they were created through investments: through the presentation of a physical image (hair, body, endowment) and the creation of a persona—straight, aloof, strongly masculine, and sexually dominant—that appealed to the men who consumed porn. And in an age when AIDS put limits on the sexual liberty of gay men, Stryker, Idol, and Ryker were designed to be men who would not be infected. They were not anally penetrated, they were not sexually versatile—they were men who would not be vectors of disease.

The gay porn industry's reigning superstars between 1985 and 1997, they were all "made" by directors (Matt Sterling and John Travis for Stryker) or agents (David Forest for Idol and Dan Byers for Ryker), all of whom stood to earn something from the success of their protégés. They consciously sought to build a mystique around each of the prospective stars and heavily promoted their name recognition. These efforts paid off in sales (as far as one can gauge without reported earnings) and industry awards. In each case, the mystique rested on a calculated strategy of aloofness, presumed heterosexuality, and a constricted sexual role that helped to sustain an air of mystery.

Idol and Ryker found it is difficult to maintain that aloof Garbo-like presence over an extended period of time. In addition, both Idol and Ryker contended with personal problems and experienced ambivalence about their roles in gay porn. Neither appeared able to achieve an economically secure career. Only Stryker seemed able to achieve any kind of economic security and maintain a strategy of aloofness over the course of a decade-long career—enhanced, in part, by working in the straight industry.

The two leading performers of the early twentieth-first century, Jason Adonis, a performer who has evolved from gay-for-pay into a self-acknowledged bisexual, and Matthew Rush, a "Lifetime Falcon Exclusive" and self-identified gay man, managed to approach, though not achieve, superstar status. Both of these men adopted the aloof role adopted by Stryker and Idol; however, unlike these superstars of the 1980s, neither Adonis nor Rush were able to sustain the superstar role. They were not able to refrain from a wide variety of sexual activities—in part because the generation of performers that came between Stryker, Idol, and Ryker and the era of Adonis and Rush had "professionalized" the role of the porn star; they had managed to generate charisma and a burst of sexual energy that made the 1980s superstars seem stiff and wooden rather than merely straight and aloof.

Jeff Stryker's incredible success created the niche within the gay porn business for straight male performers. Ryan Idol and Ken Ryker followed in his footsteps and paved the way for straight-identified performers who are less than superstars. Today, some 30 to 40 percent of performers in gay porn are said to be "gay-for-pay." Nevertheless, the era of the *superstar* is over.

HOW TO BECOME A PORN STAR
IN THE NINETIES

The gay men in their twenties who "came out" in the 1990s had created a new gay aesthetic style: new ways of dressing, new music, and new drugs—Special K (ketamine, a cat tranquilizer) was a favorite. By 1995, *New York* magazine reporter Craig Horowitz had noted:

> "The change in attitude is clearly visible around the city. The return of vintage seventies promiscuity has sparked a small boom in theaters, dance clubs, bars and variety of other venues that have back rooms and private cubicles for sex." [33]

"[A] generation of post-AIDS babies seemed to rediscover the lost joys of gay sex," observed Michael Callen, one of the "inventors" of safer sex. [Horowitz, 33]

One harbinger of the new sexual upsurge was retired porn star Scott O'Hara's sex 'zine *Steam,* which rated alleys, tearooms, and clubs around the country on the quality of sex encountered there. Another sign was the publication of a new edition of *The Joy of Gay Sex* (1992)—the first edition had been published before AIDS and was part of the bestselling *Joy of Sex* franchise published in the seventies at the height of the sexual revolution.

In the nineties, gay adult film producers experienced an economic boom as many gay men turned to porn as a substitute for casual sex. The number of films in production increased dramatically, production budgets grew, and production values improved among the major companies. In addition, as condom use gradually became the norm for anal intercourse among gay men and in gay porn films, younger gay men sought to become "porn stars."

Unlike the masculine, aloof, and ostensibly straight stars of the eighties and early nineties, the gay porn star of the late nineties was something new—a professional. Whether gay or straight, this new kind of gay porn star showed variety in his sexual performances, could top or bottom, kissed, sucked cock, rimmed, and used sex toys.

• • •

The first sign of the professional's arrival was visible at the 1996 AVN Awards ceremony in Las Vegas. The poster boy for the new generation was Kurt Young. Dark and classically handsome, Young won an AVN triple crown: Best Performer (for his role in *Flesh and Blood*), Performer of the Year, and Newcomer of the Year. In the same year, at the Gay Erotic Video Awards, he won Best Actor (again for *Flesh and Blood*) and Newcomer of the Year; and at the 1996 Men in Video Awards he won Best Actor, again for his role in *Flesh and Blood*. Six awards in his first year as a performer.

In 2003 he was inducted into the GayVN (Gay industry/Adult Video News) Hall of Fame. "Kurt Young is the most talented, intuitive actor I've worked with," said Jerry Douglas, noting as well that "He's the most dependable sexualist I've worked with ... I adore him as a person." [Lambert 9/30/96, ret. 4/27/08] Douglas went on to cast Young in two other films, *Family Values* (1997) and *Dream Team* (1998).

As a teenager Kurt Young's ambition was to become an Olympic gymnast. Through high school he wasn't aware of any attraction to men, but while in college at the University of Maryland, he and his girlfriend frequently went to Trax, a gay disco club in Washington, D.C., on "mixed nights." Since Trax "was the best club in D.C.," he started going on his own or with female friends and fraternity brothers on the gay nights. Men frequently hit on him or asked him out, and while he was flattered, he refused, explaining that he was straight. Yet when he went, "I'd like to be all pumped up and look my best. And I'd wear gay clothing ... something tight... short shorts, cutoff shorts, the big socks and the boots..." He told his friends,

"Eventually, I would sleep with a guy ... just to experiment."
[Young, *Manshots*, 6/96, 67]

Young ended up sleeping with one of his female roommate's
ex-boyfriends, Matthew Easton. Though he continued to date
women for several months, he had sex regularly with Easton.
He preferred sex with a man and gradually admitted to his
friends that he was gay.

Soon Young and Easton moved to Los Angeles, where they
rented an apartment in Santa Monica and began to look for
work. Young took a job as a lifeguard and also taught swim-
ming at two different gyms. Easton was a frequent viewer of
gay porn and was interested in seeing if he could get work performing in porn films. When he saw an ad in *Frontiers*, a local
gay paper, placed by veteran porn agent Johnny Johnston, he
met with Johnston—with some trepidation. "I was scared,
actually, I thought I'd go in, some old guy would want me to
suck his dick or try to suck me, and it would be a scam. But it
was pretty professional."

Easton's first shoot went very smoothly. The director was
longtime veteran Jim Steel. "I didn't know how many people
were going to be there," he told Jerry Douglas. "I didn't know
if I could do it. They told me that they'd like me to get fucked.
I'd be doing some sucking, and it shouldn't take that long."

After his first shoot, Easton was elated.

> "In my head, I said, 'This is great.' and I said,
> 'This is bad news 'cause this is something I could
> get trapped in.' I was happy to have the money.
> I couldn't wait to go home and show Kurt and
> say, 'Look, I worked today and I got this much
> money.' And I couldn't wait to get furniture and
> stuff for our house. But I knew it would be bad
> news, because it was, in my opinion, easy
> money." [Easton, *Manshots*, 8/98, 57, 78]

After four hours of work, Easton came home with "a nice
check." That spurred Young to consider doing porn as well.

[Lambert, 9/30/96]. They discussed whether or not performing in the porn movies would affect their relationship. "It's only business," Easton explained. "It's just work. It's not that big of a deal. You go in there and kind of do it. And it's like you think about the money." Easton's explanation reassured Young. "That made it good," he told *Manshots*. "If he could do it, then I could do it. That's what I thought." Within days, Young met Easton's agent, and almost immediately Image Video offered him an exclusive contract—after they'd shot a trial scene to see how he performed.

Within a few months, Image Video lent Young out to the legendary Matt Sterling to shoot *Tradewinds* with Derek Cameron. Compared to the director of his early scenes shot for Image (at the time they were called Man's Best), Sterling was very demanding and knew exactly what he wanted:

> "[He] wanted it *exactly* like this, *exactly* like that. And do this again, and do that again. It was good though. 'Cause he told me *exactly* what to do, *exactly* what he wanted. I do like that and not having to wing it, improvise on my own.... He is very, very strict about dialog, and wants you looking in the exact same place. You do it over and over and over again until it's exactly how he wants it."

Sterling also was strict about choreographing the sex.

> "He had everything written down," Young recalled. "He's like 'I need this shot. This position with this shot, this shot, this shot, and this shot, this position from this angle.' It was all written down and just basically checked it off as the day went on. And I liked that 'cause I knew exactly how much longer I needed to be there." [Young, *Manshots*, 6/96, 78]

Tradewinds was a smash hit, and Young emerged from it as

a major star. Winfred Scott wrote that "Director Matt Sterling, the undisputed king of glamour, has done it again, *Tradewinds* is filled with beautiful men, intense sex, and spectacular videography. In fact, the last seventeen minutes of this film may well qualify as the best sexual scene in Sterling's long and memorable career." That last scene starred Young and Derek Cameron. [Young, *Manshots*, 6/96, 44] The Gay Video Guide Awards named the final scene of *Tradewinds* 1996's "Best Sex Scene."

After launching his career with *Hot Summer of Sex* and making *Tradewinds* with director Matt Sterling, Young went on to make *Beverly Hills Hustlers,* which featured Andy Warhol "superstar" Holly Woodlawn in a nonsexual role, *Heat of Passion* in a scene with Easton, *Men Only, On the Prowl,* and Jerry Douglas's porn noir masterpiece *Flesh and Blood* in his first year in the business.

Eventually, by the end of 1996, Easton and Young split up.

> "The industry played a part," Easton told Jerry Douglas, "as far as just pulling us apart. We were both going in different ways in the industry. I think he started really liking all the attention he was getting, and I was looking at it from a stand-point of just fucking and getting a check. I think I was being more of a money whore and he was Young,being an attention whore." [Easton, *Man-shots,* 6/98, 79]

Young became involved with fellow porn performer and director David Thompson, and together they formed a dance company that toured the country.

Despite Young's success, he was ambivalent about working in porn.

> "Every now and then," he explained, "I do get this little thing—it's just totally ingrained in my mind that it is wrong with a guy. I was raised in this

way. So it's still there, and every now and then I just get a little shock. Oh, they're very rare. But every now and then I just get these little thoughts: 'Wait a second. This isn't supposed to be.' But then I realize I do like it. I'm very comfortable with it. I am now." [Young, *Manshots*, 6/96, 79]

One reason he enjoyed traveling and performing in his dance company was that "it's something I like to do, it makes me happy, and it has nothing to do with sex." [Lambert, 9/30/96]

By the time Kurt Young left the business a mere two years later (in 1998), he was the most award-winning actor in the history of the gay porn industry. Jim Buck, who followed Young into the industry one year later, did almost as well in his three years as a performer.

Modeled on *Midnight Cowboy*, *Mardi Gras Cowboy* (All Worlds, 1996) the low-budget porn parody made by local film-maker Vidkid Timo in New Orleans, launched Jim Buck (who took his professional name from the lead character of John Schlesinger's X-rated Academy Award–winning film) on his short but spectacular career as a porn star.

Buck was born in 1969 and grew up on farm in Louisiana. He was the oldest of four boys. Until he left junior high school, he was very religious. "It's sort of an easy way of allaying the fear of homosexuality," he explained, "because it precludes the possibility of it. 'I'm devoutly religious, I'm a Southern Baptist; ergo, there's no way I can be homosexual.'" [Buck, *Manshots*, 2/98, 55] By the time he was fourteen, things had begun to change. Buck met another teenager who was openly gay, the brother of one of his sister's friends. They met at a party, made out, and had sex. They soon started going, at the age of fourteen, to a local gay bar outside of town using fake IDs.

About the same time, Buck also discovered public rest-rooms, which as he said "really appealed to my tawdry side. I always have had this fascination with the sordid." [Buck, *Man-*

shots, 2/98, 55] He had discovered the possibility of sex there while at a high school football game. While he stood at a urinal, an older man came up to him and started playing with himself, and Buck clued into the fact that sex could be had there. After that he started hanging out in public restrooms. [Buck, *Manshots*, 2/98, 55]

He came out while at college. At a local gay bar (he was still underage) he met and fell in love with a former porn star, Drew Kelly, who lived in the town where his college was located. Eventually, his friends caught on, and Buck came out to his girlfriend before anyone else could tell her.

Vidkid Timo, a local amateur filmmaker who had been making non-pornographic comedy shorts for years before he made *Cowboy*, was inspired to make a porn movie set in New Orleans by the experience of Wash West, who had made his first film about a well-known local drag performer called Squishy.

Buck was in his mid-twenties when Timo approached him in the gym and asked Buck to star in *Mardi Gras Cowboy*. Even though being in porn had "Never, ever, ever... occurred to me," he immediately replied, "Sure!" [Buck, *Manshots*, 2/98, 57] When the film was done, Timo sent a copy to Wash West, who had just moved to Los Angeles to pursue his career as an adult filmmaker. West was impressed, and considered *Mardi Gras Cowboy* a "perfect parody" with a great porn story. He put Timo in touch with Rick Ford at All Worlds, who released *Mardi Gras Cowboy*. But more than anything, West was especially struck by Buck's performance and proposed to Buck that they make a movie together.

It was the first time since West had starting making porn in L.A. that he felt he was "working with a model who has this great erotic vision" interacting with his own. "Kind of like the camera and the model having sex. Basically he became my muse.... [H]e could not only look beautiful and perform sexually in incredible ways, but he could carry a story line, he could develop a character. It was just like a gift." [West, 9/00, 14] Buck was not only an electrifying sexual performer, but also a superb character actor with a great sense of comic timing. He was primarily an actor who was able to incorporate sex into his repertoire.

Over the next year, West cast Buck in three movies. The first was *Dr. Jerkoff and Mr. Hard* (BIG, 1996), less a strict parody of Robert Louis Stevenson's novel than a tale about the transformation of a nerdy, frumpy, sexually repressed and closeted young professor into a hot young gay man. This was followed by *Tool Box* (1997) and *The Naked Highway* (BIG, 1997).

Buck also worked with Chi Chi LaRue on *Gold Diggers*, which LaRue counted as one of the top forty films of his career (which had begun in the late 1980s). "I loved working with Jim Buck," LaRue recalled. "He and Jay Anthony play bitchy queens who are forced to have sex together. They take turns fucking each other, then come together on a glass table." [AGV LaRue 1999, 30]

The 1997 AVN/GayVN Awards marked Buck and Wash West's triumphal arrivals. Following almost exactly in Kurt Young's footsteps from the previous year, Buck won the award for Best Performer for his role in *Naked Highway*, and for Newcomer of the Year. He also won that year's Gay Erotic Video Awards as Best Performer for his role in *Dr. Jerkoff and Mr. Hard* and as Performer of the Year.

Buck wasn't available to receive his Performer of the Year award at the AVN Award ceremony. "Jim can't be here tonight," explained his twelve-year-old brother, "because he's performing in a Shakespeare festival in New Orleans. But I'm here to thank you on his behalf, to say I taught Jim everything he knows." The audience laughed and gave him a huge ovation. [optic.livejournal.com, ret. 5/4/08]

Kurt Young, Matt Easton, and Jim Buck represented the new generation of young men who had migrated to the large urban gay centers like New York, San Francisco, and Los Angeles and were often labeled "Chelsea boys," "Castro boys," or "Weho (for West Hollywood) boys." The generation of the mid-nineties did not put limits on what kind of sex they would perform. They became porn performers largely to make some extra money, but also because they were comfortable with the sex. Since all the major producers of gay porn were using condoms, performing on a porn set was not itself a high-risk sexual activity anymore.

Neither Jeff Stryker nor Ryan Idol were their role models—as porn stars or sexual ideals. The one performer whom many young gay men of the nineties named as their favorite porn star was Al Parker. Jim Buck, when asked whom he would like to work with in a porn movie said, "Al Parker. Al Parker was the first man I ever had a crush on. Al Parker is sort of my ideal. Beautiful man. Sexy, versatile, hot and kinky. I never met him. I wish I had." [Buck, *Manshots*, 2/98, 73]

Even though porn careers typically lasted no more than three years, they were professionals. They treated their jobs like serious work—as a kind of acting, as communicating something about sex, as something important. Near the end of Matt Easton's career, he characterized the professional attitude when he explained: "At first I started doing it for the money.... If you're going to do something, you might as well do it your best." [Easton, *Manshots,* 8/98, 79]

Among other performers demonstrating a professional ethic were Chad Donovan, previously a horse trainer who was an excellent actor and an energetic top with an extraordinarily long penis; Doug Jeffries, a former opera singer who has performed in more than a hundred videos and is currently a leading director; Dino Phillips, a popular and versatile performer who left college to pursue a career in porn; Dean Phoenix, a notable top from San Diego; Tanner Hayes, a cowboy from rural Montana who made his reputation as a power bottom; and Harper Blake, a popular drag performer in the Bay Area who transformed himself into a well-built, sexually versatile, masculine body builder. In addition, there was Logan Reed, who built a career around the flip flop (when two performers alternate between top and bottom); Clay Maverick, a straight man who was introduced to the gay porn industry by his girlfriend; and Travis Wade, a Texas-born bisexual gym trainer who was one of the most successful "Exclusives" signed by Falcon Studios. These performers were among the most popular porn stars in the late nineties. Most of them were sexually versatile and performed both top and bottom roles at some point in their careers.

There was another development that reinforced the professionalization of the gay porn stars of the late 1990s. In March 1998, Pfizer Pharmaceuticals introduced Viagra, a small blue pill designed to stimulate erections in impotent men. It was a perfect remedy for those hours that both performers and production crews waited for performers to regain erections after a break or after taking a new position. But as performers soon discovered, finding the proper dosage was a learning process. A full pill might not have the desired effect; it sometimes produced headaches or made it more difficult to achieve an orgasm. For some performers, a half pill was more effective. But even so, it would not produce an erection unless the performer "desired" the sexual interaction he was engaged in. Nevertheless, Viagra and other pharmaceuticals designed to treat erectile dysfunction have been increasingly used in the both the gay and straight porn industries. [Loe, 7–27]

In recent years, a number of the performers from the midnineties have assumed important roles as directors for a number of the leading studios. Four members of this generation have taken their place as leading directors: Michael Lucas, who founded his own company, Lucas Entertainment, in New York City has directed more than seventy videos; Doug Jeffries, long a close associate of Chi Chi LaRue, has directed more than sixty-five movies for All Worlds Video, Studio 2000, and Rascal/Channel 1 Productions; Chad Donovan has made more than thirty movies for a handful of companies since 2000; and Chris Steele, director of production at Falcon Studios and Jet Set Productions, has directed more than twenty-five videos.

NOT STRAIGHT OR GAY

Many of the men who entered the business at the time displayed a professional attitude: in particular straight men like Rod Barry, Travis Wade, and Clay Maverick. The *2000 Adam Gay Video Directory* noted, "Rod is one of those remarkable performers who was so good from the beginning, it was difficult to believe he was just a beginner." [12] All Worlds' director Mike Donner—who directed Barry at All Worlds— considered him to be "one of the best sexual performers in the history of gay porn." Twelve years after entering the industry in 1996, and still performing in videos and online, Barry was inducted into the gay porn industry's Hall of Fame in February 2008.

Barry became a gay porn star almost by accident. After a year of college, he joined the Marine Corps in 1994. But soon after joining, he got his high school girlfriend pregnant. Within months he was living in a small apartment in San Diego in a contentious and miserable marriage. During this period, his drinking spiraled out of control and his Marines career soon came to an abrupt end. He had to find work quickly and responded to a photographer's ad looking for models. When he found out that the photographer was scouting for gay porn, he tried unsuccessfully to find work in straight porn. Eventually, someone recommended that he go see Dirk Yates.

Yates invited Barry to come in for a solo masturbation shoot. While Barry masturbated, Yates asked him, "Tell me one of your sexual fantasies?"

"I think a sexual fantasy for me.... Whenever I jerk off or masturbate, I think about being kidnapped and sold as a sex slave in some foreign country. "

"You're not alone in that."

"So come kidnap me."

At the end of the session, Yates told Barry, "Well, I think you've got a future with us." Barry's tape was released as part of Yates's premier line of video tapes, *The Few, the Proud and the Naked #6*. Within weeks Barry was paired for his first sexual encounter with a man on the gay porn set of *White Hot*.

Several years later, reflecting on his experience working with Barry, Yates still expressed a feeling of amazement:

> "Rod Barry is a sweetie. I never felt he was genuinely mine. I mean when I take these military guys and make them into ... he seemed pro from the first day I met him.... He did twenty-nine scenes in a year. He started right off the bat. And I believe the guy's straight—maybe I'm wrong—but I've never seen such a performer. He would never turn you down on anything." [Adam, 68]

White Hot was directed by Chi Chi LaRue. His distinctive directorial style of shouting out instructions to the performers like "Fuck it. Suck it. Harder! Now lick it!" amused and energized Barry. While his directorial style intimidates some performers, "I thought it was hilarious. I couldn't stop laughing, Chi Chi's personality makes you forget any nervousness that you may have." [Douglas, *Manshots*, 6/98, 57]

Barry's porn career took a giant step forward in early 1997 when LaRue persuaded Yates to let Barry make several videos for Falcon Studios in San Francisco. LaRue was to direct one (*The New Coach*, Mustang, 1996) and John Rutherford would direct the other, *Maximum Cruise* (Jocks, 1997). Together LaRue and Rutherford were instrumental in the transformation of Rod Barry from an enthusiastic but minor sexual performer into one of the top porn stars.

LaRue was important to Barry's development not only because his energetic style of direction spurred Barry's own enthusiasm and pushed him to expand his sexual repertoire, but also because he helped hone his persona as a baby-faced, dirty-talking sex pig. Together with the Falcon aesthetic—of shaved bodies and high-gloss videography—they created a glamorous and beautiful male icon. The ideal Falcon porn star is an aggressive top, and working at Falcon pushed Barry to elaborate his dirty talk into a significant component of his porn persona. Barry, who says he's "not a very loud person in [his] private life," was encouraged by LaRue to talk during his sex scenes. Under LaRue and Rutherford's tutelage, Barry's dirty-talking ways flourished and he added drooling, spitting, and playing with saliva, creating a distinctive top style that included playing with his own anus, getting rimmed, kissing, spitting, sucking, and fucking.

There is no question that Barry's best early performances were in the videos produced by Falcon Studies (and their Jocks and Mustang lines), especially *Maximum Cruise* (1997), *The New Coach* (1997), *Cowboy Jacks* (1997), *Mercury Rising* (1997), and *Current Affairs* (1997)—directed by either Rutherford or LaRue (one under the name Lawrence David). The Rutherford videos (*Maximum Cruise, Mercury Rising,* and *Current Affairs*) thoroughly exploited Barry's persona as a shameless sex pig, while some of the better LaRue videos show a more romantic or easygoing side (*Gold Digger, Show Your Pride, Cowboy Jacks, Tall Tails, The Complexxx,* and *Beach Buns*).

Barry soon joined the revolving retinue of LaRue associates who traveled with him on cross-country tours giving live performances—stripping and dancing—with performers such as Doug Jeffries, Joey Hart, and others. By early September, *Gay Adult Video News* columnist Rod Sklyer reported that LaRue was "obsessed" with Barry and that they were engaged in a "torrid affair." Categorizing Barry as a tranny chaser, Sklyer also noted that Barry was two-timing LaRue with another tranny. Barry and LaRue both claimed that there was no affair, only a "torrid friendship." [Barry, *Sex Drive,* unpublished]

Eventually, any successful top in the gay porn business comes under pressure to bottom. Fans frequently fantasize strong tops bottoming, and the fantasy appeals on a number of levels. One is the potential transgression of the masculine code, which a top, to some degree, represents. As one of the industry's most successful tops, Barry was constantly questioned as to whether or not he would bottom. He finally agreed to bottom, but only if he was well paid for it. His willingness to bottom was widely heralded in the business. One reviewer wrote, "Either Barry is one hell of an actor or he does delight in bottoming.... [H]is pleasure seems downright palpable. His energetic response to the rutting, the sparkle in his eyes, his joyous grin, and his rockhard erection all confirm that he is indeed as exciting a bottom as he is a top." [Douglas, *Manshots*, 11/98, 38–39]

While bottoming was a significant public move for him, Barry had already begun to bottom at least six months before he did so on the video set of *Beach Buns*.

In an interview in *Manshots*, Jerry Douglas asked Barry: "Was this a big step or just another step?"

"Another step," Barry said. "Obviously, it's a big step, because in the industry, everybody makes a big deal out of it.... [T]hat day was, to me, like any other day. Except for the fact that I was 'getting fucked.' ... It's different from what I was doing, but it's just like any other day at the office."

Douglas asked: "Did you feel that you were playing a feminine role at that moment?"

"No. No. No. And if you watch the movie, I don't think so, because I'm an aggressive top and I was also an aggressive bottom, playing the same way, like reaching around and grabbing his ass and pulling him. 'Do it right!'" [Douglas, *Manshots*, 6/98, 73]

In March 1998, Barry bottomed again in *A Lesson Learned*—this time flip-flopping in the final scene with Dino Phillips. Barry plays a college student in Phillips's Shakespeare class. While preparing his lecture on *Hamlet*, Phillips falls asleep and dreams of Barry reciting Hamlet's "Alas, poor Yorick" speech holding a skull aloft while completely naked. When Phillips enters the scene, they stage an intense sexual performance while barely touching one another.

In 1998 after two years in porn, Barry announced his retirement. The sex and drugs had grown tiresome, and he had never really been able to think of himself as a gay porn star. He wanted badly to lead an ordinary life, and he continued to be involved with women sexually and emotionally. Although he'd left porn, he continued to perform as a stripper in gay clubs throughout the Midwest, where he fell madly in love with a young women who was with a gay male friend. They married soon after.

Finally, in March 2001, he appeared in series of movies that dramatically sparked his comeback: *Seven Deadly Sins/Gluttony* (All Worlds, 2001), in which his scene received a GayVN nomination as the Best Sex Scene; *Deception, Part 1* (Falcon, 2001), which marked his return to the prestigious Falcon Studios after a three-and-half-year hiatus; *Bringing Out Brother* (All Worlds, 2001), in which he was one of the two leading stars; and most importantly, *White Trash* (2002), a wildly popular sex comedy which earned him the GayVN award for Best Supporting Actor.

Toward the end of 2002, Dirk Yates lured Barry back to San Diego to manage Adult Depot, his company's retail porn outlet. The return to San Diego—after the collapse of his short-lived second marriage—was a homecoming. While he managed Adult Depot, over the next year and half, he continued to strip dance at local bars and clubs and work as an escort. He launched his first website, which featured a live webcam that allowed his fans to view the sexual activities (mostly with women) in his bedroom twenty-four hours a day. On the website, he also regularly scheduled shows during which he masturbated, used dildos (including a full-size baseball bat), and had sex with male and female partners—while earning tips.

Toward the end of 2004, Barry was cast in *Coming Out* (which wasn't released until 2007), a bisexual movie for Metro, a leading producer of straight adult videos, with a number of mainstream porn actresses—Shy Love and Arianna Jollee. Jollee (Barry's costar in one of his two scenes), Shy Love, the film's director, and the videographer found Barry's sexual performance remarkable. A number of them felt that they'd rarely seen anybody "fuck like that"—and they compared him to the young Rocco Siffredi, a leading straight performer and director. Jollee and the others provided Barry with contacts on the straight side, and he went on to perform in numerous straight scenes, many of them for Devil's Films. Since in the straight industry there is strong resistance to hiring performers from the gay side of the business, Barry adopted "Billy Long"—later changed to Little Billy—as his straight porn name.

Barry's versatility and sexual range also led to performing in transsexual films as well as female-to-male strap-on videos. Entrepreneur, producer, and director Tom Moore, himself a sexually complex figure with a sexual orientation very much like Barry's, cast him in a series of transsexual videos, shot mainly in Argentina. Moore and Barry shot more than eighty transsexual scenes.

As Little Billy, Barry developed a new persona as an adventurous and wacky sex-driven sidekick of "Uncle Tom"—fucking and getting fucked by trannies, as the bottom in female-to-male strap-on scenes, topping twinks, and in heterosexual creampie videos. These videos were made and distributed outside the standard gay distribution networks. It is one of the odd facts of the porn business that some mixed or marginal genres, such as bisexual movies, are classified as "gay" while others like transsexual or she-male videos are considered "straight."

Little Billy became widely known as an energetic and adventurous performer in fetish and BDSM circles. In early 2007, Barry was invited to perform for kink.com, the leading producer of BDSM pornography on the Internet. He made a series of videos for kink's *TS Seduction* and *Men in Pain* websites in which he took the submissive role. One of the most popular series was one he did with Gwen Diamond in which they played a suburban couple. Businessman by day, Billy played the sexually submissive man at home; he was tied up, humiliated, whipped, and fucked in the ass in each episode of the series.

In his career Barry has appeared in more than three hundred scenes in all genres. "For ten years, I've been making porn, stripping and escorting." He may have started out as gay-for-pay, but he evolved into a more complex sexual per-former—and a more complex sexual person.

> "I am very strange. I would never say or do most
> of those things at home. Once that camera rolls ...
> I unconsciously live out my fantasies in movies. I
> think because it's safe for me. One fantasy I used
> to have whenever I masturbated, was about being
> kidnapped and sold as a sex slave in some foreign
> country. Working in the porn industry is a little
> like that old fantasy." [Barry, *Sex Drive*]

Although he has been married twice and is predominately involved with women in his private life, Barry defines himself as "sexual" rather than "straight" or "gay." "I'm not gay or straight," he said, "I'm a freak. I like all kinds of sex. I love to fuck women and guys, but I'm a total bottom slut too. I enjoy an orgasm any way I can get one." [Barry, *Sex Drive*]

THE COMING OF THUG PORN

Since the early seventies, black performers were relatively rare in mainstream gay porn videos—and then black performers almost always performed as tops. By the mid-1980s, hardcore films featuring black performers were a specialized niche. Director Frank Ross made a series of films featuring black per-formers for Satellite Video. Black Forest Productions achieved a certain visibility as the only company that exclusively released all-black films. Catalina launched a subsidiary called Black Gold Productions, which briefly offered a number of high quality all-black films. [Parrish, *Manshots*, 8/89, 20–21]

The first black performer to achieve any broad recognition in the gay adult industry was Joe Simmons. Appearing in more than thirty videos between the early eighties and his death from AIDS in 1995, Simmons starred in films produced by New York–based PM Productions and the black films of Satellite Video and Black

Gold as well as in the videos of Christopher Rage, the leading gay director of extreme porn and kink. [Bell, 6–16].

Simmons also posed for Robert Mapplethorpe, and his portrait was published in Mapplethorpe's *Black Book*. "Robert and I had good *rapport*," Simmons recalled. "There was a connection the very first day. He saw that I was a hard-working model and had what it takes to be one." Art critic Kobena Mercer compared Mapplethorpe's portrait of Simmons to the Carl Van Vetchen's photographs of black celebrities and artists of the Harlem Renaissance in the 1920s. "The sculpted pose of Joe Simmons in one frame," wrote Mercer in his essay on Robert Mapplethorpe, "immediately recalls the celebrated nude photographic studies of [actor and singer] Paul Robeson by Nicholas Murray in 1926." [Mapplethorpe, 79–83; Bell, 12; Mercer, 206–208]

Simmons believed that the market for black actors in gay videos was more dynamic than most companies realized.

> "Most of my videos are black videos, so I'm put into this category that Joe Simmons only does black videos. But Joe Simmons has done so much other stuff, with blacks, whites, Puerto Ricans and so on. I don't want to be categorized. I'm a person who is open to a lot of ideas. That is what I want to see in the video industry. Among black videos, everything is *black* this, *black* that. They don't have the *white Stryker Force*…. the way they're advertising them is very marginal. You don't see them doing bigger ads for black videos. They're usually small and a lot of them are on the last page [of magazines]." [Bell, 15]

Like many recent black and Latino performers, Simmons identified as bisexual. "It's not that I'm closeted," he explained. "I do have intimate relationships with women. But because I am a bisexual man, I am also attracted to men…. I can't explain it any further." [Bell, 16]

• • •

In August 2006, Deadlee, an openly gay hip-hop artist and rapper, challenged fellow rappers 50 Cent and DMX to "Suck Muh Gun!" While Deadlee's lyrics are peppered with words like "bitch," "pussy," and "faggot," he is nevertheless committed to challenging homophobia—in the world of hip hop and in the world at large.

Hip-hop artists have long celebrated violence, homophobia, and misogyny. Today, there is a thriving gay hip-hop culture, though many hip-hop artists and rappers continue to lead secret gay lives. "Rejecting a gay culture they perceive as white and effeminate," observed Benoit Denizet-Lewis, "many black men have settled on a new identity, with its own vocabulary and customs and its own name: Down Low."

> "There have always been men—black and white—who have had secret sexual lives with men. But the creation of an organized, underground subculture largely made up of black men who otherwise live straight lives is a phenomenon of the last decade.... Many of these men are young and from the inner city, where they live in a hyper-masculine 'thug' culture.... Most DL men identify themselves not as gay or bisexual but first and foremost as black." [NYT, 8/3/03]

In 1997, Enrique Cruz set out to do for gay porn what hip hop had done for urban black culture. "Hip hop music has given urban culture more allure," Cruz explained.

> "White people buy videos, especially affluent white gay men, who make up over 75 percent of the gay adult market. But there's also a gray area that hasn't been tapped yet—young gay blacks and Latinos who watch music television but keep their sexuality on the down low and may

not have bought any gay videos yet. I want them to look at my videos the same way they look at a rap video. Black gay and bi men are not just surrounded by rap music, but by all the things that it espouses and talks about. It's hard not to feel a part of that world, because you're growing up in it." [Suggs, 85]

Cruz grew up in Spanish Harlem and the Bronx. He attended Hunter College in Manhattan. "I came out to myself when I was 19, but it wasn't until five years later, after my father had died, that I actually started going out to gay clubs. [My father] was very strict, very old school. Being gay was not something I felt I could be open about." During those five years, Cruz watched a lot of porn. "I liked the Duo series from a black company called Black Forest. They had no plots, but they were about couples having sex and also being romantic." [Suggs, 86]

The first video put out by Cruz's La Mancha Productions was *Learning Latin* in 1997. Set on a college campus, it featured a cast of black and Latino performers that captured the gay and bisexual Blatino sex-party scene. The hip-hop music on the soundtrack of Cruz's videos reflected their connection to the urban lifestyle and music scene. The video was a runaway bestseller. In a business where successful videos sold a thousand to fifteen hundred units, *Learning Latin* had sold over seven thousand copies in its first two years.

Cruz followed up with *Tiger's Brooklyn Tails* (1998)—another multiethnic extravaganza that takes place in cruising spots and sex clubs ranging from abandoned Brooklyn subway stations to private sex parties. The video stars Cruz's discovery Tiger Tyson.

• • •

Over the ten years since Tiger Tyson headlined in *Tiger's Brooklyn Tails,* he has become the best-known public representative of "thug porn," the new gay porn that caters to and represents young black and Latino men. Of black and Puerto Rican heritage, Tyson got his start dancing at The Web on East 58th Street—a funky little gay bar with an Asian clientele and the men who were attracted to them. Tyson had just gotten out of prison. He had served fourteen months for grand theft auto and was looking for employment when he approached The Web.

"People liked what I did onstage, and it was really a lot of fun at the time.... [I]t was an easy way to make a living. One of the other strippers asked me if I'd like to be in an X-rated movie. He said it pays better than stripping ..." [Straube, 68; Carnage, *Unzipped,* 47] Malice, one of the other dancers at The Web, gave Tyson Enrique Cruz's phone number.

Tiger's Brooklyn Tails (1998), his breakthrough video, was only Tyson's second film. "I didn't know I was going to become this whole character." The character Tyson developed for his screen persona was one that overlapped with those black and Latino men who had sex with men but who primarily identified as heterosexual. He defined himself as unequivocally bisexual, but said he did not date men—he also said that he would never bottom: "I wouldn't feel right being on the bottom."

He was engaged, but had no plans to stop dancing or working in the gay porn business. He also said that he preferred "dancing" for male audiences.

"My fiancée is beyond cool," he explained. "I met her at Magic Touch [a gay bar in Queens] while I was dancing for gay men, and she knows all about the videos. My mother is even supportive. I guess that's why I don't bother to think I'm doing something wrong. If my mother doesn't feel disgraced, I feel good about it." [Straube, 68]

After making four films for La Mancha, Tyson went to work for the Latino Fan Club, at the time La Mancha's main competitor producing for the "ethnic market." He left the business for several years because "working for any company that you're not financially invested in is frustrating after a while. Since my name and image were being used to sell the movies,

I wanted to have more control over how I was being portrayed. I wanted to make movies that had good production values." [Carnage, 48] For several years after 2000, Tyson sought to launch his production company, finally joining with Jalin Fuentes to launch Pitbull Productions in 2003.

With Pitbull, Fuentes coined the term "thug porn" to characterize the genre and market niche they sought to develop—and for their product line.

According to Tyson, "I discovered we had the same vision about the adult business, by using only authentic thugs, paying performers well, and practicing safe sex." [Carnage, 45, 48] Since their launch in 2003, Tyson and Fuentes's Pitbull Productions has released more than fifty videos. One estimate puts thug porn sales at more than 20 percent of the gay porn DVD market. [Carnage, 48]

Ten years after Tyson's first big hit as a porn star, he is now a celebrity. On a recent visit to Paris where he shot *Tiger's Eiffel Tower: Paris Is Mine*, his two-part thug porn spectacular, he posed for the gay French artist duo, Pierre and Gilles. They portrayed him in a tiger-striped kitchen cooling himself in front of a refrigerator packed with raw meat—the portrait sold shortly afterward for $65,000.

"Tiger Tyson is probably the most popular Latin porn performer ever," said Brian Brennan. "Tiger has an incredible star presence and dynamic personality. He's got all the ingredients of a major talent: great looks, huge uncut dick, and sexual energy that won't quit." In February 2008, he was inducted into the GayVN Hall of Fame. [Carnage, 47]

• • •

Three companies dominate "thug porn" today—Pitbull Productions, Big City Video, and Latino Fan Club, the daddy of them all. Latino Fan Club was founded by Brian Brennan in 1985. Brennan had worked as the art director for a porn magazine, but was disappointed by the lack of Latinos in mainstream gay porn.

"In 1985 no one was shooting porn with my favorite kind of men: young urban Latinos. I lived around the corner from a Latino hustler bar in Manhattan, and I found my first models there." Many of Brennan's models identified themselves as straight. Like G.Q., one of Brennan's models in the late nineties: "I consider myself to be bisexual, or just sexual."

Brennan's *cinema verité* style has helped to define the style of thug porn—a rough, homemade look. "The location set is lit and prepped beforehand, and the actors and myself are the only ones getting the scene made." [Carnage, 47]

The original Latino Fan Club members, who got a newsletter and Brennan's amateur videos, served as the basis for an extensive mailing list. He started with simple videos of solo masturbation scenes and eventually produced ambitious narrative films like *New York Street Boys* (n.d.), *Boys of El Barrio* (1988), and his best-selling two-part feature, *Spanish Harlem Knights* (1991). Movies set in a rehab center or prison have been some of Latino Fan Club's most popular titles. According to Brennan, "Those were the gay fantasies that were most popular. Straight men who were confined or restricted and need some kind of sexual release." [Suggs, 86]

Today Big City Video, the third company, produces more black, Latino, and Blatino videos than any other New York–based company. "I love the macho behavior," says Big City CEO Robbie Glessman. "I love their sensuality—they have a sexiness that drives me crazy."

Over the years, Big City has discovered or promoted many of the most popular and successful black and Latino stars: Manuel Torres, Enrico Vega, Jason Tiya, Tiger Tyson, Viper, and Ricky Martinez. Many of these performers have also worked for the mainstream gay porn companies in California. Ricky Martinez proclaims, "I feel that the beauty of blacks and Latinos is not fully represented in the porn industry." [Carnage, 49] Martinez, in particular, has worked for most of the major California companies.

The success of Enrique Cruz, Latino Fan Club, Tiger Tyson's Pitbull Productions, Big City Video, and a host of smaller companies has made New York City the capital of gay "ethnic" porn. "New York has the corner on the thuggish, roughneck market," Brian Brennan told Donald Suggs. "They have the bodies, the attitude, the charisma—everything."

MAKING A LIVING

Most porn-star careers are relatively short. Porn director Kristen Bjorn observed that "the longer you are in [this business], the less money you are paid. Once you are an old face, and an old body, forget it. You're through as far as your popularity goes."[DeWalt, 55] In the porn industry, a performer who is considered an "old face" or an "old body" is either too sexually predictable or "overexposed"—too many movies in too short a period of time. Viewers become bored and do not expect the performer to provide anything new. Every performer in the porn industry must contend with this ruthless dynamic through which they exhaust their potential to generate fresh fantasies and keep their erotic appeal alive. A star's durability and appeal can be prolonged only if he offers new sexual possibilities, makes new fantasies possible, and reinvents or renews himself without closing off the original fantasies that inspired his fans.

On a practical level, most performers worry about "overexposure." Falcon exclusive Travis Wade sought to avoid overexposure by limiting the number of movies in which he appeared. Discovered by Falcon Studios, Wade signed a contract to make five movies over one year. When he completed his contract, he re-signed after a short break because the "money is way too easy to make [at Falcon] for me to be … doing 20 films with all these different companies" and being forced to leave the business because 'nobody cares who you are.'" [Holden, 2000]

Over the course of his career, Wade also expanded his sexual repertoire from his original stance as a trade top and eventually bottomed in *The Crush*, his last movie for Falcon. Wade believed that bottoming "increased my overall worth in the business. It appeals to a different audience. Some people just want to see me as a top. And then there are those people out there that have been saying how beautiful my butt is.... I wanted *The Crush* to take me to that next level, so that when I'm ready to stop making movies, I'll still have the option of another year or two of performing in clubs, doing video signings, and doing appearances." [Holden] Throughout the period he performed in porn movies, Wade also danced and escorted. When he left the business, he worked as a gym trainer—a common post-porn career for many of the more gym-conscious performers.

• • •

For most performers, acting in porn is not a full-time job. In order to earn higher incomes, many porn stars also work as escorts. "I don't think that porn stars really make a living doing porn, they have to have some kinds of other income," notes director Kristen Bjorn. "They just cannot make that much money. So those who are totally into just doing porn movies are, basically, prostitutes who use the porn movies as publicity for what they really do." [De Walt, 55] Appearances in porn movies become akin to infomercials, and the dancing and stripping in the gay club circuit become a modern triple-X version of the traveling salesman.

Performing live, dancing, or stripping—all different names for the same activity—are probably the most common remunerative activities porn stars engage in to supplement their income. As Travis Wade noted, the porn star comes with an advantage: his name recognition, or merely his status as a performer in porn, serves as an attraction for the club putting him on stage. The porn star, by virtue of national distribution of porn videos and adult sites on the Internet, has a reputation that reaches beyond the local gay community. In the clubs, he is a "featured entertainer" in contrast to the local talent or the relatively anonymous dancers who routinely perform. Travis Wade asserted that: "The money is not in the movies really. The money is good for movies, but if you're a dancer at the same time— which is what I was before I was a film star—it quadruples your money when you're performing in a club." [Holden]

Many models are satisfied with the combination of performing in movies and live performances. However, such a combination of activities is difficult to sustain if one has a "regular job." It is difficult to schedule the travel required to appear in clubs and bars around the country, and the time needed to perform in movies, if one has regular employment. And unless one has achieved considerable popularity upon entering the industry, it is unlikely that performing in gay porn and stripping will provide a stable income for long.

It is necessary in porn and in all kinds of sex work to continuously up the ante. Several years ago, at Cherry's in Cherry Grove on Fire Island, Rod Barry reenacted the aggressive "sex pig" persona he portrayed in his videos. He came onto the stage and stripped relatively quickly, then presented his ass to the audience, spreading his cheeks to show his anus, allowing spectators near the stage to finger it. Then he inserted a beer bottle in his ass and penetrated himself (and then afterwards, drank the beer that had remained in the bottle). After that, he moved along the perimeter of the stage reaching out and pulling in the oldest or less attractive men to him, rubbing himself up against them. He spat on the bald head of one man dressed in leather, spreading the spittle out affectionately over the man's naked scalp, and kissed the man's head. Then, swinging from the pipes along the ceiling of the bar, Barry moved over the heads of the audience, landing and planting his naked ass on the faces of patrons who sought his attention. It was an extremely provocative and even shocking performance; the audience, however, was delirious with excitement and surprise.

Stripping as a supplement to a career in pornographic movies can be, as Travis Wade suggested, quite lucrative. By itself, however, even when combined with performing in gay sex videos, it probably cannot produce a sustainable income. "Movies and dance gigs," observed Rod Barry, "they're just a little extra cash. I can go out and do a film—and get a motor-cycle." [Escoffier, 192] Only escorting can provide an adequate full-time income. In this regard, stripping is a somewhat ambiguous enterprise. While many strippers may not work as escorts, stripping can serve as a point of contact for escorting. Traveling around the country dancing in gay clubs and bur-lesque theaters allows the porn star to demonstrate his appeal and meet clients in the smaller markets away from the gay meccas of Los Angeles, San Francisco, and New York.

Fantasy is a significant component of any sexual encounter between the porn star/escort and customer. As long as the porn star appears only in movies, he remains to some degree unat-tainable (e.g., Jeff Stryker) and exists only in a fantasy mode. However, the spectator's ability to imagine access to the star, whether by gossip, strip show, website, or escort ad, helps sus-tain the fan's desire and fosters a fantasy scenario of connection between performer and audience member. Thus, the possibility of hiring the porn star as an escort is integral to the spectator's fantasy (even if he never hires one) and to the economic link between working as a porn star and working as an escort.

REFERENCES

Adam Gay Video Erotica, *Dirk Yates*.

2000 Adam Video Guide, "Rod Barry," (Los Angeles: Knight Publishing, 2000).

Rod Barry, Interview by Jerry Douglas, *Manshots*, June 1998.

Rod Barry, *Sex Drive* (work-in-progress)

Alan Bell, "Joe Simmons: Black Gay Adult Film Actor Talks

About Racism, Safe Sex and Being a Porno Superstar," *BLK*, June 1991.

Jim Buck, Close-Up: Interview by William Spencer, *Manshots*, February 1998.

Jim Buck, "Kountry Kruisin' or: How to Fuck Rednecks in Six Easy Steps," *Unzipped*, October 2000.

Sean Carnage, "Thug Porn Takeover," *Unzipped*, November 2007.

Benoit Denizet-Lewis, "Doubles Lives on the Down Low," *New York Times Magazine*, August 3, 2003.

Mark DeWalt, "The Eye of Kristen Bjorn," *Blueboy*, January 1995.

"DFW on the Porn Awards," *www.optic.livejournal.com*. Retrieved May 5, 2008.

Jerry Douglas, "Beach Buns," *Manshots*, November 1998.

Matthew Easton, Interview by Jerry Douglas, *Manshots*, August 1998.

Jeffrey Escoffier, "Porn Star/Stripper/Escort: Economic and Sexual Dynamics in a Sex Work Career," *Male Sex Work: A Business Doing Pleasure* (Binghamton: Haworth Press, 2007).

David Groff, "Letter from New York: Fallen Idol," *Out Magazine*, June 1998.

Bryan Holden, "An interview with Travis Wade," *www.radvideo.com/news/article.php?ID=130*. Retrieved July 21, 2005.

Craig Horowitz, "Has AIDS Won?" *New York*, February 20, 1995.

Lucas Kazan, "Production: Diary: The Making of *Matinee Idol*," *Manshots*, April 1996.

Meika Loe, *The Rise of Viagra: How the Little Blue Pill*

Changed Sex in America (New York: New York University Press, 2004).

Robert Mapplethorpe, *The Black Book* (New York: St. Martin's, 1986).

Kobena Mercer, "Black Masculinity and the Sexual Politics of Race," *Welcome to the Jungle* (New York: Routledge, 1994).

Vincent Lambert, "Porn Star Interview: Kurt Young," *www.vicentlambert.blogspot.com/2007.03/porn-star-interview-kurt-young.html*. Retrieved April 27, 2008.

Christopher Parrish, "Afro-Disiacs: A History of Blacks in Sex Films," *Manshots*, August 1989.

Preston Richie, "Idol Country," *Manshots*, August 1995.

Mickey Skee, *The Films of Ken Ryker* (Los Angeles: Companion Press, 1998).

Trenton Straube, "Porn Star Profile: Tiger Tyson," *HX Magazine*, May 14, 1999.

Donald Suggs, "The Porn Kings of New York," *Out Magazine*, June 1999.

"Wash West, Behind the Camera:" Interview by Jerry Douglas, *Manshots*, Part II, September 2000.

Kurt Young, Interview by Jerry Douglas, *Manshots*, June 1996.

CHAPTER ELEVEN

Lost in Fantasy

...through fantasy we learn how to desire.

—SLAVOJ ZIZEK

Porn is a pervasive part of everyday life in the gay male community. Straight porn personalities, adult businesses, or images are still relatively rare in mainstream media, but in the gay media they are pervasive. Porn stars, producers, and adult websites are frequent advertisers or sponsors at gay bars and club parties and in tourism, as well as non-porn publications, community events, benefits, and gay pride parades. Most gay men are familiar with brands like Falcon and names like Chi Chi LaRue and Jeff Stryker.

Porn and its role in the life of gay men were changed dramatically by the AIDS epidemic. In the 1970s, the gay sexual subculture exploded in the wake of the sexual revolution and the Stonewall riots. Casual sex in the baths, the backrooms, the sex clubs, the parks, and on the streets was more exciting and adventurous than anything shown in the porn movies of that era. Yet during the seventies and eighties, many gay men in the process of coming out initially explored their sexuality through pornography. Because pornography can ignore social conventions and allow viewers to play at new forms of behavior, it validated gay sex and facilitated acknowledging gay identities.

During the AIDS epidemic, when sex turned deadly, many men switched to porn as a substitute for the wild and raunchy sex they had previously enjoyed. Pornography let them live out those fantasies without the complications—social, psychological, and physiological—of real interactions between people. It allowed them to enter a fantasy world where sex was not fatal, but which still allowed them to explore their most secret desires and violate the sexual norms of a homophobic society.

FINDING PORN

Three days after arriving in New Orleans, Wash West met a young Bourbon Street stripper who went by the name Squishy. He decided to stay in New Orleans. Within days he moved in with her. And he soon decided to make a movie about porn and the "queer" sexual subculture of New Orleans. [West, *Manshots*, 7/00, 16]

> "New Orleans," he observed, "is a very special place in America. It's like an island that drifted up the Caribbean and stuck to the mainland. The town was founded by whores and pirates, and only certain types of people are attracted to that town.... It's a great place to experiment with lots of different identities.... Everyone's going insane, people are screwing, everyone's getting drunk, everyone's sweating, different things are biting you all the time." [West, *Manshots*, 7/00, 16]

West loved the spirit of the city. "New Orleans is the kind of place you can bump into someone on the street who'll change your life." He became obsessed with Squishy and the effect she had on people. "[I] just met her on the street," he said, [West, *Manshots*, 7/00, 16]. Squishy would trek across town to the predominately African-American Ninth Ward (an area later devastated by Hurricane Katrina), where the children would run around in circles pointing at her—because she often wore underwear as her street clothes. Very soon after he met her, West began to fantasize about trying to capture on film the effect Squishy had on people.

"Another ingredient," West explained, "that got thrown into the mix was that I found, on the street, a box of old Seventies porno mags and I found that they captured something that I hadn't seen anywhere else—the kind of looks of the models, the styling of the shoots ... everything I just found incredibly appealing aesthetically. I also started to get into them ... erotically, in terms of ... fantasy." [West, *Manshots*, 7/00, 17] That box of seventies porn magazines had a deep impact on West's films—scenes appear throughout his work that seek to recreate the fresh but rough look of that period's pornographic films.

• • •

Like many children, Wash West was both fascinated and repelled by porn when at the age of thirteen he found his parents' collection of porn and sex toys. His parents' porn didn't turn him on, and years later when he first came out, gay porn didn't arouse him either.

West grew up in Leeds, a working-class town in the north of England, during the 1970s. He was a dreamy boy who managed to escape the battles between his parents—as he later explained, they had "a very lively and active hatred for each other"—by inventing stories before going to sleep at night. Many of them were vaguely homoerotic. But it was years before he thought of himself as gay.

At eighteen, he left home, first traveling to Yugoslavia where he fell love with a young shepherd and joined a religious cult that tried to exorcize "the evil gay spirit" that possessed him. He hitchhiked to Israel and across North Africa. At age twenty-four, West moved to the United States to find the American Dream—or the cracks in the American Dream, as he told Jerry Douglas. He settled briefly in New York, where he worked as a busboy in a so-called "British pub," mostly because of his accent. But he quickly left the city when he realized that New York had "chewed me up and spat me out again." Soon he was on his way to New Orleans.

While West was living in New Orleans, a feminist friend gave him a copy of Andrea Dworkin's book *Intercourse* (1987), in which she argued that heterosexual intercourse was a form of violence against women. Building on poet Robin Morgan's claim that "pornography is the theory, rape is the practice," Dworkin argued that pornography is not merely an expression of abstract fantasies, but literally a form of torture, abuse, and the male domination of women. Thus the making of pornography is a form of torture and abuse that promotes the belief among men that women are inferior, that they do not deserve their civil rights, and that they should be always be sexually available to men.

Dworkin's writing about pornography provoked a series of bitter political and cultural battles in the eighties and early nineties over the regulation of pornography, the funding of sexually explicit or "obscene" art, sex education (especially "safe sex" and AIDS education), reproductive freedom for women, and the rights of lesbians, gay men, and transgendered people. This interlocking set of political battles—known as "the sex wars"—profoundly shaped the way gay male sexuality and gay male pornography were viewed.

Gay male sexuality was not exempt from Dworkin's disapproval; it posed as much a problem for Dworkin as heterosexuality or straight pornography. According to John Preston, author of *Mr. Benson*, the classic BDSM novel considered the gay male equivalent of Pauline Réage's *Story of O*, Dworkin used "to deface any poster or other material that promoted male homosexuality: 'THIS OPPRESSES WOMEN,' she'd write all over the place." [Preston]

West reacted against Dworkin's vitriolic and dogmatic approach. He felt that the anti-porn position was largely an "over-reaction," a form of panic created by female readers' lack of familiarity with pornography. "This doesn't really fit gay pornography," he thought, "and it certainly doesn't fit a lot of straight pornography, and it doesn't fit my life." [West, *Manshots*, 7/00, 16]

Pornography's function, West believed, is more complicated; it is a passport to fantasy, a ticket to an imaginary erotic world. Desire is shaped by the fantasies pornography portrays, but pornography also serves as a substitute for real sexual action. While the pleasures of masturbation and the achievement of an orgasm are often part of the experience of watching pornographic films, both grow out of "the wish to be aroused and the wish to fantasize a scenario of sexual activity" that pornography offers. [McNair 1–15, Cowie 137]

Such complex and ambivalent views make West unique in the world of gay porn filmmaking. Because of his awareness of both its pros and cons, his films demonstrate the power of fantasy as well as how it can harm us.

PORN FABLES

Ironically, despite West's ambivalence, he soon found work in the porn industry. After *Squishy*'s successful premier in New Orleans, Bruce LaBruce, a director of avant-garde erotic videos who was in New Orleans to show his most recent film, invited West to Los Angeles to work on his next film. Titled *Hustler White*, it was about the hustlers who worked along Santa Monica Boulevard.

> "I was the entire technical crew: the assistant camera, grip and gaffer." West explained. "I worked really hard for two-and-a-half weeks— and that was my introduction to Los Angeles. It

was also how I got my first job as a director in the porn industry. I met the porn star Kevin Kramer, who gave me the phone number for an adult video company.

"After *Hustler White* finished filming, I had basically no money, nowhere to live, no job, no car, couldn't drive—disaster looming. But I have this phone number on this little piece of paper and I rang up it up. I said, 'I make films and I'm really interested in doing porn really differently 'cause porn is so boring and it can be done in a much more creative and interesting way, I want to create a revolution in porn.' For some reason they took me on, and literally three days later I was directing my first movie." [Hays, 140]

West's ambition was to try to make a porn film that viewers could "relate to pornographically, but was ... something that I could relate to artistically—art that you can wank to." He started working for Image Video (which soon changed its name to B.I.G. Video) shortly after he arrived in Los Angeles. He made a series of eight and a half movies, some of them low-budget quickies, among them *Taking the Plunge*, *Plugged In*, *Tool Box*, *Dr. Jerkoff and Mr. Hard*, and *Naked Highway*. He left B.I.G before he was able to complete *Beverly Hills Hustler*.

On his first shoot, he was brought in at the last minute and given only three hours to film the video's orgy scene. He was happy to discover that "porn can be made in a free form, non-exploitative way. The models in the warehouse were encouraged to pair up with whomever they wanted and do whatever they wanted. There was no pressure on anyone to do anything. Luckily the group had chemistry and they all started really having sex." [West, private correspondence] He edited the videos using the same method he had employed while working on *Squishy*—editing to the music. B.I.G Video put out the movie without even looking it, as they did with several of his later efforts. Nevertheless, the company's haphazard style of operating opened up enormous artistic opportunities for West.

In 1995, West saw *Mardi Gras Cowboy*, which starred Jim Buck. Deeply impressed by Buck, West felt he had found a performer who was not only a gifted character actor but someone who had "this great erotic vision." Buck became his muse, and West cast him in a series of films. The first of them, *Dr. Jerkoff and Mr. Hard* (1996), is a comic takeoff of Robert Louis Stevenson's *Dr. Jekyll and Mr. Hyde.* "The movie is right there in the title—nerdy professor takes magic potion and transforms into porno stud—a high concept!" West explained, laughing. "I wrote the script as a comedy, and knowing I had Jim Buck allowed me to develop the character and the scenes in an interesting way. Sure enough, when he turned up on set, he knew his lines, he'd thought out the character, and he'd perfected a Milwaukee accent for Dr. Jerkoff." The video was less about good and evil, the theme of Stevenson's short novel, than a tale of sexual transformation.

Dr. Jerkoff and Mr. Hard was the first of Wash West's porn fables—allegorical stories about porn as a passport to fantasy and about the way porn affects its viewers. "This is where I really started to develop my pro-plot feelings about porn," West recalled. "My theory was that the buildup and the context of the sexual act could tremendously heighten the eroticism of the scene. That what was traditionally 'the bit you fast forward through' could be the key to pushing the eroticism to a higher level." [West, private]

Buck dominated West's movie, appearing in three scenes—one exclusively oral, once as a top in a three-way with Dax Kelly and Jack Simmons, and a third climactic scene with Matt Easton, who is the other star of this film. He plays a young homeless man and is in two scenes: one with gay-for-pay performer Mason Walker and the final scene with Buck.

The transforming mechanism of Buck's character is a "magic potion" that functions, much like porn, to liberate his sexual fantasies and free him to play them out. Under the influence of the potion—his "passport to fantasy"—he goes out on the town and plays the sex pig. Buck eventually discovers that it is not the potion but his own sexual imagination that is key to his coming to terms with his homosexual desire. The film challenges Buck's *dependence* on the potion (or "the passport"), not the fantasies or the sexual desires themselves. Like pornography itself, the potion helps Buck's character discover what his sexual desires are.

West's next major project at B.I.G Video, and the second with Jim Buck, was *Naked Highway*, the movie that won West recognition as an original and successful director of erotic films. *Naked Highway* is a road movie shot at various locations on the road between New Orleans and Los Angeles: an epic journey across a mythological landscape. It replays the archetypical stories of American literature—two young men, outsiders, bound together as outsiders against society. The film owes much to the history of gay porn films and to mainstream film history: to William Higgins and John Travis as much as to Samuel Fuller and Terrence Malick.

It is the tale of two desperate young men on a quest to realize their fantasies. It's also a love story. And it has an autobiographical component for West.

> "It had to do with my experience of my coming to America, and discovering America. The road movie. My feeling of the freedom you get when you travel, and also the element of being outside the law, which is a recurring theme for me... two people who are outside society, but who found each other.... The journey from New Orleans to L.A. was very similar to my own journey." [West, *Manshots*, 9/00, 14]

In the film, Jim Buck plays Colorado, a gay man living in New Orleans who is obsessed by a former boyfriend who refused to go "all the way" (i.e., get fucked) and then left him in order to go to California to get into movies. When Buck comes across a porn video in which his ex-boyfriend bottoms, he feels betrayed. He decides to track his boyfriend down in California. Hitching his way across the country, he is picked up by Joey Violence, who is driving a stolen car.

Buck's costar, newcomer Joey Violence, had street-punk good looks, which like his last name, match the character he plays. West had met Joey Violence in the waiting room of agent Johnny Johnston while he was there to interview another performer for the role that West eventually offered to Violence.

> "[Joey] and I found ourselves waiting in an outer room together. We got talking and he told me he was just starting in the industry. On his eighteenth birthday he had gone to the Tomcat Theater and seen *Dr. Jerkoff and Mr. Hard*. He had developed a huge crush on Jim Buck and had decided to go into the porn industry to find him. I was astonished by this quirk of fate and told him I was actually there to cast for Jim Buck's new movie." [West, private]

Violence's attraction to Buck and his attempt to break through the barrier between porn's fantasy world and real life matched West's understanding of how porn worked: it promised and at the same time withheld something the viewer desired. This was a theme that West would return to in some of his other movies.

Buck and Violence have a series of adventures, including a Thelma and Louise–like adventure with a Highway Patrol officer, an unsuccessful attempt to hustle local redneck pool players in which Joey gets gang-banged, and the robbery of a convenience store. As they drive across the western highways, both young men are guided by their fantasies—Buck by the fantasy that his boyfriend must be saved from working in porn and Joey by a childhood fantasy based on a newspaper story of two escaped convicts shackled together. West recreates Violence's fantasy in the style of a 1970s porn loop.

When Colorado becomes aware of Joey's feelings for him, he wonders if they had known one another in a previous life, and he fantasizes about a couple in a black-and-white segment in the style of an old AMG loop of two body builders having sex (at the time, real life partners Kurt Young and David Thompson). When at last Buck finally fucks his old boyfriend, he finds that he no longer wants him, and while he is fucking him Buck fantasizes that he is instead fucking Joey Violence.

Like Jerry Douglas, West brought a sophisticated cinematic imagination to his movies.

> "I tried to have every shot reinforce what was going on in the story. The kind of filmmaking I admire from other people is when there's a perfect link between the story and the visuals, when the cameras or the lights are doing something that boots the narrative.... The scene that immediately springs to mind is the one where J. T. Sloan plays a traffic cop who stops the two runaways—Jim Buck and Joey Violence—and it's sort of a classic suspense set-up. I established that Joey Violence is hiding in the back of the car, voyeuristically watching the scene as it unfolds, which adds a suspenseful element to the sex....When will the third party come into play? When we shot the blowjob (between Buck and Sloan), which is very charged, we shot it deliberately like *NYPD Blue,* very flashy and fast-moving, and very quickly edited. We had Joey Violence in the back of the car, and then we also had the gun on the top of the car. The cop had taken it out of his belt so that Jim Buck wouldn't get at it while he was giving the cop the blowjob. I tried to keep the audience aware of all these things during the sex, so that by the end of the scene when Joey gets hold of the gun and pulls

it on the cop, it's all been perfectly set up."
[Suglia]

Toolbox (1997) was the last film in what might be considered West's "Jim Buck trilogy." Not as ambitious as either *Dr. Jerkoff and Mr. Hard* or *Naked Highway*, *Toolbox* is a tribute to the classic 1970s loops of companies like Nova Studios *(Under Construction* or *The Boiler Room)* and the movies of Joe Gage that were shot in blue-collar settings such as construction sites, boiler rooms, and locker rooms. The film is made up of four loops, each with its own titles and credits; one, with Jim Buck, takes place between two house painters; another among Mexican mechanics at an auto repair shop; in the third a plumber is played by a West favorite, performer Sam Crocket; and the fourth explicitly refers to seventies porn loops and shoots in a style directly imitated from the period. Unlike *Dr. Jerkoff* or *Naked Highway*, *Toolbox* does not offer any self-contained parables, but instead contemporary recreations of and a tribute to the founders of the gay porn film industry.

Over time, story and plot became increasingly important to West.

> "What I'm always interested in is the story part—that's what excites me. When I'm planning a movie I don't think, 'Oh, I'll get a great shot of a cock going up an ass' ... I'm thinking, 'I can create a power dynamic that leads to this particular situation where they have sex. And what if they fall in love? What if there's some element of crime? ... So I'm always more interested in the story. I think in my early movies, I felt, if you don't like it you can fast-forward through it. Porn is different from mainstream cinema in that it's edited twice—it's edited once by an editor, and again by the viewer with their fast-forward button. But what I did eventually get into

> [exploring] was the idea of having a story that people didn't have to fast-forward through. I think the closest I've come to that is *Gluttony*.... I honestly don't think there's a slow moment in the 80 minutes of the movie. And for porn it's a short movie." [Suglia]

"If you look back at the early days in the 1970s during the 'golden age' of porn," West explained, "people were really interested in making 'films.' For example, *Kansas City Trucking Company* (1976) and *LA Plays Itself* (1972) were the work of real filmmakers—well-constructed, beautifully shot, visually experimental, and sexy.... They were my biggest influences. I wanted to return to elements of '70s filmmaking and bring that up to date." [Hays, 141] West's recreations give an almost mythological status to the early loops and films of the seventies. The re-creations serve as parables or fables about the important place of porn in gay men's lives—and how they have shaped fantasies and instilled new desires.

The historical re-creations set in *Naked Highway* and *Toolbox* illustrate that pornography, as writer Laura Kipnis suggests, is "an archive about both our history as a culture and our own individual histories—our formations as selves." The early loops offered fantasies of a liberated gay male sexuality beyond the shame and repression of the years before the late sixties and early seventies.

PORN STRUCK

Pornography exerts enormous power because, according to West, it is "ultimately inaccessible to the viewer."

> "There is always a glass screen in between the viewers and the object of their desire. That distance is part of the appeal, but [it] never fully satisfies them. It is like an obsessive relation-

ship; it gives you a little bit, enough to keep you in a needy state, but never enough to completely fulfill you." [Hays, 143]

It helps make porn a breeding ground for obsession.

Wash West's most ambitious films often show the role fantasy plays in self-discovery. While pornographic films often serve as a passport into a fantasy world, West observes that some men only had one-way tickets—finding themselves emotionally trapped in the fantasy world pornography created.

In everyday life, we maintain a sharp distinction between social reality and fantasy, but due to the film medium's basic "photographic realism," the line between reality and fantasy is blurred in porn movies. Porn films portray a seemingly "real world" where the improbable and the desired take place— when, for instance, straight men drop their clothes and have sex with other men in the locker room.

West's 1999 film *Technical Ecstasy* is about a young man who has found a company that offers a way to enter a digital three-dimensional computer-simulated environment—something like *Star Trek*'s Holodeck—that allows the user to inhabit another person's identity and body. When he is in the simulated environment, he has more intense sexual experiences than he would otherwise be able to have in his own life. But the program has risks: a customer can only enter the world a limited number of times before he becomes trapped there, unable to return.

The young protagonist, played by Dean O'Connor, becomes obsessed with the simulated experience and increasingly uninterested in sex with his boyfriend, Derek Cameron. Eventually, O'Connor finds himself trapped in the fantasy environment, unable to return to "real life." West offers no happy ending; the addictive simulated fantasy becomes the place where O'Connor must live permanently.

• • •

West made two films about the way porn feeds obsession and enlarges it: *The Fluffer*, an independent nonpornographic feature, and *Gluttony*, his porn adaption of Oscar Wilde's *Picture of Dorian Gray*, released as part of All Worlds' series on the Seven Deadly Sins.

Even before West had left New Orleans to work with Bruce LaBruce on *Hustler White*, he had conceived of a feature-length movie about the porn industry during a drunken conversation at 3 a.m. in a bar. He had read the autobiography of *Deep Throat* star Linda Lovelace and came across a comment "about a fluffer on the set of *Deep Throat* and I just thought, 'Oh, my God, what a ludicrous job description. The idea of fluffing interested me because it is an exaggerated version of a common power relationship—someone gives everything and the other receives everything. I thought: What would happen if a fluffer fell in love with a porn star?'" [Hays, 141–142]

He didn't pursue the idea until he moved to Los Angeles and began working in the porn industry. "I worked on ... *Hustler White* and met [porn star] Kevin Kramer," West recalled. "He gave me a number to call. Four days later I got a job directing a movie called *Taking the Plunge*, which had 10 guys in a warehouse. I shot it guerilla style and had two bodybuilders fucking with a plunger. That was my window into porn." [Lambert, 30]

Over the next five years, West and Richard Glatzer, a television producer and director of *Grief*, an independent film, with whom he had become involved, worked on the film together. West absorbed a lot about the industry while working as a videographer and director—mostly for B.I.G. but also for Men of Odyssey (*Technical Ecstasy*) and All Worlds. "I kept a diary of interesting quotes and thoughts." he recalled, "I also did interviews.... From that, I came up with characters and the idea for the story." [Lambert, 30] Johnny Rebel, the gay-for-pay porn star who is one of the film's main characters, was modeled on the many straight performers West encountered in his work.

One scene, for example, is based on an incident involving Rod Barry, the prominent "gay-for-pay" performer whom West had cast in *Red, Hot, and Safe*, a video made to promote HIV prevention and condom use in which everyone involved donated their services. "I shot lots of super-8 of Rod driving [his motorcycle] up 101, in the sunshine, looking super hot," West recalled.

> "I thought it would be great for the title sequence of the picture. We got to [the location] and there was no Rod. We were hanging out and setting the shoot up, when he turned up grinning.... He had been driving up the freeway and this woman in a sports car—a blonde of course—saw him and signaled him to turn off on the exit. They both went up the road and made a date for that night. So he was happy about that—he was going to do his gay porn in the afternoon and the blonde in the Porsche at night. Later I lifted that little scene and used it in *The Fluffer*—for the character of Johnny Rebel, who is a gay-for-pay porn star. I thought it shows that being this guy has its perks—being a sexual symbol, that is, to both men and women." [unpublished interview]

By 1999, he and Glatzer were ready to make it. "It took about a year of pitching it around and trying to raise the money. We actually cast it before we had any money." In addition, West cast many of the people he had met while working in the industry. "I wanted to have a lot of people from the industry in the movie—people like Chad Donovan, Thomas Lloyd, Derek Cameron, Cole Tucker—because they're the real thing," West explained. "We even ran our production out of the Men of Odyssey porn offices. The party scene has Chi Chi LaRue and the Johnny Depp Clones, which is a band made up of porn stars and drag queens—and they rock." [Lambert, 30] In 2001, *The Fluffer* was finally released.

• • •

The Fluffer is Sean McGinnis, a film student who moves to Los Angeles to pursue his dream of Hollywood movies only to find the reality much harsher than he had imagined. After seeing a porn film, Sean is captivated by gay-for-pay porn star Johnny Rebel. In order to get closer to Johnny, Sean takes a job at the porn company that has Rebel under contract. But Johnny Rebel counts himself as heterosexual, though in fact his sexuality is more ambiguous; he makes gay porn for money, but he exploits his sexual appeal to engage with both men and women. After Johnny and his girlfriend Babylon break up, Johnny becomes unmoored. He has begun to lose his appeal as a gay porn star. In a desperate attempt to get drugs, Johnny kills one of the men in the porn business who has befriended him. In a panic, he decides to run away to Mexico—and takes Sean with him.

Seven Deadly Sins: Gluttony (All Worlds, 2001) was made almost immediately after *The Fluffer* and continued West's exploration of porn-inspired sexual obsession. *Gluttony* tells the story of the obsession of a young film student (played by Tanner Hayes, one of gay porn's finest sexual performers) for the porn star Dorian (played by Eric Hanson), whose photo he has found hidden under his father's mattress.

Presented as the young filmmaker's "personal documentary," the film follows Hayes's obsession with Dorian and his discovery that the 1960s porn star, like his namesake Dorian Gray, never seemed to age. But *Gluttony* is more than a simple retelling of *The Picture of Dorian Gray;* it is also a history of gay porn, brilliantly realized in a series of torrid and passionate sex scenes done in period styles—the classical poses and whimsy of the early sixties, the grainy, unpolished naturalism of the seventies, the queer avant-gardism of the early nineties (a politically incorrect tribute to phallocentrism), the postmodern mixing of sex and food set in the late nineties, and the present, in which at last the film student consummates his sexual obsession with the permanently youthful Dorian.

Gluttony pushes the film techniques used in gay pornography to new limits, potentially creating the basis for a new porn aesthetic. In it, West weaves together themes of the gay man's obsessive preoccupation with youth and his obsession with porn stars and with sex itself. Yet it is also a detective story, an exploration of beauty and desire, and a vivid, sexually exciting porn film. The film won the 2002 GayVN Awards (the "Oscars" of the gay porn industry) for Best Video, Best Director, and Best Screenplay—and one of its scenes (with Rod Barry and Troy Michaels) was nominated as Best Sex Scene.

Porn, as West points out, offers "[a] tease ... that will give a sexual experience without really giving emotional satisfaction." [West, private] For most viewers of porn, the glass screen of the TV or the computer is a barrier that will ensure that result. In *The Fluffer* and *Gluttony*, the protagonists break through the glass barrier and pursue their sexual obsessions to the outer limit. The films represent two different ways of escaping from being "porn struck." Eventually, Sean comes to terms with his obsession with Johnny Rebel by following it through to the bitter end, when it becomes clear that his role as "the fluffer" offers no solution to his fundamental loneliness and his sexual insecurities. In *Gluttony*, the student filmmaker finds his release from his obsession with Dorian by following his career and encountering the hidden film of Dorian as an old man—meeting him in person and having sex with him.

CONDOM FANTASIES

Since 1990, the gay porn industry has adopted condoms as the standard practice in the production of all new videos. The straight industry had left condom use optional—leaving it up to individual performers and producers. But eventually, it established a rigorous testing policy: while condoms were not required, no performer could work in a production without having had a series of tests for HIV and other sexually transmitted infections.

These differing policies had very different impacts on performers. In the gay industry, the HIV status of the performers was private. They could be either HIV positive or negative and still perform in hardcore videos, while in the straight side of the business no one who was HIV positive or had an STD could perform in a sexual scene.

• • •

Bill Gardner and John Singleton owned a company that produced safety videos for the transportation industry. They had both been HIV positive for years, and decided in 1998 to invite some friends who were also HIV positive to a sex party at their Palm Springs home. Since they were all positive, they chose not to use condoms. The parties became a regular thing, and soon, sixty to seventy men were coming to each party. After several of them, someone at one of the parties suggested making a "fuck video." (Hick, White, 37)

That same year, they started Hot Desert Knights to produce and distribute their bareback sex videos, and numerous other companies have also made and distributed "bareback" porn videos. Since 2003, bareback videos have been among the fastest growing segments of the gay porn market; many of the top-selling videos are bareback titles. Retail stores have expanded their bareback sections into the front of the store and moved videos from the traditional leaders to the back. Old-line producers have marketed their "pre-condom" classics to the same audience; for example, Falcon has recently marketed its early videos as "bareback."

The rise of bareback video has challenged the industry as a whole. Policies on monitored testing are being reexamined. Many performers, especially those like Rod Barry or Wolf Hudson, who also work in the straight industry, would like to see greater attention paid to testing for other sexually transmitted infections. Bareback producers charge the mainline producers, who continue to market their pre-condom classics, with hypocrisy. Bareback producers have been excluded from certain aspects of the industry; for example, bareback videos are not eligible for GayVN awards. Only recently have certain publications such as AVN and its gay publication *GayVN* and websites like Cybersocket begun to review bareback titles.

Critics and some activists see porn as an educational medium as well as escapist entertainment. Porn is ambiguous; it is both a "passport to fantasy" and a "documentary" of real sex. How directly does the sex portrayed in porn influence the behavior of its viewers? How does the condom play in the erotic imagination of gay men? Does it signify safety or death? Does bareback porn foster an erotic fantasy that is dangerous if acted upon in real life? Paul Morris, one of the founders of Treasure Island Media, claims that "the condom isn't about safety or survival, it's about apology, guilt and relinquishment. Condom use in gay porn is a sexualized way of saying, 'Look, we're good boys, normal and responsible just like straight folks.'" He considers the condom an "epidemiological fetish." [White, 37]

Condom use is both about the safety of the performer and the influence of fantasy on the viewer. Does the straight industry encourage the fantasy and the viewers' practice by insisting only on monitored testing rather than condom use? Gay producers who use condoms seek to eroticize safer sex, and by allowing HIV-positive performers to appear in hardcore movies, positively stress the erotic lives of those who are HIV positive. As most porn viewers know, porn as the passport to fantasy isn't always a practical guide to unfettered pleasure in real life.

REFERENCES

Kathee Brewer, "The Condom Conundrum," *GayVN Magazine*, May 2008.

Cowie, "Pornography and Fantasy," in Segal and McIntosh, *Sex Exposed*.

Matthew Hays, *The View from Here: Conversations with Gay and Lesbian Filmmakers* (Vancouver: Arsenal Pulp, 2007).

Jochen Hick, Interview with Will West, Ray Butler and Bill, "Hot Desert Knights," *Sex/Life in L.A.2* (Hick, dir. TLA, 2005).

Laura Kipnis, *Bound and Gagged: Pornography and the Politics of Fantasy in America* (New York: Grove Press, 1996)

John Preston, "Whose Free Speech?" Boston Phoenix, October, 1993.

Vincent Lambert, "Fluff Daddy," *HX magazine*, November 16, 2001.

Brian McNair, *Striptease Culture: Sex, Media and the Democratisation of Desire* (London: Routledge, 2002).

Mickey Skee, "Bareback on Top," *Cybersocket*, February 2008.

John Preston, "Whose Free Speech?" Boston Phoenix, October 8, 1993.

Ben Suglia, Interview with Wash West, *www.nightcharm.com/habituals/video/wash/index.html*. Retrieved 9/7/03.

"Wash West, Behind the Camera:" Interview by Jerry Douglas, *Manshots,* Part I, July 2000; Part II, September 2000.

Wash West, private correspondence, 1/3/08.

Dave White, "Video Companies That Produce Bareback Porn Are Thriving, but Do They Change the Way Gay Men Have Sex?" *Frontiers*, October 24, 2003.

The End of Gay Hardcore Films

As an art form, the gay video feature is over.

—JACK FRITSCHER

The history of porn is full of accidents that have a huge impact. The sexual revolution of the sixties and seventies created an atmosphere in which porn would be acceptable, but the United States Supreme Court had already created an economic opportunity in 1947, when it forced the Hollywood studios to sell off their theater chains. Television had already cut into their business, and suddenly theaters had no guaranteed content. In the late fifties, exploitation movies—cheaply produced films that featured tabloid topics like drugs, abortion, adultery, and incest—moved into the breach. Russ Meyer launched the "nudies," which showed bare breasts. That worked for a while, but by 1969 hardcore porn—both straight and gay—was in the theaters.

Boys in the Sand (1971) and *Deep Throat* (1972) were the

first hardcore features that attracted a wider public. Bernardo Bertolucci's *Last Tango in Paris* (1972), a mainstream feature imported from Europe that starred Marlon Brando, was a landmark film for its explicit sexual content, though it contained no hardcore sex. The emergence of the commercial porn industry followed in the wake of these films.

Since that time the porn film industry has grown enormously. From an underground business worth $10 million in 1972, it has become a giant industry today, earning more than $10 billion. While the gay component of the industry is relatively small, it has grown as well. [McNair, Lane]

The advent of video technology and the AIDS epidemic in the 1980s produced immense changes. The emergence of video led to the demise of adult theaters and moved the viewing of porn away from a social and public setting to a more private one, the home. The AIDS epidemic reinforced that shift. Sex in the theaters was dangerous; watching porn at home was safer, a substitute for risky sex—especially in the early days of the epidemic when there was uncertainty about its cause and how to protect oneself from it.

The growing importance of the Internet and other new media is only the latest revolution in the commercial development of the industry. But the porn industry has also contributed to the commercial development of the Internet. Pornography has been a part of the World Wide Web since its creation. The porn industry itself has pioneered the development of the software and technology necessary to make secure purchases on the Internet, display images and streaming videos, and transmit live interactive web sites. Pornography is estimated to account for 5 to 10 percent of all online purchases.

These developments are dramatically altering the landscape of the gay porn industry as we currently know it—and as I have described it in this book. Gay porn websites have made porn even more widely available than the mail order businesses or video rental stores of the past. DVDs will probably no longer be produced by the end of the next decade. Adult materials in all the various Internet media compete for direct sales and rentals of porn videos. As the number of broadband subscribers surpass those using dial-up, video-on-demand (VOD) offers a more convenient form for viewers to see and sample porn videos. The live sex shows or amateur videos available on many sites have changed the narrative and sexual expectations presupposed by most porn movies—whether they are plot-oriented or wall-to-wall sex videos. [Ray]

Gay porn websites vary from live sex shows by ordinary people to the individual websites of porn stars, and include specialty sites like Naked Frat House, Leather Bound Sex, Sexy Men at Work, gossip sites like Gay Porn Blog, porn company sites like Falcon TV or Live and Raw, and megasites like BadPuppy.com, NakedSword.com, or RandyBlue.com that carry links to many specialty sites. Most of these websites charge viewers monthly fees to have access to live shows or new material.

Recently, the Internet has come to dominate the way in which sex workers attract customers. Websites for escorting agencies and individual escorts abound. These typically include information about the escorts' appearance, endowment, sexual roles and interests, and rates. There are even websites in which the sexual performances of escorts are reviewed and discussed.

In addition, the proliferation of chat rooms, webcams, voyeur sites, and interactive websites allow fans to engage in conversation and have contact with amateur performers, escorts, and porn stars. For example, on a website that offers one-on-one sessions, fans can purchase "exclusive" time with the performer, interact with him, and together enact a fantasy scenario—while voyeurs, who pay a lower fee, can watch the interaction but not interact with the performer. This is the cyber-fantasy equivalent of an escorting encounter. Thus, increasingly, the Internet has taken the place of face-to-face contacts, interactions, and marketing for male sex workers. Some escort sites have review sections for clients to review the men they hire; *male4malescorts.com* is one the most popular. In the case of well-known porn stars, reviews often seem to navigate between the fantasies clients may have entertained before they hired the performer and the quality of the sexual encounter itself.

After slightly more than forty-years, the gay porn industry is in the midst of a major transformation—it lives almost entirely in cyberspace. The Internet has changed how gay porn producers portray sex, just as the transition from film to video changed how sex was seen in porn. Sex as it appears on websites with live sex shows differs from that portrayed in gay videos—it does not establish a sexual fantasy or frame a sexual encounter through a set-up. Without scripts, directors, or post-production or online editing, accidents, lack of chemistry, and boredom are more likely to determine the course of the sexual encounter on the internet than in videos. Sex in the "real world" will change and that will shape Internet sex, just as Sex 2.0 will change how we choreograph our own sexual encounters. But the kind of stories—whether sexual adventures, romantic tales, or just plain orgies—that gay porn films tell, will emerge in new ways.

REFERENCES

Frederick S. Lane III, *Obscene Profits: The Entrepreneurs of Pornography in the Cyber Age* (New York: Routledge, 2001).

Brian McNair, *Striptease Culture: Sex, Media, and the Democratization of Desire* (London: Routledge, 2002).

Audacia Ray, *Naked on the Internet: Hookups. Downloads, and Cashing in on Internet Sexploration* (Emeryville: Seal Press, 2007).

INDEX

S

Sadownick, Don, 197, 203

Safer Sex Comix, 191

safe-sex campaigns, 181–204, 231–32, 235, 316

Sailor in the Wild, 164–65

St. Clair, Sheri, 195

San Francisco, 117–46

San Francisco Examiner, 124

Sayles, Shan, 50–62, 74, 80, 95, 100–101, 112, 129

Scarborough, Steven, 258–65, 267, 277–79, 281, 287

Scavullo, Francesco, 36

Schaefer, Eric, 50, 87, 125, 146

Schlesinger, John, 34–35

Schnitzler, Arthur, 107

Score, 107

Scorpio Rising, 12, 13

Scott, Jeremy, 164

Scott, Steve, 160, 233, 236–37

Screw, 4, 40

Seagers, Will, 155

Sears, James T., 120, 123, 146

Self-Portrait, 257

Settle, Tom, 284

Seven Deadly Sins, 309

Seven in a Barn, 128, 132, 198, 233

sex, and story, 235–37

Sex, Death and God in L.A., 47

sex factory, 20–31

Sex Garage, 75, 154

sex, in city, 91–95

sex, in ruins, 177–204

Sex Magic, 112

sex, on beach, 96–101

Sex Tool, 75–76, 154, 230

sexual freedom, 14, 94, 177, 181

sexual liberation, 2, 91–95

Sexual Outlaw, The, 84

sexual revolution, 1–5, 14, 48, 142, 153, 156, 170, 185, 295, 325, 345

sexually transmitted diseases, 166, 177–204, 248, 250, 256, 280, 326, 346

Sgt. Swann's Private Files, 184, 192

Shagley, Earl, 125

Shamama, Jack, 215, 236, 251, 284

Shilts, Randy, 120, 146

Show Your Pride, 307

Shulman, Marvin, 98, 101

Siebenand, Paul Alcuin, 50, 52–54, 57–60, 62–63, 66–69, 72–73, 76–78, 83–84, 86–87, 124

Siffredi, Rocco, 310

Silver Factory, 24

Simmons, Jack, 331

Simmons, Joe, 230, 311–12

Sinclair, Mick, 146

Sinema, 23

Singleton, John, 342

Sizing Up, 169

Skee, Mickey, 293, 323, 344

Skyler, Rod, 307

Slade, Joseph, 7, 79, 258, 287

Slater, J. D., 188

Sleep, 35, 38

Smith, Jack, 4, 13–14, 16, 20, 42, 47, 51

soft-core films, 4, 23, 28, 40, 47, 50,

ACKNOWLEDGMENTS

I wrote this book because I wanted to read one like it. It was many years in the making. It didn't start out to be a history of gay porn cinema. I had originally planned to write a book-length profile about the gay porn world as a community and an industry; I especially wanted to write about the people who worked in the industry and how it functioned. But it soon became apparent that I would not be able to give an account of that world without understanding its history—its evolution from the world of all-male adult theaters to the VCR, the impact of AIDS, and the arrival of the Internet. Writing about the early years was like putting together a jigsaw puzzle without any idea of what the picture was. I slowly built up the picture with dozens of obscure stories and fragmentary facts. I could not have written this without the help of the many, many people who agreed to be interviewed and who willingly talked honestly and candidly about their lives and work.

I would like to thank my agent Lori Perkins, who proposed that I write this book, Don Weise, who acquired it for Carroll & Graf (and edited it), and Lisa Clancy and Jon Anderson who took it over at Running Press, when Carroll & Graf was absorbed by Perseus Books.

Many others encouraged me and helped me: Linda Williams, whose wonderful books *Hard Core: Power, Pleasure and the "Frenzy of the Visible"* and *Screening Sex* enlightened me and showed me why it's important to take porn seriously; Eric Schaefer, who solicited a contribution on the history of gay porn from me for his book on the sexual revolution and popular culture; the editors of *GayVN* who helped to arrange for passes to the *GayVN* award shows; and to Rod Barry, Chris

Bull, John Gagnon, Matthew Lore, and Eric Schaefer (again) who read parts of the manuscript in draft form and made valuable comments.

This book would never have been written, nor could any such book have been able to be written without the amazing work of Jerry Douglas, who, as the editor of *Manshots* magazine from 1989 to 2000, literally created an historical archive of the industry's evolution. This book would not have been possible without the interviews of directors, performers, and other people that were published in *Manshots*. He was one of the first people I interviewed, and he was my mentor and guide throughout.

Finally, I would to thank my family for their understanding and support—and I especially want to thank my mother for her forbearance and patience. She was always willing to hear about my adventures in the world of porn, and graciously accepted my excuses for the many times I was unable to visit her.

ABOUT THE AUTHOR

Jeffrey Escoffier writes on sexuality, gay politics, history, music, and dance. He is the author of *American Homo: Community and Perversity* (University of California Press, 1998) and of *Sexual Revolution* (Thunder's Mouth Press, 2003). He has also written a biography of John Maynard Keynes (Chelsea House, 1995) and edited, with Matthew Lore, *Mark Morris' L'Allegro, il Penseroso ed il Moderato: A Celebration* (Marlowe, 2001) on the choreography of Mark Morris. Long active in the LGBT community in Philadelphia, San Francisco, and New York, he is one of the founders of the San Francisco Gay History Project and of *OUT/LOOK: National Lesbian and Gay Quarterly*. He has written for *The New York Times Book Review*, *The Nation*, *The Utne Reader*, *The San Francisco Chronicle Book Review*, the *St. James Encyclopedia of Popular Culture*, and *Out Magazine*. He worked as a freelance developmental editor, "book doctor", and literary agent. He has taught economics, lgbt studies, and sexuality at San Francisco State University, the University of California in Berkeley and Davis, at Rutgers University, and at the New School University. For the last decade, he has worked in health communications and marketing in New York City.